S 4
Bdno

12/50.

An Ever-Rolling Stream

The White Rabbit put on his spectacles. 'Where shall I begin, please your Majesty?' he asked. 'Begin at the beginning,' the King said gravely, 'and go on till you come to the end; then stop.'

Lewis Carroll,
Alice's Adventure in Wonderland

Dr Eric Ogilvie, BSc (Econ), MEd, PhD, FRSA

An Ever-Rolling Stream

**The Ongoing Story of the Development
of Higher Education in Northampton
and Northamptonshire**

Compiled by David Walmsley

 Pinter Publishers, London

First published in Great Britain in 1989 by
Pinter Publishers Ltd,
25 Floral Street, London WC2E 9DS

British Library Cataloguing in Publication Data

A CIP catalogue record for this book is available from the
British Library

ISBN 0 86187 787 X

Typeset, printed and bound in Great Britain by Biddles Ltd., of Guildford, Surrey.

Contents

List of Plates and Other Illustrations

Frontispiece: Dr Eric Ogilvie

Plates

Other illustrations

Acknowledgements

Many of the photographs are of historic interest and the help given in particular by Messrs Beedle & Cooper and by the *Chronicle & Echo* of Northampton in tracing these is very much appreciated since the photographic record is an integral part of this book. The Author and Publishers are grateful to the following for permission to reproduce copyright material.

David Mackenzie (official College photographer); Jacket illustration, Frontispiece and Plates 24, 34, 45 and 59

College Records: Plates 1, 10, 11, 13, 16, 17, 18, 19, 21, 32, 33, 43, 49, 50, 52, 53, 58

Beedle & Cooper, Northampton: Plates 2, 7, 12

Chronicle & Echo, Northampton: Plates 3, 6, 20, 23, 36, 46

V. Hatley: Plate 4 (old print), Plates 5 and 8

Borough Records: Plate 9

British Timken: Plates 22, 54, 55, 56

Northamptonshire County Council: Plates 29, 30

John Roan, Northampton: Plate 31

The Leathersellers' Company: Plates 47, 48

Leslie Skelton: Plate 37 and 57

David Walmsley: Plates 27, 35, 38, 39, 41, 42, 44 and 51; and on loan to him Plates 14, 15, 25, 26, 28 and 40

Plate 10 is reproduced with the permission of HM The Queen Mother; Plates 49 and 50 are used with the permission of HRH Prince Michael of Kent.

While every effort has been made to trace the holders of copyright material reproduced in this book, in a few cases this has proved impossible. We would be grateful for any information that would enable us to correct any omission.

Preface

One day a 'considered' History of Nene College will be written. At that time one hopes that this book will be a help for such a venture. This is not intended to be a formal academic exercise which explores the various implications of the development of higher education in the area. On the other hand, this is something more than a collection of anecdotes and gossip. It comprises two elements namely (a) source materials; and, (b) a series of essays written by local historians or by those involved in the developments described.

Primarily, this book has been generated because of the retirement of Dr Eric Ogilvie (Director of Nene College from 1975 to 1989; and before that the first and only Principal of the Northampton College of Education). The occasion of Dr Ogilvie's retirement at the end of the academic year in June 1989 will also be marked by Nene passing out of Local Authority control on the 31 March 1989. There is therefore very much a beginning and an end to the story of Nene and this is what this book provides.

My own involvement with what became part of the College goes back to 1932. As a boy of five I recall being taken by my father on a 'grey' November day to stand in St George's Avenue (he lifted me onto his shoulders at the appropriate moment) to see the Duke and Duchess of York pass by on their way to the opening of the new buildings.

I cannot claim to have 'known' the formidable John Blakeman who was Principal of the College of Technology from 1911 to 1941. I did meet him and I remember the nervous twitch from which he suffered, but I knew his son (another John Blakeman) better. The John Blakeman I knew worked for the County Borough and then for the County as an Education Welfare Officer. In the old days he would have been referred to as the School Board man who pursued truants but the nature of these duties changed in the 1950s and 1960s. 'My' John Blakeman retired as the County's Senior EWO after thirty-four years' service. He was committed to the care of young people and taught in the Sunday School at Park

Avenue Methodist Church for over forty years; in attitudes and concerns, I am told – like son, like father.

Another Methodist intimately involved in the affairs of the 'Tech'. was David Woodroffe who became Head of the College Leather Depart-ment in 1920 when this functioned in very cramped quarters behind the buildings in Abington Street. David Woodroffe doubled as Head of the College Boot and Shoe Department until 1948 when a separate post was created for this position. Mr Woodroffe retired in 1957 and died in 1962. He was a member of Kingsley Park Methodist Church, a Methodist Local Preacher and a past President of the Northampton Rotary Club. His memory is kept alive by the annual award of the David Woodroffe Prize for excellence in Leather Technology.

As a teenager I attended student functions in the old wooden hut behind the 'Tech.' and became involved in The College Players. John West and Marie Chapman were leading lights in this amateur dramatic company and I remember a fine performance of Bernard Shaw's *Pygmalion* in which they were involved, with Iris James as Eliza and Geoffrey Brightman as Dolittle. John West played Professor Higgins and Marie Chapman was a stunning Mrs Eynsford Hill. My contemporaries were the next generation and I used to play opposite an attractive stage-struck Welsh girl, Sybil Williams, who lived round the corner from my home with her married sister, Elsie Newell, in Collingwood Road. Elsie in turn was a school teacher at Stimpson Avenue Junior School and (prior to our marriage and indeed for a time after it) my wife served on the staff of the same school. Sybil and I appeared together in *The Two Mrs Carrolls* and the Emlyn Williams thriller *Night Must Fall*. One weekend Sybil's boyfriend came down from London and waited until we had finished either a rehearsal or a performance before walking her home. This must have been the autumn of 1948 and of course the young man was the young Richard Burton. What a charming young man he was and what a wonderful voice he had! Other old Northamptonians of that era will have similar happy memories of a gifted actor. Also in the company at that time were Elizabeth Dolman, Robert Shaw, Graham Ashley and Barbara Mitchell (who so sadly was just beginning to make her name on the professional stage when she was struck down by a wasting illness and died).

It was the 'Tech.' which landed me into my first major political difficulty. I had just become the Chairman of the Education Committee and had to introduce an emergency resolution to the full County Borough Council to authorise the purchase of a piece of engineering equipment which the College urgently needed (and which the Principal had the opportunity of buying at a substantial discount). Tongue-in-cheek, Councillor Ron Dilleigh asked me why I wanted the Council's authority to buy when the equipment had already been delivered. Of course in my innocence I denied this but Councillor Dilleigh was right and I was wrong. The machinery in question was on site at the back of a workshop under a tarpaulin. Although the Council gave its permission to buy, there were repercussions! However, even such events have a happy side. For my wife and myself it was the beginning of a friendship which lasts to this day with Alex Parthenis (then the Head of Engineering Studies and afterwards the first Dean of Technology at Nene). What a story Alex could tell! He survived (as a civilian) one of the submarine disasters of the 1940s. A confirmed bachelor he surprised us all by marrying a charming Maltese lady who took charge of him and his 'cars' – and they both lived happy ever after.

Other friendships followed – with Eric Jewitt (the then Principal) and with Dr Walter Siddall and his wife, Jessie.

On the occasion of the opening of the extension to the 'Tech.' in 1970 there occurred a gathering which could be regarded as unique. Amongst the guests on this occasion was my father and he supported that afternoon:

— his son, who was Chairman that day in his capacity as Chairman of the Education Committee – and one of his former pupils (1940);
— the opener, Gerry Fowler, MP, the then Minister of State at the Department of Education and Science – and one of his former pupils (1950);
— the mover of the vote of thanks, the then Mayor Councillor John Poole, OBE (later Chairman of the Northamptonshire County Council) – and one of his former pupils (1930); and
— the seconder of the vote of thanks, Alderman Harold Cockerill, who substituted for Miss Phyllis Hennings who was ill, and who spoke on behalf of the Governors of the College of Technology – and one of his former pupils (1920).

Four people. Four decades of schoolmastering locally.

My principal recollection of the Opening Day of the College of Education (10 November 1972) was that it was a very long day indeed! Mr Henley (the Chief Education Officer for the County Borough) went off to greet Mrs Thatcher and to take her round the Duston Upper School. I went off to the Moulton Park Campus of the College to see how the work to make good the recent fire damage to the Drama Theatre was getting on. There was a contingency plan to switch the opening ceremony to the main hall of the College of Technology if necessary. I found that the decorators had moved in and everything was in hand. Miller Buckley promised that the work would be complete by the afternoon.

I then went across to Fairfields School for the Physically Handicapped to join up with the Chairman of that school (Alwyn Hargrave) and the Vice Chairman (Mrs Ivy Short) to welcome Mrs Thatcher when she arrived. Perhaps my strongest memory of the day is that of Mrs Thatcher getting down on the floor to talk to and to play with one of the pupils aged 6 or 7. For a short space of time she gave her whole attention to this child and nothing else mattered – not even the official party.

Afterwards we all moved off to Lumbertubs Lower School for lunch. This school was in the process of enrolling children from the first housing area in the eastern district of Northampton. Consequently, the school was not full and we were able to use one of the empty class rooms for dining. I had decreed that we should be served the standard school lunch being provided that day in the County Borough Schools. It was served by the School Dinner ladies. It was not only a very good lunch but the arrangement did wonders for morale within our local School Meals Service. However, I did get into trouble with the Treasury. If a Local Authority provides a meal for a Cabinet Minister then the bill (for the Cabinet Minister and his/her entourage) is sent to the Treasury. When the Borough Treasurer sent in a bill for half-a-dozen people for this occasion of less than £5 we had the greatest difficulty vouching this to the appropriate officials in Whitehall. They seemed very suspicious (a) as to what we had done; and (b) as to our motives.

After lunch we all adjourned to the College where the Opening Ceremony duly took place concluding with Alderman J. T. Lewis (the Chairman of the Sites and Buildings Sub-Committee of the County Borough Education Committee) 'breaking' the College flag for the first time – blue for the East Midlands' sky (of which John Clare so eloquently wrote), green for the hills and valleys of the county and silver for our river. Coincidentally, blue, green and silver had been the college colours for Kirkby Fields, too.

Mrs Thatcher then departed by car to keep an appointment with a teachers' group in Luton. The rest of us regrouped, changed and made our way to Wicksteed Park, Kettering, where the Northamptonshire County Association of the National Union of Teachers had arranged a dinner dance in aid of their Benevolent Fund. There we joined up with Lord Belstead (then the Under Secretary of State for Education but now a Cabinet Minister in his own right and Leader of the House of Lords). His purpose in coming to Kettering was to be the principal after-dinner speaker on this occasion. Our purpose in attending was not only to enjoy a pleasant evening as guests of the local teachers but also to book Lord Belstead for the future as opener of the College of Further Education, Booth Lane, Northampton.

Around 10.30 pm Mrs Thatcher arrived back from Luton and went round each of the tables to speak to as many teachers present as possible. I suppose that there were around 900 people there. Her energy left most of the rest of us completely exhausted but we gathered that her programme for the day was no more than she normally tried to fit in whenever she had the opportunity to get out of London, away from Parliament and go visiting. Eventually she departed well after midnight, having been presented with a copy of *The Harpole Report* – a novel about the work of a teacher written by the Northamptonshire Head Teacher and author, John L. Carr. This presentation was made by that year's President of the NUT and of the Northamptonshire Association, Mr C. W. Elliott. The function was also part of the Centenary Celebrations of the NUT. Northamptonshire had supplied the first President of the Union (J. J. Graves, the Head of Hanging Houghton Village School). It also supplied the hundredth President in the person of C. W. Elliott (the Head of Exeter Junior School, Corby).

It was a bit of a shock for me when the Labour Party secured a majority on the County Council in the elections in 1974. I had expected to step down as Chairman of the Education Committee (the Borough Council ceased to exercise any functions as an Education Authority and these passed over to the County Council) and since it was only right and proper that the Chairman of the new County Education Committee should also be the Chairman of the Governors of the College of Education, I had to step down from this post as well. The new Chairman was Mrs Dora Oxenham (a former Chairman of the County Council and a formidable 'County' figure).

It was agreed between the political parties that as the opposition spokesman on educational affairs on the County Council I should be the Vice Chairman of the College Governors. Coming from the 'other' political party and coming from the Borough rather than the County I think Mrs Oxenham viewed me with some suspicion at first but we were able to establish a relationship very quickly, which developed into friendship and, certainly on my part, into a considerable respect even when we held different views on particular matters, as inevitably we did from time to time.

Mrs Oxenham took up the challenge of the three-college situation in Northampton from the very beginning of her Chairmanship. She was convinced that higher education needed a local base and that this could be best secured by an amalgamation of the College of Art, the College of Education and the College of Technology. To this end she directed the tremendous force of her personality and steered the amalgamation scheme through. I suspect (looking back now) that she was the right person in the right place at the right time. There was some opposition both over the principle of amalgamation (especially in so far as a major centre for higher education in Northampton had implications for other further education colleges in the County) and also over some of the financial aspects but in the debates in the Education Committee, and later in the County Council, Mrs Oxenham spoke brilliantly and crushed those who disagreed with her.

I have always regretted the fact that because at the time I had to earn my living as a lawyer I was engaged on a case in the Victoria Courts, Birmingham (which case was spread over eight weeks), so I missed the ceremony on the 14 October 1975 when Lord Crowther-Hunt inaugurated Nene College. I got back in the evening and heard of the success of the occasion to which my wife had been very kindly invited as my 'stand-in'. I heard also that there had been a difference of opinion between the Chairman and the Mayor of Northampton (Councillor John Gardner) as to the pronunciation of the name of the College!

I was never quite sure whether it was Mrs Oxenham herself or someone else who was inspired to suggest this name. I have always attributed it to Mrs Oxenham personally. Certainly, the name 'Nene' promoted conversation with visitors official and unofficial, although some people retreated from the field and just called Nene 'the College'. But the name was much more than a brilliant public relations stroke, it stressed the unity Mrs Oxenham was seeking. Just as the river served both town and county (and belonged to both) so she believed that 'Nene' should serve both town and county (and belong to both).

One of the subsidiary themes of this book I believe underlines this truth. Technical education (out of which higher education grew in our local context) started in the closing days of the nineteenth century as a joint County Council/Town Council venture. After 1911 it became very much the prerogative of the County Borough Council (although supported by the County Council), but after 1974 once again the joint County Council/Borough Council involvement was restored.

I suppose that the most hilarious connection I had with the old 'Tech' occurred during my Mayoralty in 1978–9. I had been invited by the students to open the extension (and much needed improvements) to their Avenue premises. I duly accepted but the builders fell behind schedule and by the end of the summer term the only part of the work which had been completed were the ladies' and gentlemen's lavatories. The Students Committee, which had done all the hard work in planning the extension and in raising the money to pay for the same, was due to disperse at the conclusion of the academic year, so His Worship the Mayor found it 'convenient' to attend in his robes to open that which had been completed and to pay tribute to everyone's endeavours to date.

Again it was at the old 'Tech' that my reign as Chairman finally came to and end on 15 May 1981. I had not sought re-election to the County Council in the elections earlier that May and the voters had determined that the Conservative Group should no longer enjoy a majority at County Council level. The day of the Annual Council Meeting coincided with a visit to Nene College of the then Minister of Education, Rhodes Boyson. I spent the morning with the Minister but at lunchtime, Councillors Jimmy Kane and Jack Morrish arrived hot foot from County Hall to take over. It was a sad moment for me though generously I was enabled even as a non-Council member to remain involved in the affairs of Nene College to a lesser degree thereafter. Obviously, I will never cease to watch the development of the College with interest but there is a difference between this and having responsibility for decision making. Nevertheless, I cannot grumble. I had a longer spell than is given to many people when I could really influence affairs.

I have been asked about my view over the future for Colleges of Higher Education (such as Nene) aspiring to be Polytechnics, aspiring eventually to University status. Some things do concern me. First of all, the moral which I think emerges clearly from this book, is that Nene began and was sustained by local 'patriotism' and local endeavour involving both the town and the county. This was expressed through Local Authority involvement in educational affairs over a period of more than a hundred years. For the immediate future Local Authority involvement in Nene is no longer to be encouraged and the links with the Borough Councillors appear to have been severed. This saddens me. Furthermore the new College Governors are 'appointed' – they do not have to face election to justify their 'alleged' sins of omission and sins of commission to local voters in the way most of the College Governors of past days had to do. Thus there has been a significant change of direction here.

Secondly, I fear for the lack of continuity. The three local firms who in the past have given most support to the old 'Tech.' and to the newer 'Nene' have been Blackwood Hodge, British Timken and (in more recent times) Robert Horne. Without this backing and that of the Leathersellers' Company from the City of London the story set out in these pages would have been very different. One can welcome the greater involvement of industry in the College and at the same time regret that representatives of two of the firms most concerned in the old days have not been appointed to the new governing body by the Secretary of State. New blood is always desirable but so is a degree of continuity, especially if the previous local authority input at councillor level is virtually taken away.

Thirdly, the Board of Governors has been streamlined. Again there is a lot to be said for this but I wonder if the 'new' people realise exactly what they are taking on. In terms of time and commitment it will be a major personal involvement. I was always anxious in my time to invite major figures in local industry to serve the College. The response was gratifying but I felt that it was wise to see that the College did not demand too much. 'Involvement' in future will mean involvement with the students, with the staff as well as with others (not least other educational bodies). For some Governors, there could well be involvement at regional level. One hopes that this will happen but if it does the College 'involvement' can become almost a full-time job. In addition, I have found in the past that leaders of business are used to saying to their subordinates 'do this' and 'do that'. The academic mind does not work that way – it analyses, it discusses and it questions. Because colleges work best through co-operation and participation, I hope people are not going to be in for shocks.

None of this is intended personally. Many members of the new Governing Body are known to me individually, several are friends, and indeed I am sure that all the appointees are worthy. I would emphasise that nothing I have to say here is intended as an attack on those who will continue the story of Nene – these comments are simply intended to convey in general terms those concerns which I feel and which I know are shared by others. I only make them out of a general love and affection for Nene, its welfare and in the hope that it will continue to prosper. The world is a cold, cold place and the world of higher education is no exception. Nene will need all the friends it can win if it is to sustain that place which it has so far secured.

However, this is not 'my book' or a record of my personal opinions. My part is to have been responsible for the selection of material, the linking of passages when necessary and a few of the essays. Basically my role has been that of a co-ordinator and I am grateful to those who have helped me. Behind the scenes, Miss Gywneth Hood, BA, MA (the Senior Tutor at Nene) has gathered numerous press cuttings to which the rest of us have been able to refer; the well-known local Historian, Victor Hatley, BA, FRHistS, ALA, has checked our historical references; the Chief Administrative Officer, Alan Riley, has supplied most of the facts and figures incorporated in the appendices; and the Head of Learning Resources, Maurice Wilson, BA, MEd, ALA, has advised on the book list and prepared the index. I have been able to refer to Professor G. Bernbaum, BSc (Econ), FRSA, and Professor A. N. Newman, MA, DPhil, FRHistS, of Leicester University for advice.

As will be obvious from the extensive source material used, the local press have been most co-operative and have helped over research, particularly with reference to tracking down suitable photographs. I believe that the illustrations included here are an important part of the total record. The whole exercise has enjoyed the benevolent support of Jeffery Greenwell, MA, FRICS (the Chief Executive of the Northampton-shire County Council) and R. J. B. Morris, MA, LLM (the Chief Executive and Town Clerk of Northampton). But especially we all have to thank Leslie Skelton, MA (formerly the Chief Administrative Officer, Nene College, but now the Hon. Secretary to the Northampton Record Society), who has acted as the Administrative and Finance Officer for 'The ERS Project' with the assistance of Mrs Jean Hall. I also have to thank the long-suffering Mrs Anita Hickman who has typed much of the draft manuscript.

Finally the contributors to this book have all had specialist knowledge of the background in respect of which they have written and I am most grateful to them – not least for their forbearance with me. They are: Derek Brooks, MEd, on the School of Technology and on the School of Art; Richard Foulkes, BA, MA (the Warden of the University Centre, Northampton) and Ron Greenall, MA, BSc (Econ) (the former Warden) on the influence of the Leicester University Centre in Northampton; Phyllis Annis, MEd, Trevor Scholey, George Kitson, MA, and John Wilson, BA on the 'Scraptoft Influence'; Ron Smith, MA, on the Kirkby Fields Teacher-Training College; Leslie Skelton, MA, on how to move a College of Education; Richard Alcock, BA, on Dr Eric Ogilvie; Eric Ogilvie, BSc (Econ), MEd, PhD, FRSA, on 'Glorious Ad-Hocery'; Michael Henley, MA, on the formation of Nene College; Richard Fox, MA, on Nene College from 1975 to 1989; David George, PhD, MSc, CBiol, on the National Leathersellers' Centre; Sir William Shapland, LLD, FCA, and Tony Berry, PhD, BSc(Econ), M.Biol, Cert Ed, on the Sunley Management Centre; Michael Furminger, MSc, CEng, MIEE, on the Timken Business & Innovation Centre; Linda Merriman, SRCL, MCLS, Cert Ed, on the Chiropody Centre; John West and Tony Rounthwaite on Memories of the Student Bodies; and J. Stuart Maclure, CBE, MA (editor of *The Times Educational Supplement*, 1969–89), who has contributed the 'Envoi'.

I struggled for some time to find a title for this book. 'A History of Nene College' seemed not only inappropriate but also rather dull. Something after the style of 'The Beginnings and Development of Scientific and Technical Education in Northampton' (after the booklet by Beeby Thompson FCS, FGS published in 1931) would have been pretentious. I chose the title 'An Ever-Rolling Stream' because (a) it suggests a link with the River Nene; and, (b) it comes from a verse in the well-known hymn 'O God our Help in Ages Past' namely:

> Time, like an ever-rolling stream,
> Bears all its sons away;
> They fly forgotten as a dream
> Dies at the opening day.

So many people have had a hand in the story of Nene College and its build-up over a long period of time – some are remembered and some are forgotten. All have contributed to the ever-rolling stream which makes up the story of Higher Education in this part of England's fair and pleasant land.

David Walmsley
January 1989

1 From the Battle of Northampton 1264 to the Mechanics' Institute and After

David Walmsley

There were two Battles of Northampton, or perhaps one serious skirmish and one battle. The more important of these two events took place on 9 July 1460 and was fought in pouring rain in the water meadows between Delapre Abbey and the River Nene. King Henry VI and his Lancastrian allies had constructed a strong point outside the town with marshy land in front and the river behind; but they had reckoned without a traitor in their camp. When the Yorkist rebels (allied with Warwick the Kingmaker) swept down at dawn from the direction of Hunsbury Hill, Lord Grey on the King's right wing changed sides and the Yorkists overran the King's camp, gradually forcing the Lancastrians back into the river where many were drowned. It was said that some 10,000 lives were lost that day and if this is true then the Battle of Northampton was one of the major killing-fields of the Wars of the Roses. In any event the King was captured and the Lancastrian cause was for the time being overthrown.

In terms of the history of this country the 1460 Battle of Northampton is important but in terms of the story of Higher Education in Northampton and Northamptonshire the other Battle of Northampton on 5 April 1264 is more relevant. It is described in the Victoria County history as follows:

In or about the year 1260 a 'town and gown row' at Cambridge, of the bloody kind then usual, led to an exodus of scholars to Northampton. In 1263 the Oxford schools were stopped, and emigrants from the older university flowed thence also to Northampton. Next year the Oxford scholars did yeoman service with their bows and arrows from the walls of Northampton against the king, and narrowly escaped hanging when the town was taken. After the battle of Lewes the scholars were ordered to return to Oxford, and in 1265 a royal writ ordered the entire cessation of the university of Northampton.

In *Northampton Past and Present*, Volume 2 No.2 (published by the Northamptonshire Record Society) there is an excellent article on the 1264 Battle which is identified as the beginning of the Baron's War

(1264-5) between King Henry III and Simon de Montfort. In this earlier encounter the King's Army attacked the town from the south west and west (over the same water meadows of the later battle). Having drawn most of the defenders of the town to the walls at this apparent danger point a strong body of the King's force under Prince Edward attacked a weak section of the north walls adjacent to St Andrew's Priory. Afterwards there were stories circulating of treachery on the part of the Prior of St Andrew's admitting the King's men but significantly there had been reports in 1258, 1259 and 1260 to indicate that the walls of the town and castle at the point of attack in 1264 were close to collapse and temporary patching with timber had been ordered until more substantial repairs could be put in hand. Other stories alleged that the King was engaged in a parley with the defending forces at the South Gate of the town when the Prince and his friends mounted their attack. Whatever the truth of these stories of foul play the fact was that Northampton was taken and both 'town and gown' suffered for it.

Following the Battle of Lewes in 1265 the King signed a Royal Decree dissolving 'the heretical universities of Northampton' (and Stamford) and directed that the Scholars who had emigrated to Northampton from Oxford and Cambridge should return to their former universities. So ended the short-lived 'University of Northampton' and it is arguable that an Act of Parliament would be needed now to set aside the royal decree if ever there was a proposition to set up a twentieth century university in the town.

Another account of the events of 1264 is set out in *The Story of Northampton* by A. P. White, originally published in 1914 but recently re-issued. This differs in detail from the account quoted above but the means by which the town was taken and the after effects of the battle are confirmed. White says that following the return of the students to their former universities and the dissolution of the University of Northampton a general pardon was issued and that King Henry III (like so many of his predecessors) spent a great deal of time at Northampton Castle. So far as the town was concerned if this was so then it was something of an Indian summer following the great days of Norman and Plantagenet times. The town was heading for decline, confirmed by the consequences of the 1460 Battle and the effects of the plague (the Black Death).

In the Middle Ages for many years 'education' was provided through the monasteries and religious houses, especially so far as the beginnings of academic learning were concerned. 'Training' in the sense of what later became technical or further education, was provided through the apprenticeship system. With the dissolution of the monasteries it became fashionable for Protestant merchants in the days of Queen Elizabeth I to demonstrate their piety and loyalty to the State by founding Grammar Schools, e.g. Thomas Chipsey founded the Northampton Grammar

School in 1541. This School flourished for a limited number of pupils alongside various dame schools in the town and various charity schools (such as the Bluecoat School and the Becketts and Sergeants School). All this schooling was of very mixed quality and the level of academic learning in the town did not amount to anything which could be regarded as higher education until the eighteenth century when for a period the Revd Dr Philip Doddridge ran a Dissenting Academy in Sheep Street for the sons of Nonconformist gentlemen barred from the 'establishment' Anglican Universities of Oxford and Cambridge. But in fact this welcome activity locally merely confirmed the view of the town held by outsiders that Northampton was basically:

— an anti-establishment town;
— a radical town; and
— a Nonconformist town.

The 'apprenticeship' system as it worked in Northampton was coloured by the nature of the staple trade, namely boot and shoe manufacture. Boot and shoe-making had become established in the town during the Civil War but it was very much an individual trade carried on by individual shoe-makers in their own houses. Each would have perhaps one or two apprentices learning the craft and living with the family. William Carey (the Baptist missionary to India and translator of the Bible into Asian tongues) was born in the village of Paulerspury, near Towcester and initially he was apprenticed to Mr Clarke Nichols, a shoe-maker at Hackleton just outside Northampton. There he and a second apprentice shared in the life of the home and the village.

In all this Northampton was little different from many other places until the industrial revolution intervened. The discovery of steam as a source of power and the development of machinery as a means of manufacture coincided with the impact of the agrarian revolution on the economy of the countryside. It meant a movement of population to towns and a concentration there of labour. Factories were built. This new age demanded a literate (or at least semi-literate) work-force in large numbers to work the new machinery and the inadequacies of the educational system, such as it was, were exposed. So called 'Mechanics Institutes' sprung up all over the country and one was started in Northampton in 1832, meeting in rooms at George Row. However, in Northampton this was not a success in the way it was intended to be.

The town was fortunate in that it escaped the evils of the first factories. Boot and shoe manufacturing continued to be carried on by individual shoe-makers working from home. Consequently, the impact of machinery was not felt in Northampton in respect of its then major industry until the latter part of the nineteenth century when factories had become to some degree 'humanised'. So the Northampton Mechanics' Institute became an evening out for non-mechanics – very often just an 'improving' evening lecture for shop assistants, clerical workers and church/chapel goers. There was another problem in that these lectures had to be self-financing. Consequently, they had to have the widest appeal and this often led to superficiality. Moreover, the lectures themselves tended to be discontinuous and unsystematic.

In education terms, therefore, in the first half of the nineteenth century Northampton was 'drifting', since the pressures being experienced in other towns were not felt locally. However what was happening elsewhere was given tremendous publicity by the Great Exhibition in Hyde Park in 1851. Northamptonians travelled to London on the railway and some of these citizens began to wake up. Some of them realised that opportunities were being missed by the town because the local labour-force was so largely untrained. Pressures grew and 'technical' education in Northampton is generally regarded as dating from 1867, when the Museums Committee of the Borough Council (out of very limited and meagre financial resources) inaugurated 'classes' under the guidance of Mr Charles Lees, who at that time was the Headmaster of All Saints' Church of England School.

ALL SAINTS' COLLEGE

I wrote the following in 1889, and I feel sure it appeared in print somewhere. I can give no further particulars. From the communication by J. W. there appear to be two versions as to the period of the immigration of Cambridge students into Northampton.

Where were the Oxford students domiciled when they immigrated to Northampton in the thirteenth century? This question naturally arises on examining the old houses now in course of demolition at the bottom of College Street. It is generally regarded that College Street, formerly College Lane, obtained its name from the fact that the Oxford students' college stood adjacent; but Whellan says that the name came from the proximity of All Saints' College, which was founded in 1459:

'At the south-west end of College Street groined arches were found in some cellars. It has been supposed that this was the site of All Saints' College, from which this lane, recently . . . promoted to the rank of street, derived its appelation.'

Some of these groined arches are now about being demolished, and it is very gratifying to find that they are being carefully drawn by Mr Matthew H. Holding, A.R.I.B.A., Northampton, so that their appearance will be preserved. Even a cursory inspection, however, reveals the fact that they are considerably older that 1459, and the question arises having regard to the situation of these arches, 'Are they a portion of the original college of the thirteenth century?' That a college, if not colleges, was built soon after 1258 is certain, and the period of the arches of College Street – transition between Norman and Early English – coincides with that date.

It is recorded in 'History and Antiquities of Oxford' and in Bridge's History of Northamptonshire, that in 1258 a quarrel broke out among the Oxford students which rose to such a height that a battle was fought outside the city. The following year there were further disturbances and on February 1st, 1260, the king, by licence, granted to the masters and scholars the liberty of removing to Northampton, with permission to erect public schools. By a precept of the same date the mayor and bailiffs of Northampton were directed to receive immigrants with becoming respect, to provide them with what necessaries they should want, and to see that no wrong or injury was offered them. In 1263 more students came an immense multitude in fact, and when the king invested Northampton he found the students very plucky and very harassing foemen. Henry captured the town, the students all hurried back to Oxford, and the king abolished all the privileges he had granted them at Northampton, and ordered that for the future no scholar should be permitted to reside there. Soon afterwards some students from Cambridge settled at Northampton, but owing to the jealousy of Oxford they had to leave.

All Saints' College does not come into existence until nearly two centuries later; and though it might occupy the site, or even the building of all or part of the former college, and that at the 'south-western corner of College Lane,' the crypt at least was not built for All Saints' College. Of course the arches are much older than the rest of the building. The erection on the top of them, whatever it was in 1675, was burnt to the ground in the Great Fire; and the houses now in course of demolition were built subsequent to that.

F.A.W.
Extract from the *Northampton County Magazine*, Vol. 4, 1931, p. 48

'FACTORIES NOW HIDE THE SITE OF A ROYAL PARK'

History is all around us, and in the most unlikely places. Take Moulton Park, a bustling modern industrial estate of box-like factory units. It may be an improbable site for a Royal park, but that is what it was.

Most of the Royal Moulton Park was surrounded by a high stone wall enclosing 450 acres. It followed roughly the line of today's Boughton Lane from near Northampton Lane along the south side of Boughton Green Road to about where Nene College now stands. It then ran almost due south across the area now called Parklands, towards the Kettering Road, near Manfield Hospital. As early as 1250 Henry III issued a writ ordering the sheriff to fence the park and, when done, to inform him of the cost.

Many villages in the county were responsible for a section of the wall and keeping it in good repair. The village name and the length of wall in its care was engraved on stones built into it. Among the 120 villages supposed to look after the wall were Clipston, Crick, Deene, Drayton, Byfield, Litchborough who paid 4d, Walgrave, Cransley, Moulton, Orlingbury, Hannington and 'dyverse other townshippes.'

The wall was important, to keep in the King's deer and other animals. Kings actually stayed at Moulton and two lodges existed in the park. The Great Lodge being roughly where Nene College stands today.

The villagers of Kingsthorpe certainly suffered at the hands of one of the park keepers, Robert Latham. He claimed the rights of freewarren, that is the right to hunt conies and hares on common land outside the estate. To make sure he had a worthwhile bag, he knocked holes in the wall allowing rabbits, etc. to establish themselves in common lands at Kingsthorpe, Moulton and Pitsford. These lands became so infested that beasts were famished and up to a quarter of the corn was eaten. The rabbits even dug a warren in Boughton old church yard, scratching up human bones. Latham was a violent man, too, cutting the throats of villagers' dogs, even when they were on a leash.

It seems the estate went out of Royal ownership during the reign of Charles II and by 1791 was in the hands of the Thursby family, who also owned Abington Manor. From the Thursbys it passed to Lord Lilford, until in 1908, we find it is in the occupation of St Andrew's Hospital. The ancient ivy covered wall still marks the boundary of the estate and some of the stone from the lodges is incorporated in buildings in the area.

Other names also provide a link with the past: there was a shelter in the thicket called Summerhouse Spinney, now Summerhouse Road, and there is still a Deer Park Road.

'County Tales' by Alan Burman,
extract from the *Chronicle & Echo*,
11 September 1985

THE EXPANSION OF THE ENGLISH UNIVERSITIES

In the history of the European universities there have been three great ages of expansion. One was in the twelfth and thirteenth centuries, when universities, as we know them, began, first in Italy and then, soon afterwards, in France, England, Spain and Portugal. In the fifteenth century came a second expansion, different but hardly less remarkable, which involved the creation of more than 30 new universities.[1] Lastly, the past 150 years have seen an even greater development, reaching out from Europe into almost every part of the world. In the course of the nineteenth and twentieth centuries, universities have multiplied and their scope has widened far beyond the conception of any earlier age. And yet, in essentials, many of their ideals and purposes remain the same as those of their earliest predecessors, 800 years ago.

This course of development is strikingly illustrated, on a small scale, in Great Britain. Its two senior universities, Oxford and Cambridge, belong to the first great age of foundation. The fifteenth century brought the establishment of three out of the four Scottish universities – St Andrew's, Glasgow, and Aberdeen; seven major colleges were founded at Oxford and Cambridge between 1429 and

---

[1] See the table in H. Rashdall, *Universities of Europe in the Middle Ages*, ed. F. M. Powicke and A. B. Emden (1936), vol. i p. xxiv.

1496;[2] an effort was made by Owen Glendower to set up universities in Wales. This momentum, indeed, continued. The first half of the sixteenth century saw further lavish foundation of colleges – including the two most magnificent of all, Christ Church and Trinity. Before the century was out there was a fourth university in Scotland, at Edinburgh, of a kind quite new to these islands; and Trinity College, Dublin, had been founded, the first university in Ireland. Then, for more than 200 years, the work of expansion ceased.

It was taken up again in the nineteenth century, with all the accustomed furious energy of that age. When the battle of Waterloo was fought, there were still only two universities in England, seven in the whole United Kingdom. A century later, at the outbreak of the first World War, the two English universities had grown to fifteen (including five university colleges); and in the British Isles altogether the number of university institutions was now 31. Or, to employ another comparison, whilst in 1815 there had been some 2,000 undergraduates in the English universities, in 1914 there were more than 18,000.[3]

Such figures are of no great value, in themselves. They provide nothing more than an outward sign of change. But at least they show that there *was* great change: most striking in England and Wales, but also in Scotland and Ireland. How did so many new universities come to be founded during these years?

Extract from *New University*
by Jack Simmons (Professor of
History in the University of Leicester)

NIGHT SCHOOL IN THE EIGHTEENTH CENTURY

Notice *is hereby given*
THAT THOMAS CRASS, who was six Years Assistant to Mr John Smith, Writing-Master, deceased, and three Years since to his Widow, Joyce Smith, is disengaged from thence, and has opened a School at the Bottom of Saint Giles's Street in this Town; where Youth are taught Writing, Arithmetic both Vulgar and Decimal, Geometry, Surveying, Trigonometry both Plain and Spherical, [Sun] Dialling, Architecture, and other Sciences Mathematical. And he takes this Opportunity of returning Thanks to his Friends for their particular Favours, hoping for the Continuance of the same, which he will endeavour always to merit.
N.B. The said THOMAS CRASS continues his Attendance in the Evenings as usual, that those Artificers and others, who cannot attend in the Day-Time, may learn the above Sciences.
Land survey'd, and neatly plann'd, at reasonable Rates.
Northampton Mercury, 22 March 1762

---

[2] Four more might be added, by including those at Oxford (like St Mary's) that have not survived to the present day: Sir C. E. Mallet, *History of the University of Oxford* (1924–27), i. 405–7.
[3] Sources: *Calendars* of Oxford and Cambridge Universities; *Universities of the United Kingdom* (Board of Education: Educational Pamphlet 33, 1918).

On Friday, the 30th inst. December, will be held at the Dolphin Inn [now the Grand Hotel], in Gold Street, Northampton, A MEETING of SCHOOL-MASTERS, to consult on proper Measures for the Improvement of Knowledge, especially in the conveying Instruction to Youth: Those that please to encourage this Undertaking with their Presence and Advice, will be so good as to be at the said Inn at Ten in the Forenoon of the same Day, bringing with them such Regulations and Articles as they think will tend most to promote useful KNOWLEDGE; that, from their various Schemes, proper Information may be obtained, and such Regulations and Articles made as may best answer the End.

Northampton Mercury, 19 December 1774

MECHANICS' INSTITUTES

Incalculable are the advantages which must inevitably flow from these truly excellent institutions. By means of these the *arcana* of learning are thrown open to all classes of the community; and we are happy to find that this great blessing seems duly appreciated by the inhabitants of Northampton. The *Mechanics' Institute*, situated in the George row, where it occupies commodious premises, which supply the necessary rooms for a library, museum, reading, classes and lectures, was established in 1833, and has for its primary object the dissemination of scientific, mechanical, and other useful knowledge, among the operative classes. This institution is in a more flourishing state than most establishments of the kind in the kingdom, and is liberally supported by the literary gentlemen of the town and neighbourhood. It comprises about 600 members. The library contains about 9,000 volumes, for which the members are indebted to the munificence of John Litchfield, Esq. who at different times has contributed nearly the whole of them, together with a considerable supply of apparatus in the several departments of Mechanics, Electricity, Pneumatics, and Meteorology, and several valuable curiosities for a museum. The library and reading room are open daily; lectures on scientific and other subjects are delivered during the winter season; and mutual improvement classes, in music and the languages, are continued throughout the year. The Most Noble the Marquis of Northampton, who is always foremost in every laudable institution in the county, is the President, Mr William Rice, Secretary, and Mr Wm. Slater Sheppard, Librarian. The amount of subscriptions to this invaluable institution is 1s. 6d. and 2s 6d. per quarter, and a ticket admitting a family, 21s.

'It may not be uninteresting to state,' says a local writer, 'that somewhat more than a century ago, a Philosophical Society existed at Northampton. It originated at a small meeting held September 17th, 1743, by Messrs. S. Paxton, G. Paxton, — Poole, B. Goodman, and — Woolley, who resolved to assemble statedly once a week for improving each other in natural knowledge. The association was soon afterwards joined by Sir Thos. Samwell, Bart., who became the president; Dr Doddridge, John Ferguson, Esq., and Jos. Jekys, Esq., upon which the parties proceeded to a course of philosophical lectures, illustrated by experiments. A report published in the Gentleman's Magazine states:- "Mr Poole, in one of its first meetings after it had grown to any considerable number, entertained the society with some remarks which he made on the comet that appeared in 1743. He has also kept a register of the state of the barometer and of the weather, in order to compute as exactly as possible the quantity of rain which falls here, and to illustrate by comparing the observations of succeeding months and years, how the changes of the barometer correspond to those of the weather. Dr Doddridge also exhibited two papers, the one on the doctrine of pendulums, and other on the laws of the communication of motion, as well in elastic as non-elastic bodies, in which the most material propositions in relation to both were set in so plain and easy a light, that he was requested to transcribe them, and lay them among the papers belonging to the society."'

> Extract from Whelan's *History,*
> *Gazeteer and Directory of*
> *Northamptonshire* (1849)

RELIGIOUS AND USEFUL KNOWLEDGE SOCIETY

This is another useful and interesting institution, formed in 1839, its object as its title implies, being the diffusion of religious and useful knowledge. Its depot in St Giles's Street, contains a library of about 2,500 volumes, a reading room, which is supplied with periodicals, and a small museum. The society consists of about 300 members, who pay, some, 5s., others, 2s. 6d., and a third class (mechanics) 1s. per quarter. Mutual improvement classes, in drawing, writing, music, the languages, &c. are also held here, and the lectures of the society are delivered monthly at All Saints' parochial school room. The Lord Bishop of Peterborough is the President of this society, the Archdeacon of Northampton, Vice-president, P. Phillips, Esq. Secretary, and Mr Charles Wright, Librarian.

> Extract from Whelan's *History,*
> *Gazeteer and Directory of*
> *Northamptonshire* (1849)

RULES OF THE NORTHAMPTON MECHANICS INSTITUTE

As amended at the Quarterly Meeting of the Members, Dec. 30, 1833.

---

1. The object proposed to be obtained is the instruction of the members in the principles of the arts they practise, and in the various branches of science and useful knowledge.
2. That every subscriber of SIX SHILLINGS per annum, ONE SHILLING and SIXPENCE per quarter, or SIXPENCE per month (to be paid in advance), shall be a member of this institution, so long as such subscription be continued.
3. That members making a donation of one pound, and subscribing six shillings per annum, shall, so long as they continue such subscription, be trustees of this institution.

4. That donors of five pounds and upwards, or of approved books or philosophical apparatus to that amount, shall be members of this institution for life.

5. All persons shall be received as members of this Institute upon payment of the subscription as above, and of one shilling as an admission fee.

6. Every annual subscription shall be considered as made on the 1st of January; every quarterly subscription on the 1st of January, April, July, and October; and every monthly subscription on the 1st of every calendar month. Members omitting to renew their subscriptions within fourteen days after they become due will cease to be members; but they may at any time afterwards resume their standing as members on payment of their arrears, or be re-admitted on payment of the admission fee.

7. That every member on paying his subscription shall receive a card, which is an acknowledgement for the contribution paid, and will admit him to all the privileges of the institution. But the members' cards shall be personal, and not transferable.

8. That a library and lecturers be provided under the following regulations:-

1. That a library be formed to consist of such books as may be approved by the committee, after having been submitted to them at two of their meetings.
2. That the library shall consist of two distinct branches – a circulating library, and a library of reference; and that a room be provided for the reception of books and for conducting the business of the institution.
3. That the committee shall have the power of purchasing and exchanging books, and of establishing such regulations as they may deem necessary for affording the members the free use thereof, as far as may consist with their safe keeping and the general convenience.
4. That the committee be empowered to make the requisite arrangements for the delivery of lectures on natural and experimental philosophy, practical mechanics, astronomy, chemistry, literature, and the arts.
5. That not less than twelve lectures be delivered in every year, of which the committee shall give due notice.
6. That persons not being members may be admitted to attend the lectures on such terms of payment as shall be appointed by the committee.

9. That the officers of this institution shall be a president, vice-presidents, treasurer, secretary, a committee of management, and librarian; any vacancy occurring in which offices by death, resignation, or otherwise, is to be supplied by the committee until the next general meeting, when the appointment must be submitted to the sanction of the body of members.

10. That the managing committee shall consist of 20 persons, 10 of whom shall be chosen from the trustees of this institution, and 10 from the general body of members; and five shall be a quorum.

11. That an occasion of the election of any officer of this institution such election shall be by ballot.

12. That the committee shall have the power of expelling any member who may misconduct himself, but the person so expelled shall have a right of appeal to the first general meeting of the institution thereafter.

13. That the committee shall meet every month, on a day appointed by themselves, and the secretary shall summon a special meeting whenever requested to do so by seven members. The secretary shall read at every meeting the minutes of the preceding meeting, and also the propositions, if any, of altering the rules. The committee shall cause the accounts to be made up four times a year, and lay them, together with the minute books and all orders, bills, receipts, and other documents, in the room of the institution, for the inspection of the members, for fourteen days after the quarter day of auditing the accounts.

14. That there be four general meetings in every year, which shall be held the second week in January, April, July, and October; that the business shall commence at eight precisely, and shall on no account be continued later than ten, when, if its business be not finished, the meeting may adjourn. All questions shall be determined by the majority of the members present (by ballot if required by three members), reserving a casting vote to the chairman. But no member shall be entitled to vote while his subscription is in arrear. That the following reports shall be presented at the four quarterly general meetings:-

1. Of the total amount of all moneys received and expended since the last meeting.
2. Of the balance in hand.
3. Of all donations and the names of the donors.
4. The number of new members since the last meeting.
5. The number of persons who have ceased to pay their subscriptions.
6. The total number of members.
7. Of all other matters which the committee of management may be desirous to communicate.

15. That at the meeting in January the officers for the ensuing year shall be appointed, the accounts audited, and the general business of the institution attended to. All payments on account of the institution shall be made by the secretary; who shall pay no money without a draft drawn and certified by three of the committee. The secretary shall collect, or cause to be collected the subscriptions due to the institutions, and shall not retain in his hands more than five pounds, but as often as the sum collected amounts to five pounds, he shall pay it to the treasurer to the account of the institution.

16. That every proposition for altering the rules and orders be in writing, and signed by at least 10 members of six months' standing – that it be delivered to the secretary at least one calendar month before the day on which the next quarterly general meeting be held, and be immediately copied by him and hung up in the public room of the institution.

17. That every proposition for altering the rules and orders which shall be carried at any quarterly general meeting, be copied by the secretary, and hung up in the public room of the institution until the next quarterly general meeting, when if again carried it will be incorporated with the rules and orders.

18. That no resolution for breaking up the institution, or alienating any part of its property, shall be passed unless it is not only proposed in the manner above provided, but consented to at two general meetings by at least nine-tenths of the members present, in which case the property shall not be sold, but given over to some similar institution elsewhere.

NORTHAMPTON & NORTHAMPTONSHIRE

MECHANICS' INSTITUTE.

SIR,

I am directed to inform you, that owing to a considerable falling off in the Single Subscriptions since the terms of Subscription were raised, it has been deemed advisable by the Committee to pass a resolution, by which Mechanics, Artizans, Working Men, Apprentices, Shopmen, and Young Persons under 16 years of age, will, from 24TH JUNE NEXT, be entitled to all the advantages of the Institute, on payment of an Annual Subscription of 4s., payable quarterly, or of 3s. if paid in advance.

The Committee would take this opportunity of urging upon the friends of the Institute the importance of their liberally subscribing to its funds, in order that its design may be more fully carried out, and the means of Mental Culture placed within the reach of the poorest of the Working Classes.

With this view, the Chairman of the Committee, JOHN BECKE, Esq., has liberally offered £5 as a Prize to the Working Men of the Institute, for the best Essay on the following subject :—

"SCIENCE AND LITERATURE THE HANDMAIDS OF RELIGION."

In addition to this Prize, the Committee, *on their own account*, offer £3 and £2 for the Second and Third best Prizes on the same subject.

The conditions to be observed by those who may become Competitors are as follows :—

1. "No person will be entitled to compete but *Mechanics and Working Men*, resident in the Town and County of Northampton, who are either already Members of the Institute or shall have become so by Midsummer next.

2. "The Essays must be sent in by the 25TH DECEMBER, enclosed in a sealed cover, and signed with initials, or in cypher only, each Essay being accompanied with a sealed letter, stating the name and address of the Essayist, and containing a counterpart of the initial signature. The letter to be addressed to the Chairman of the General Annual Meeting."

The Rev. C. H. HARTSHORNE, J. E. RYLAND, Esq., and Mr. DE WILDE have kindly consented to act as Adjudicators, and their decision will be declared at the next Annual Meeting.

WILLIAM RICE, Secretary.

Northampton, May 12th, 1852.

N.B. The Library and Reading Room are now open daily from 10 a.m. to 10 p.m.

2 The College of Technology

Derek Brooks

The industrial revolution did not give rise immediately to a similar surge in the sphere of education in general, or technical instruction in particular, in the early part of the nineteenth century. Demand was there but it remained inarticulate. In addition, there was a craft hierarchy whereby the skilled craftsmen would only transmit their accumulated skill and knowledge to their own apprentices. They did not wish labourers to become craftsmen.

However, as early as 1800 lectures were being given at the Anderson Institution in Glasgow by George Birkbeck and later by his successor Ure. Their aim was to give artisans some scientific and theoretical background to the work in which they were involved. By 1823 several Mechanics' Institutions were established, and were the forerunners of the Institutes of Technical Education. Indeed some of them grew directly into Technical Institutes, notably that in Birmingham, and one more locally at Wolverton. By 1850 there were 610 Mechanics' Institutes in this country with a membership of over half a million. Unfortunately, the lack of general education seriously hampered them. They lost their artisan flavour and became instruments of the clerical and middle class. Many are remembered only by their libraries, often their most important contribution to the growth of technical education.

An early move in the history of technical education was the inspiration of William Ewarts, MP for Liverpool, and his Select Committee of 1835. This committee was established to enquire into the best means of extending knowledge of the arts and principles of design among the people. Their report prompted a government grant, and a School of Design was established in Somerset House in 1837. Other schools of design were later established, which at first were under the direction of the Board of Trade, and prepared for examinations run by the Society of Arts.

The Great Exhibition held at the Crystal Palace in Hyde Park was the mirror which reflected not only the industrial power of this country, but also showed to thinking men the technical illiteracy of the bulk of industry's manpower. Schools of Design came under the aegis of a new department, the Department of Science and Art, which grew directly from the Exhibition and came into being in 1852–3. It was merged into the Department of Education in 1857. Another important venture arising directly from the 1851 Exhibition was the School of Mines, which opened in South Kensington in 1851.

After 1851 the impact of the industrial revolution was really felt. Nevertheless, the changes were made reluctantly and it took time for the reverberations to take effect since technical education was contrary to the Victorian 'self help' ideals. In the early years progress was slow; few classes were started prior to 1859 and even the School of Mines had only fourteen full-time students and fifty-one part-timers.

The structure of classes was altered radically in 1859 by a new minute whereby the Department of Science and Art allowed classes to be established anywhere in suitable buildings, provided the local municipal authority contributed an amount equal to the grant made by the Science and Art Department. Classes could be in geometry, mechanical drawing, building construction, physics, chemistry and natural history, and were to be aimed at the working classes. Annual examinations were a condition of the classes, and indeed successful results were essential for extra payments for the teachers. Classes were started by Mechanics Institutes, by local library committees, and various *ad hoc* bodies. The scheme began in 1860 with thirty classes and 1,340 candidates, and by 1873 had grown to 1,182 classes and 24,674 candidates. Among these were early classes in Northampton, where like few other towns, the school of science was formed within the framework of an endowed grammar school.

Tuition under this system was stale and unimaginative. Classes were entirely theory and demonstrations, and no practical work was included. Indeed the Royal Committee on Technical Instruction of 1884 heard much evidence that the instruction did not meet the needs of the artisan.

The 1870 Education Act removed the big impediment to the growth of technical education in that it created a basis for a more literate population. With machines becoming more refined and trade more competitive, it became necessary for workers to be more technically efficient. As a result technical education expanded.

In the year 1860 Northampton adopted the Public Libraries Act but because of the smallness of income produced by the penny rate allowed by the Act, only a museum was opened at first. Notwithstanding, thoughts of science and art classes were in the air; but when a representative of the government Science and Art Department came to the town in 1862, there was such a small audience to listen to him that no action was taken.

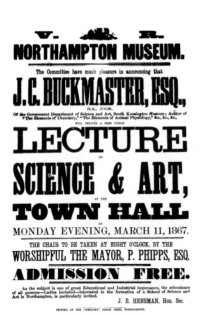

1 The advertisement for the 1867 Public Meeting which led to the establishment of the art and science classes, the forerunners of technical education locally.

2 The old Technical School and Grammar School buildings on Abington Square

3 The Technical School when it was situated on Abington Square. Also seen is Mutton's book and paper-shop and further along the Bantam Cock Hotel. The gap between the College and the Hotel was used as a playground for the pupils of the Grammar School and the junior members of the College

4 The old School of Art in Abington Street, Northampton (from a print in the possession of Mr Victor Hatley)

5 Beeby Thompson, FCS, FGS, a former student of the Technical School and later a master of the Technical College

6 Osborne Robinson, OBE, an old student, theatre designer and local celebrity who presented his Poster Collection to the College of Art

7 Alderman S. S. Campion, DL, JP, HF

8 Keightley Cobb, LRIBA (Architect of the St George's Avenue premises)

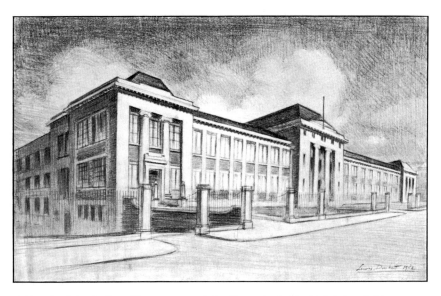

9 Sketch of the College Frontage as originally projected by Keightley Cobb

10 The Duke and Duchess of York with the Mayor (Councillor P. F. Hanafy) at the Opening Ceremony, 17 November 1932

11 The College of Technology and School of Art before the College Frontage was added in 1961

12 John Blakeman, MA, MSc,
Principal of the College of
Technology, 1911–41

13 Oliver Bailey, BSc, MIEE,
Principal of the College of
Technology, 1941–55 (from the
painting by G. B. H. Holland)

Four Principals

14 Eric Jewitt, BSc(Eng), MIEE,
Principal of the College of
Technology, 1955–73

15 Arthur Beavan, ARCA, ATD,
Principal of the School/College of
Art, 1949–75 and Assistant Director
of Nene College, 1975–77

16 An ATS clerical training class (standing on the right at the back of the class is Miss L. G. Redley)

17 Room D.11 and D.10 in use for a Ministry of Labour training scheme for centre lathe turners

18 Training radio mechanics

19 The 'NORTEKS' Concert Party with Myer Cipin as the Schoolmaster (playing the drums is Mr Wilf Sharman, one of the senior staff members at the College in the 1940s)

20 Jack Longland with the Mayor and Mayoress (Councillor Mrs E. E. Wilkinson and Miss C. Causebrook), Alderman Arthur Chown and Mr H. A. Skerrett on 26 January 1961 on the occasion of the opening of the College of Technology frontage

21 The completed frontage to St George's Avenue in 1961

Five years later on the evening of 11 March 1867 a meeting was held at the Town Hall in Northampton under the auspices of the Museum Committee. The speaker was J. C. Buckmaster Esq., BA, FSS, of the South Kensington Government Department. He was to deliver a public lecture on science and art. The Mayor was in the chair and admission was free. This lecture was well attended and the speaker was cheered.

What had happened in the period between the two meetings? Interest in technology had been fired. Machinery, once the problem of other industries, had now reached the boot and shoe industry, and had obviously come to stay. There had been an abortive strike against the first machines in the town in 1859 but over a thousand machines were in use by 1864. This then was the incentive for the attendance at the meeting in 1867.

By September posters were published and classes advertised in the local papers. The science classes were in magnetism and electricity and commenced on Tuesday, 8 October 1867, meeting in committee room No.9 at the Town Hall. They met on Tuesdays and Thursdays, the Junior Class from 7.15 to 8 p.m. and the Senior Class from 8.15 to 9 p.m.

'Fees for Junior Artizan Classes are fixed at one penny per week and for Adult Artizan Classes at 6d. per month payable in advance.' The science teacher was Mr Charles Lees, a certificated science teacher, who was also at the time Headmaster of All Saints' School, Northampton. Examinations were to follow in May 1868, with prizes for successful students according to the standard – Queen's Prizes, medals, honorary certificates and scholarships to the government School of Mines.

Drawing classes were similarly established, under the direction of Mr Abram S. Taylor, Keeper of the Museum, who was also a certificated drawing master. Classes were to be held in the Grammar School Rooms at the Corn Exchange on Mondays, Wednesdays, Thursdays and Fridays, with fees of one shilling per month. Instruction was in freehand drawing, geometry, perspective, model and mechanical drawings, flower painting and painting in oils and water colours.

The classes got off to a good start. The rate provided ample equipment for both classes, before the public library was opened, and the salaries of the teachers were paid out of the grant for the classes from the central government. During the first season, the science classes had sixty-five senior students and fifty junior students, and there was a total of eighty-five altogether in the art classes. The first prize-giving took place on 31 October 1868, when Earl Spencer presented the awards. For a new school the results were excellent. Of the thirty-two senior students who presented themselves for examination, twenty-eight were successful – nine first class, thirteen second class, five third class and one fourth class. One student, Mr Beeby Thompson, took a bronze medal and was placed third in the United Kingdom. Six juniors were successful out of twenty-seven examined in science. According to the examiner, Professor Tyndall, they made the mistake of choosing the harder questions. In art thirty-five pupils submitted papers and together collected forty-one passes. The age range was 13–32 years.

The classes changed their venues several times in the course of the next few years, meeting in All Saints' School, St Giles' Working Men's Club, the Corn Exchange and the Trade School, Waterloo. The science classes broadened their scope in these years too. In 1869, heat, light and sound were taught and the following year inorganic chemistry and physiography. The inorganic chemistry classes were not popular with council officials because pungent smells often filtered down to the public part of the building. Beeby Thompson, himself the star pupil of the first year, was awarded a Whitworth Scholarship tenable at the School of Mines in South Kensington.

In 1870 Mr Lees, the science teacher, who could see the popular movement growing, broke away from the Museum Committee classes and, believing in private enterprise, established on his own account a Trade School. This met in a large room in the Mechanics' Institute at the Corn Exchange. The classes were a success from the start, and Beeby Thompson became assistant to Mr Lees, so beginning his teaching career. This private 'Trade School' soon required room for expansion, and was removed to premises in Waterloo, Northampton. The Museum's science classes were also held there from 1874 onwards. There was far more room here and individual experiments could be performed in addition to the lecture-demonstrations.

NORTHAMPTON SCIENCE SCHOOLS

By 1876 the Waterloo College, as it was then called, had begun to decline in popularity, possibly because Beeby Thompson had left two years previously to go to Truro School. That year the science classes were removed to the Grammar School on Abington Square, and a master in charge was to be appointed. His duties were to include science teaching in the Grammar School as well as the evening classes. Beeby Thompson successfully applied for the post. He supervised the fitting out of the science extension, the art classes were housed in a large upstairs room under the direction of Mr Henry Hill, and a new chapter in the story of technical education in Northampton began. Science was really in vogue. Lectures and soirées were held as fund-raising efforts, and new equipment bought with the money received. The rooms at the Town Hall now known as the Upper and Lower Assembly Rooms were used for 'Museum' purposes and the Curator's office (without benefit of any ventilation or fume cupboard) doubled at night as a chemistry laboratory.

In 1879 there was a new departure; classes in the principles of agriculture were held under the auspices of the local Chamber of Agriculture. These later spread into the County and were very successful, but science and art department regulations restricted them under government subsidy.

The Public Libraries Act had in fact led only to a Museum in Northampton, but there were several important developments in the following years. In 1876 the Library of the Mechanics' Institute was handed over to the town, and this formed the nucleus of the first Public Library. The following year it was decided to make this a free lending library and a librarian was appointed. In 1884 the Museum and Library were removed from the Town Hall to a new building in Guildhall Road and a year later the library of the Religious and Useful Knowledge Society was added. All of this meant added expense. The more spent on the Museum and Library, the less was available for science and art classes, and eventually there was no rate subsidy available for the classes. At this time the head of the art classes resigned, and Mr Alfred A. Bradbury from Derby was appointed.

Technical education in Northampton might well have died a premature death had it not been for the advent in 1885 of the scheme introduced by the City and Guilds of London Institute, whereby a system of examinations and payment by results was introduced in trade subjects. What more natural than that this scheme should apply to the boot and shoe trade? There was much opposition from the Museums and Libraries Committee, but Mr S. S. Campion and Mr Philip (later Sir Philip) Manfield managed to push it through.

The classes in boot, shoe and tanning subjects got under way in the autumn of 1885. The first year there were 171 entries, eighty-one students entered the examinations and forty-three passed. There were fifteen pupils in tanning subjects. The syllabus was extended to include plumbing in 1887. There were only seven entered for the examinations but five passed, one with a bronze medal. The small nature of the success in these early classes was due largely to opposition by both employers, who did not want educated employees, and craftsmen's unions, who wished to transmit craft secrets in apprenticeship not in the classroom. The classes pressed on under the general direction of Beeby Thompson and achieved moderate success. The science classes had continued as indeed had the art classes, but both lacked space for their work. Statistics for 1888 show 300 in science classes, 395 art students and seventy-two in the technical classes. This was a good year in which third prize in the whole country was won for science, a first prize in boot and shoe subjects and a second prize in tanning.

In 1889 the Technical Institute Act was passed by Parliament, and at the Technical School prize-giving the guest of honour, the Right Hon.

A. J. Mundella MP, pressed for its adoption by the town council. The implementation of this Act could mean up to 1d. on the rates which was discouraging to the Town Council. There was indeed active opposition. Only the fact that the Local Government (Customs and Excise) Act* was passed in 1890 saved the day, and the classes, in Northampton – although many firms (Manfields, Randalls, Allinson, Crockett and Jones among them) had already tabled a motion to give financial assistance themselves.

In 1891 the Act was adopted in the town and the first 'whisky money' amounted to £384.11s.8d. For the first time the Heads of the Science and Arts Schools had a salary – £150 per year, plus a proportion of the grants earned. The Museums and Gymnasia Act of 1891 also helped to improve the finances, and the sums allocated to the technical classes were: boot, shoe and tanning, £60; plumbing, carpentry and joinery and brickwork and masonry, £25; each. All this and a Technical Instruction Act Committee to exercise general supervision.

Several important events took place in 1892, which were to shape the course of Technical Education. Mr E. J. Swaysland came to work for the County Council, and was immediately secured by Beeby Thompson to teach the boot and shoe classes in the town. Mr Bradbury the Art Headmaster left, and no new appointment was made. Instead Beeby Thompson was made Director of the Science, Art and Technical Schools. Allied to this, but not directly connected, was the move to change the Grammar School into a Modern and Technical School. Possibly it was this change which led to the departure of the Headmaster Dr Sanders, who returned to the Church. No new appointment was made there either. Amid all this change, a science school Students Association was formed.

The master in charge of the Grammar School dropped all science from the curriculum, and Beeby Thompson was allowed to concentrate on his own classes. He now had a staff of eighteen teachers, most of them part-time, six for science, three for art, eight in technology and one in languages. The classes, now under the control of the governors of the new Northampton and County Modern and Technical School, flourished in 1894, and from the point of view of the evening classes it was the most successful year since their inception. There were over 500 students, not counting commercial classes, and over 900 entries in examinations. In boot and shoe subjects alone there were forty-three entries and forty-three passes. The Swaysland touch!

---

* The grant made in support of Technical Education under the Act was colloquially known as 'whisky money'. In the budget of 1890 the Government imposed a duty of 6d. a gallon on spirits with a view to using the monies so raised to compensate licence-holders of public houses declared to be redundant. The temperance groups opposed this and eventually the idea of compensation was dropped. the duty, however, had been voted and it was decided that the revenue should be passed on to Local Authorities in support of technical education instead.

On to the scene came the new Headmaster of the School – Mr R. Elliott Steele MA. The staff of the school was amalgamated with that of the evening classes, and both were required to teach day and evening lessons. Beeby Thompson could not tolerate the change and left teaching to found a new, and as it turned out, more glorious career.

THE NORTHAMPTON AND COUNTY TECHNICAL AND MODERN SCHOOL

This school was in fact the result of an amalgamation of the Science and Art Department classes, and an established endowed grammar school, which traced its history back to 1541. The new school was administered under a scheme sanctioned by Charity Commissioners and 'approved by Her Majesty in Council on 28th May 1894'. The school opened in September 1894.

The Headmaster, Mr R. Elliott Steele, MA, FRGS, FCS, was a typical Victorian classicist with very rigid ideas about schools and external examinations (unlike his predecessor Dr Sanders). He organised the whole range of classes. The Day School consisted of three departments. A junior school for 9–12 year olds, and a senior school in two sections. One section specialised in classical subjects and the other in modern subjects, that is commercial and science subjects. Fees were six guineas per annum for three terms. Hours were from 9 to 12.40 and 2.25 to 5.0 except Thursday and Saturday afternoons. There were some 110 boys in the school, some of whom, to the Headmaster's regret, only stayed for a year. The school studied for Science and Art Department examinations and the Oxford Local examinations. It was a typical 'would-be public school' institution.

The former Technical School was now reorganised in four departments – Science, art, technological and commercial – and it was compulsory to work for the South Kensington examinations. Classes were held in the evenings and on Saturdays and fees were five shillings per subject up to a £1 maximum for evening instruction, and Saturday classes were five shillings per session for one class, seven shillings and sixpence for two and ten shillings for any number. It was expected that the Saturday classes would consist largely of teachers from elementary schools. Certainly the classes got off to a good start, and by the commencement of the third session 1896–7 there were 297 science students, 312 in art, 165 in technology and 154 in the commercial classes. By this time it was established that the South Kensington Departmental examinations were taken in science and art, City and Guilds of London Institute examinations for technology and Society of Arts examinations for commerce. A little later pre-technical classes were begun, which aimed to prepare younger students for City and Guilds courses.

Judged on examination results Elliott Steele was a fine headmaster, but he was certainly a most autocratic one and his period of headship was violent and stormy. He interfered and argued with everyone – his pupils, their parents, his staff, the governors and even the local church dignitaries. In 1900 the inspector declared the school to be totally unsuited to technical school work, but expansion of the classes went on. By this time it was generally known as Northampton and County Technical School, and was a thriving institution in spite of overcrowding. There were added ladies' day classes in needlework, embroidery and wood-carving, and women's evening classes in dressmaking and domestic economy. The early years of this century however proved difficult ones, particularly for the day school. Numbers rose to 185 by 1903 and the building was bursting at the seams. Efforts to expand were frustrated by the failure of the Charity Commission to sanction any plans. In 1903 also the evening schools had a most unsatisfactory report following an inspection. 'The classroom accommodation was inadequate and the laboratory accommodation unsatisfactory from every point of view.' From 1904 onwards there were repeated complaints from the Board of Education about the Abington Square premises, and pressure was exerted to get the town authorities to move on secondary education; indeed in 1906 a threat was made to close the secondary school section. The following year the authority were virtually instructed to re-organise the boys secondary school and to do something about a secondary school for girls and that if they failed the Board of Education would withdraw recognition of the pupil teacher centre it now contained. In January 1907 Elliott Steele was asked to resign – a scapegoat possibly.

Through all this furore the Evening Technical College carried on. It regrouped itself, spontaneously apparently, since no one was appointed in charge, although it is certain that Swaysland had some say in matters. In 1907 it became the Northampton and County Technical and Art School, with the School of Art functioning separately under art master George C. Duxbury, ARCA, from London. The School of Art moved into separate rented premises at 100A Abington Street and the following year the institution became officially the Northampton and County Technical School and School of Art.

Plans finally were made. The Grammar School was to have a new building in Billing Road and a girls grammar school was to be built. Under these plans, the Abington Square Building was to become a Municipal Technical Institution and School of Art. Inspector W. B. Dallas Edwards inspected the technical classes in 1910 and made several points. A principal was required as the classes had had no head since Elliot Steele's departure. He suggested that a science graduate was desirable. Research into local industry was necessary in order to relate the work of the technical institution to its requirements and he thought that local manufacturers might help here, both in the supply of teachers (skilled technicians) and with the loan of machinery. Classes must cater for not only the boot and shoe industry and tanning, but for engineering too, and chemistry was essential for all of these. The buildings he considered totally unsuitable for the classes that were held and for the 604 students in the 1910 session. He advised the authority to build a new technical school in instalments, quoting the example of Leicester. In answer the authority proposed to appoint a principal at a salary of £250–£300 per annum, and to re-erect the Park Avenue Temporary School (a corrugated iron structure) at the rear of the Abington Square Schools, as a temporary solution to the overcrowding. This was to house the boot and shoe classes.

In 1911 the Grammar School moved to its new premises in Billing Road, and the Abington Square buildings became wholly technical in their content. The new principal of the Technical School was appointed, a Mr John Blakeman, MA, MSc, who was to be 'at the helm' for over thirty years. The building was refurnished, the laboratories refitted, a prospectus printed and the telephone installed. The staff consisted of some forty part-timers, teaching from 1½ to 6 hours per week; Edward Swaysland was head of the boot and shoe department. The other main sections were engineering, building and commerce, and in addition there was a wide range of single subjects such as chemistry, vehicle body building, typography and special grocery trade classes.

By 1912 Blakeman was getting the school running to his liking. A building trades instructor was appointed and grouped course certificates introduced based on three subject groupings, with performance, attendance and homework counting for the award. The prize system introduced did not greatly differ from before i.e. medals and prizes of the City and Guilds, the Royal Society of Arts and the Midland Counties Union. In addition there were Royal Scholarships and Whitworth Scholarships awarded by the Board of Education and the Dennis Prizes, in memory of the former Mayor of Northampton, three in number, one each for Boot and Shoe, Commerce and Engineering. Blakeman also had ideas of incorporating the evening schools into his technical system and proposed drawing up the syllabus for all evening school work, and completely altering the science teaching, which he considered poor. This was in fact done and many courses, particularly in the commercial section were reorganised. Applied science became essential to the boot and shoe classes too. In addition a Preparatory Technical School was established at St James' on an experimental basis, probably because St James' had proved a successful venue for technical classes earlier. This was part of the liaison with the shoe industry deemed so essential by the Committee. Another example the following year was the establishment of classes for GPO engineers.

Blakeman was obsessed with his idea of grouped courses, and it was not long before the City and Guilds examinations were being made an option, except for the teachers' handwork course which was introduced in 1912. In fact, the boot and shoe course in 1913 and the following year took the County Council examination. Certainly by 1915 the only examination taken was the grouped course certificate awarded by the Northampton Borough Education Committee. External examinations as such did not return to the prospectus until the 1924-5 session, when the pride of place was given to the examination of the East Midlands Education Union (EMEU), although City and Guilds National Certificates and Royal Society of Arts were also included. Blakeman was one of the architects of the EMEU and was bound to support its (his) examination system.

Blakeman was still far from satisfied however; he said of technical education in the town 'As regards the education of the working class in Northampton, the outstanding feature is the deplorable lack of advanced instruction. There is very little work done at the Technical School of a higher standard than would be found in the best continuation schools in the country.'

The war years 1914-18 caused difficulties for the school, but even if the evening school population went down owing to the exigencies of the armed services the loss was balanced by the introduction of 'time off' classes for young people in Northampton industries. Although these early classes were on a small scale they meant that the Fisher Act was anticipated by three years. The 'time off' scheme allowed young people of 14-16 years of age and in the boot and shoe trade an early release from work, without loss of pay, for those who were going to the Evening Continuation Schools. Day release proper, half a day at the Technical School without loss of pay, was introduced in 1918.

The day continuation scheme was the composite so dear to Blakeman's heart: the complete interdependence of the Technical School and the evening schools. Under this original day-release scheme attendance was at the Technical School for the day-time classes, but also for one or more evenings at the evening continuation school to cover the full pre-technical course. All boys under 16 years had to attend one half-day a week from 8 am to 12.15 pm and took an artisan course in either boot and shoe or engineering and allied trades. There was also a commercial and general course. The continuation schools ran complementary courses in the evenings, and also catered for girls with either clerical or domestic grouped courses. Any need for art was allowed for on Thursday evening special classes at the Art School. This system was to remain virtually unchanged from 1918 until the end of the Second World War.

The influx of ex-servicemen for refresher and training courses in boot and shoe repair and hand-sewn shoe making under the Ministries of Labour and Pensions schemes began in 1918. Up to 200 were trained at a time under these schemes. Again the school was filled to capacity, and to alleviate the situation a small factory in St Michael's Road, backing on to the technical buildings, was purchased and set up as a small tannery and boot and shoe instructional factory. As a result other courses could expand, particularly engineering, which had become really well established in the town as a result of the war. With full-time staff appointed to the boot and shoe department, it was only logical that full-time courses would follow. They did in 1919 and have since received world-wide recognition. It was in this year too that the first, premature, signs of a new building for technical education were seen, when a memorandum was drawn up by Alderman S. S. Campion suggesting a site in St George's Avenue.

The teaching staff of the school was strengthened considerably in 1921 when Mr D. Woodroffe, MSc, was appointed to the staff on a full-time basis. He was a science graduate from Leeds, and was made head of the leather department with a watching brief on the boot and shoe section also, but the boot and shoe department had become a 'pet' of the Principal and in fact no exclusive head of that department was ever appointed under Blakeman. The 1920s were years of steady work and progress. Blakeman found his ideas of closer liaison with industry reaching fruition. The Shoe and Allied Trade Research Association was formed at this time (1919–20) and took up its headquarters in the Technical School with the Principal as Hon. Secretary. He was a leading light in its organisation, as he was in the British Boot and Shoe Institution foundation in 1927–29.

The shoe industry made day continuation a condition of employment. The School undertook experiments for industry, in particular metal testing in the engineering department. This department expanded rapidly. Industry lent equipment, and a heat engine laboratory was established. The leather department expanded to cover the study of heavy leathers and did successful research into chrome tanning; the commercial department entered for London Matriculation for the first time, and two more branch technical schools were set up at St George's School and the Kettering Road School. To combat the unemployment at the time classes for the unemployed were operated. They were generally successful, and the women's classes in closing were reported guilty of 'unsatisfactory behaviour'. A further strengthening of the full-time teaching staff was made with the appointment of Mr O. F. Bailey to full-time teaching duties in 1924. There were on roll that year some 1,931 students, including nineteen full-time day students in the boot, shoe and leather department. Reports of HMIs in this decade showed two distinct trends; increasing satisfaction with the work and examination results, and increasing dissatisfaction with conditions and accommodation in the school. Plans for a new college were in the open now, and Blakeman was designated principal. In readiness for this the name was changed to the Northampton Technical College. In fairness, it was a title that was fully justified on the examination results. Students were reaching inter-degree standard regularly and many obtained professional qualifications in pharmacy and banking. The percentage of passes in the City and Guilds Leather examinations were greater than those for the rest of the country and the boot and shoe department had gained highest awards every year since 1915. At lower levels classes were being added at the request of industry – gas fitting, butchery, bakery (held in a local bakers) – and classes were recommended for teachers' handicraft certificate examinations. There were successes in the National Certificate in Electrical Engineering too.

In 1924 the Education Committee secured a site for a new Technical College in St George's Avenue at a cost of £7,000. By 1928 plans for the proposed buildings had been drafted and eventually the tender of Messrs Glenn and Sons amounting to £79,850 for the first phase of the scheme was accepted. An additional £24,000 was to be spent on equipment and machinery.

Work began in February 1931 and on 3 December 1931 foundation stones were laid by Councillor James Peach, Alderman S. S. Campion (the last survivor of the 1890 Technical Instruction Act Committee) and by the then Councillor (later Alderman) A. W. Lyne. Because of the financial recession, Geddes' Axe had been applied and the original scheme had been substantially modified. Instead of a complete College of Technology and Art being ordered, only the Technology section was to be built, and even this was to be without certain features such as assembly hall and administration block. Contracts were eventually placed and the new Northampton Technical College was opened by the Duke and Duchess of York on 17 November 1932. The town was *en fête* for the occasion, and the newspaper resounded with eulogistic phrases, about the new building in St George's Avenue, of hopes for university status, and other castles in the air.

Certainly the new building raised Northampton from the bottom of the secondary education league in that one of the first material benefits was a Junior Technical School. This recruited from the intermediate schools largely, and commenced with a first entry of thirty-one boys and nine girls. Mr O. F. Bailey assumed responsibility for this side of the Technical College, ably assisted by a new appointment, Mr P. F. Tomkins, in charge of general subjects. The boys and girls were pledged to certain technical departments, but all received their general education together. They also had the use of a new library presented by the Northampton Footwear Manufacturers Association.

A return to depression in Northampton in 1933 led to classes for the unemployed again, but these were held in the old Technical School on

Abington Square and consisted largely of classes in boot and shoe repair. Examination results that year were very good. The top honours were seven Ordinary National Certificates, two students to Nottingham University College, two gained Inter-BSc (London), two Silver Medals and one Bronze in City and Guilds Finals, and one Advanced Course Prize in the Royal Society of Arts Examinations. Despite these results, or because of them, in 1934 Intermediate City and Guilds examinations were dropped, and the Authority's own Craftsman's Certificate was substituted.

The Unemployment Act of 1934 stipulated that there was to be an extension of the provision of classes for the unemployed. All boys had to attend day classes, and girls were directed to evening continuation schools. There were not many in Northampton affected by this law, and it was largely avoided by insisting that no young persons be allowed to leave school until they had a job to go to. Demand was so small in Northampton in fact that the unemployed classes were dropped in 1935, and the few persons affected were incorporated in the day-release classes.

It had been obvious for some time, particularly to the inspectorate, that the large thriving boot and shoe department needed a full-time head of department. The Principal was still reluctant to part with this sphere of influence, and effected a compromise by appointing the head of the leather department to be head of the boot and shoe department also. In order to relieve him somewhat for his new duties he was given a full-time assistant in the leather department. Woodroffe inherited some trouble with his new responsibilities. All was not well in the boot and shoe education sphere. The day-release system was not receiving the full backing of the industry and had become ineffectual. There was a general reluctance among parents to let their brighter children enter the shoe trade, and there was a new Education Act (1939) in the drafting stage. The outcome of these difficulties was that a deputation from the College went to the shoe manufacturers. As a result of this deputation the manufacturers agreed to release their 14–16 year olds on two half days per week. This system began very successfully and by 1938 there were ninety-eight boot and shoe day-continuation students, forty-five boys and fifty-three girls. They did half-time trade training in their own factory trades and half-time general education. This for the boys consisted of English, calculations, drawing and science, and for the girls arithmetic, English, needlework and cookery.

It was clear that Blakeman was greatly preoccupied with the general lack of education among young people, for in 1937 he proposed the abolition of all National Certificate Courses in favour of an all-out assault on adolescent general education, but to maintain courses for professional bodies and general courses for EMEU and RSA. This was the direct result of a disagreement with the Board of Education, and National Certificates did not reappear in the prospectus until 1945.

In spite of the success of the day-continuation classes, 1938 proved a very unsettled year. Enrolment was 1,721 students including 165 Junior Technical School (JTS) students and 133 day-continuation students. The state of international affairs was depressing, but there certainly was positive progress. The Northampton Chamber of Commerce provided an advisory committee for the Commerce Department, and Nottingham University commented favourably on the graduates from the College. On the debit side, however, instructions on blackout and air-raid precautions were issued, enquiries as to accommodation for evacuated institutions were made, and classes requested for Royal Air Force reservists, and some instruction for members of the Women's Land Army. In 1939 the portents were grave: the only new class started was one in English for refugees.

THE WAR PERIOD, 1939–45

In September 1939, the storm burst, and the College swung straight into a new role as part of the war effort. The buildings begun in 1938 were hurriedly finished, basements and bicycle sheds were utilised for instruction, and although the true student population dropped to 639 senior students, 139 day-continuation and 184 JTS students the military moved in for the duration. The racecourse opposite the College became a hut and canvas barracks (known as Talavera Barracks) and many empty houses in the vicinity were requisitioned.

The first military class was an intensive class to produce twenty vehicle mechanics for the Northamptonshire Yeomanry, the local Territorial Army armoured regiment. The military were not the only interlopers: the College was also the billet for some 414 secondary school evacuees as well. The year 1940 saw the retirement of the deputy principal Mr W. Chater, MSc. O. F. Bailey stepped into the breach, and in November 1941, the Principal, John Blakeman, was forced to retire for health reasons. Bailey became Acting Principal, since Alderman W. Percival (the Chairman of the Education Committee) was not prepared to advise the Local Authority to make a permanent appointment in war-time conditions.

The pace of the special war-time classes stepped up early in 1941. The War Office trainees came in batches of fifty-four at a time. They were turned into carpenters, fitters or electricians in the shortest possible time. Much of the training comprised the basics of electrical engineering in order to produce technicians who understood the elementary principles behind the development of radar. A two-shift day and a six-day week was the routine, and at any one time in 1940–1 there were 285 students going through the process. The engineering department also was producing results, for in addition to the War Office students they processed up to forty-five persons at a time, converting them into lathe turners as quickly as possible. In the commerce department, women in uniform were becoming clerks. The boot and shoe students were producing ARP gloves and Army leggings, the domestic students were making nurses' uniforms, RAF pilots and observers were taking special mathematics courses, instrument mechanics courses were tucked away in an odd corner, teachers were directed to the College alongside military instructors and experts of all description. At one time during 1941 there were between 600 and 700 War Office trainees undergoing instruction at the Technical College, yet amidst all this confusion the Junior Technical School continued its way, now under the able direction of Mr P. Tomkins.

This scene of controlled frenzy persisted throughout 1942, when statistics show that output was 8,950 students hours per week. Of course it was generally speaking a 52 hours, six-day week for adults. Yet even within this total there was provision for leisure activities for some 200 soldiers stationed locally, and classes were provided in commercial subjects, automobile and electrical engineering and woodwork. At a less intensive level also twenty-four officer cadets started a two-year Army engineers' course.

By 1943 the pace was allowed to slacken somewhat. The production unit, which produced lathe turners as well as turned material, closed down having put 282 men and women into war factories as efficient craft workers. With this closure, day-continuation classes in engineering had room to function and these classes began, and convened to guide them was an advisory committee in engineering. The boot and shoe department took on a trans-Atlantic atmosphere with groups of Canadian soldiers on courses in boot and shoe repairing. The ordinary boot and shoe students were producing cadet-force boots and children's shoes at this time.

National Certificate work was re-introduced in 1944, and a measure of normality returned to the College. Uniforms were still in abundance, but life was less intense. Clerks were preparing for the administration of demobilisation; ATS officers were doing instructors courses, and were learning how to re-educate their girls to domesticity. A member of the staff was awarded his PhD for research in chemistry and day-continuation classes in commerce were introduced. On the technical side a new pattern emerged. The City and Guilds examinations were to be the goal for the day-continuation courses and the building department generally, and the Ordinary National Certificate the aim for the senior engineering students in either electrical or mechanical engineering. The boot and shoe and leather department of course had its own diploma and the BBSI awards to work for.

Compared with the hectic war-time years, the peace-time Further Education and Training Scheme for ex-servicemen caused only mild disturbance. This began with the end of the war in 1945 and continued for several years. There was training for the disabled and vocational courses for those who had gone straight to the forces without a trade. Many trade courses were run – plumbing, boot-repairing and carpentry and joinery – and in addition many full-time students attended on the strength of FETS grants.

THE POST-WAR YEARS

The County College Scheme of the 1944 Education Act was beginning to be implemented by 1946. The building trade began to send their apprentices on two half-days per week, and a Building Advisory Committee was reconvened.

Bakery classes began and a course in business administration was started. Still present were War Office students, some eighty-nine including the engineering cadets, of whom twenty-two out of twenty-three were successful in their finals. In addition there were Ministry of Labour students on vocational courses.

In 1946 O. F. Bailey was confirmed as the Principal of the College which consisted of departments in boot, shoe and leather, commerce, engineering electrical and mechanical, science, domestic and building. Numbers were on the increase once more and all departments (except leather) could claim in the region of 500 students apiece. In 1947 the boot and shoe department at last was separated from the leather department, and Mr J. H. Thornton was appointed Head of Department. This coincided with the first Recruitment and Training Scheme for the Shoe Industry. The Government-sponsored courses finished that year, and the College finally achieved a peace-time footing. By 1948 there were 3,085 students on the roll, and the College began to shape up to what had been expected of it in 1932. Even a certain amount of recreational physical activity was managed with the use of an army gymnasium on the racecourse opposite, the only building left of the army camp.

Between 1949 and 1954 the number of courses was legion: Higher National Certificate courses in engineering subjects, ONC in Commerce; City and Guilds throughout the whole range of technical classes, including fuel technology and telecommunications; quality control, management, retail distribution, catering, furnishing, teachers courses, pharmaceutical, brewing, pre-medical BSc, general science and BSc, special in chemistry – the list could go on. In 1953 3,299 students were on roll of whom 246 were full-time and 1,007 part-time day-release. There was a set-back to plans in 1952 when the College had its application for recognition as an advanced college turned down by the Ministry of Education. However, hopes were still high and with the Development Plan designating them the Central College of Further Education (with the Art School), dignity was restored and they achieved their own set of governors, who took over the functions formerly administered by the Technical Education Sub-Committee.

With the publication of the White Paper on Technical Education in 1956, plans for higher status again became paramount; polytechnic, college of advanced technology, university status? Alas, no! The abundance of courses run at craft level, on which the College had built its reputation was its undoing. Too much work of a high practical standard but regarded as of a low academic standard was being done for the College to be uprated.

SOME BIOGRAPHIES

A hundred years of technical education is a long time, and it is liberally sprinkled with outstanding personalities. Biographical details of some of them follow.

Beeby Thompson, FCS, FGS

Born in 1849 at Creaton, Beeby Thompson was first apprenticed to Messrs Abel & Sons in Northampton. It was during this apprenticeship that he attended the first science classes and on examination received the Bronze Medal and was placed third in the country. His apprenticeship finished in 1869 and he began work as a junior reporter on the *Herald*. This did not last long, however, as he was awarded a Whitworth Scholarship tenable at the Royal School of Mines. Beeby Thompson's teaching career began in 1870 when he assisted at the Trade School and also at the science classes in Northampton. In 1875 he went to teach at Truro School as science master. This was a short-term position, as in 1876 he applied for the post as master of the science school which was being built on to the Northampton Grammar School on Abington Square. This period 1870 onwards also saw the commencement of Thompson's geological surveys. No county has been so thoroughly and accurately surveyed as Northamptonshire, and his experience in this field was to stand him in good stead. In recognition of his work in geology he was made honorary curator of geology at Northampton Museum in 1884. Beeby Thompson loved teaching and although he could not suffer fools gladly, he would take infinite pains with his work. In 1879 he branched into the County with lectures on the principles of agriculture. He was well received always but most notably at Kettering. A new venture also was his introduction of City and Guilds examinations to the boot and shoe classes in 1885. This success was crowned in 1892, when he secured the services of Edward Swaysland for these classes. In that year too, Beeby

Thompson became director of all the science, art and technical classes in Northampton. Two years later he resigned over the amalgamation of the classes with the Grammar School to form the Modern and Technical School.

He lectured in the area for four or five years after that and then went all over the world as an oil and water consultant. In the 1914–18 war he found unknown sources of water for the British forces in the Middle East and added many specimens to his unique collection of geological specimens. His globe-trotting over, Beeby Thompson settled down to semi-retirement in his house in Victoria Road, Northampton. He was editor and regular contributor to the *Journal of the Northampton Natural History Society*. Upon his death in December 1931 his library and his collection of some 10,000 geoological samples were left to the town.

John Blakeman, MA, MSc

John Blakeman was born in Oldham in 1881. At the age of 10 he became a part-timer in an engineering works and finally left day-school at the age of 13. He attended technical classes in Oldham for the next four years and proved himself a brilliant mathematician. At the age of 17 he won three scholarships to Owen's College, Manchester, and three more while he was there – in mathematics, physics and engineering. He gained his BSc degree and went on to Trinity College, Cambridge, where he gained his BA with first-class honours and was also awarded his MSc by Manchester. Upon leaving Cambridge in 1904 he became lecturer in mathematics at University College, London. From London he went on to become head of mathematics at Leicester Technical School. It was while he was there that he gained his MA (1908). In 1911 he was appointed principal of the Northampton Technical School, a post he held for the next thirty years.

John Blakeman was a dedicated educationist. He said that he believed in 'education rather than instruction' and devoted his life to raising the standards of the ordinary working youth. It was to this end that he organised grouped certificate courses, to the detriment of City and Guilds and National Certificate. He championed the cause of the East Midlands Educational Union and gave the boot and shoe section of the school his especial attention. For this work, and for his work in founding the Shoe and Allied Trades Research Association, he was made the first honorary fellow of the Boot and Shoe Institution. Blakeman was much sought after as a lecturer and proved superior in many fields including that of economics. His ideals, his determination and his ability as a 'committee man' led to the establishment of the Northampton College of Technology we know today. He died in 1942.

Oliver F. Bailey, BSc, MIEE

Born in Northampton in 1889, Oliver Bailey attended Kettering Road Elementary School, and then went on to the pupil-teaching centre in the town. Subsequently he went on to St John's Training College, Battersea, where he became a certificated teacher and also took an Inter BSc. His first teaching appointment was in Northampton at St Peter's School. For the whole period of the Great War 1914–18, Bailey was with the infantry in France, and on demobilisation returned to the town to teach in elementary schools.

In 1922 he had the opportunity of doing evening work in the Technical School teaching science, and in 1924 was offered a full-time post there, which he accepted. Oliver Bailey's main work, especially upon removal to the new school in 1932, was to establish the engineering department, which with his particular delight in science and electricity he did very successfully. He also was made responsible for the Junior Technical School which began at the same time. He managed to complete his BSc degree as well.

The outbreak of the Second World War brought Bailey's organising ability to the fore. He became acting principal upon the retirement of Blakeman in 1941 and was confirmed as Principal in 1946. The organisation, administration and staffing problems would have daunted many a lesser mortal, with JTS, day and evening students and an ever-changing military student body.

The post-war period brought many changes. The end of the JTS, the running down of army courses, the increase in day-release schemes, and the gradual conversion to a College of Further Education. Sights were set on advanced work to degree level in addition to the more mundane courses and yet, when Mr Bailey retired in 1956, he had not then achieved for the college the advanced status he so desired. Oliver Bailey enjoyed a long period of retirement and died in 1986.

W. J. Chater, MSc

W. J. Chater was one of the strong silent men of education, and never really received his due recognition. A local boy, he commenced his career in technical education in 1912 as a part-time teacher in evening classes. He was appointed a full-time science teacher in 1915 and during the war years was responsible for the junior course and the 'time off' and day-release students as well as the solution of special problems due to the war. He was also acting principal during Blakeman's long illness in 1916–17. In recognition of his work he was appointed deputy principal in 1919.

For the next three years in addition to his technical teaching he did valuable work in connection with the founding of SATRA. As head of science he built up the work of the school to a good inter degree standard in chemistry. A number of his pharmacy students were extremely successful. In 1929 he was awarded his MSc (Liverpool) for a thesis on the physical properties of vegetable tanned leathers.

He designed and supervised the installation of the new laboratories in 1932, and publicised the work of the College in a valuable series of science lectures and exhibitions. The science department, achieved a reasonable standard of work in both examination and research and he was sadly missed when he retired in 1940.

David Woodroffe, MSc, ABSI

Born in Yorkshire in 1893, Woodroffe went to Leeds University and took an honours degree in science. He followed this up with a period as a research fellow. He became a lecturer for a while, but re-entered industry in 1915. In September 1920 he was appointed head of the leather department at Northampton Technical School. He set up his department as a model factory and very efficient it was, judged by examination results. He also designed the lay-out of the new leather department in 1932.

A prolific technical writer, he wrote three textbooks on leather of his own and contributed sections to several others. He also made valuable research contributions to industry, particularly on chrome tanning. He was a founder member of the BBSI, and it is certain that the Institute idea grew out of a conversation between him and Blakeman.

He was in overall charge of the boot and shoe department until 1948 and it says much for his application and adaptability that the department thrived as it did.

He was a prominent Methodist Local Preacher and a Rotarian. He died in August 1962 at the age of 69 years after a long illness.

P. F. Tomkins, BSc (Econ)

Percy Tomkins, born 1891, was a contemporary of Oliver Bailey and attended Kettering Road School at the same time. They went to the pupil-teacher centre together from 1905 to 1909. Tomkins then went as an uncertificated teacher to St James' Road School and began teaching at the evening school in 1912. During the 1914–18 war he served in the Medical Corps in Mesopotamia. After the war he returned to teach at Kettering Road Intermediate School, and while there took his Inter BSc in 1928 and his Finals in 1930, when he was awarded first-class honours.

In 1932 he went to the new Technical College to teach in the commerce department and help with the JTS. When Oliver Bailey became acting principal in 1941, Tomkins became head of the JTS department. He said of those war years it was 'like conducting a school in Piccadilly Circus'. The Junior Technical School was abolished under the 1944 Education Act and became the Technical High School. When it moved to its own building in Trinity Avenue it became a mixed grammar school as the Technical Grammar School.

John H. Thornton, MA, FBSI

Born at Kettering in 1909, John Thornton was the son of a jeweller and watchmaker and one-time mayor of Kettering. His early education was at Spencer Street Elementary School, from whence he went as a scholarship boy to Wellingborough School. From Wellingborough he went to Emmanuel College, Cambridge, to read natural sciences, and was awarded his BA, and later his MA.

The world in the early 1930s did not owe any science graduate a living, and he was out of work for twelve months. It was almost by chance, or by last resort, that he entered the shoe factory of C. W. Clarke (Thos. Bird & Co Ltd) at Kettering, as a management trainee. He attended the County Boot and Shoe School at Kettering, passing City and Guilds examinations, and gaining the Swaysland Diploma. In 1935 Thornton made a successful application for the post of assistant superintendent of Boot and Shoe Education for the County, a post which he held until 1948, when he was appointed head of the boot and shoe department, Northampton College of Technology.

Mr Thornton was a Council member and a Fellow of the Boot and Shoe Institute. He was a member of SATRA for many years. He edited and wrote sections for two textbooks for the industry, one on shoe making and the other on shoe materials. In addition he contributed regularly to the trade journals.

As a technical historian Mr Thornton was without equal. During his life time he was the acknowledged authority on the history and geography of shoes and shoe-making, and gathered a remarkable collection of shoes, implements, and old machines.

Northampton & County Modern & Technical School.

Report of the SPECIAL COMMITTEE, appointed by
the Governors on the 14th day of February, 1907

Your Committee have met on six occasions and consider that they have to report
on two distinct but allied matters.

FIRST.—As to the immediate continuance of all the Educational Work now transacted at
Abington Square in a manner which shall not increase the cost and liabilities of
the Governors ; and

SECONDLY.—The permanent provision for Secondary Education in all its branches in the
Town and that part of the County of which the town is the necessary centre.

With regard to the first of these matters they make the following recommendations :—

They have ascertained that the annual deficit on the current expenditure of the School
does not exceed £500 a year on the average, and that a saving of this amount would guarantee
financial equilibrium. Much of the deficit now existing has been accumulated by capital
expenditure upon purchases with the view to a permanent settlement, and a full statement
of the financial position is appended to this Report in the form of Appendix " A."

In advising the continuance temporarily of the existing Educational Institutions on
Abington Square on that site, and in estimating that a saving of £500 a year will be adequate,
your Committee have borne in mind that the grants from the Board of Education are vitally
necessary to the continuance of the Schools, and that there is a reasonable prospect of
securing this if certain economies are effected, and the sanction of the Board of Education
is obtained. Accordingly, your Committee have interviewed officials at the Board of
Education, and have their sanction to the proposals for the temporary arrangements now
proposed.

Briefly these proposals are :—

(A). That the remuneration of the Head Mastership, a post which becomes vacant in
July, should be £350 per annum, made up as follows :—

Salary	£150	
Capitation Fees at the rate of £1 10s. per boy up to the first 100	150	
Ditto £1 upon all above 100	50	
	£350	

This will effect an economy of £320

(B). Giving up the houses on East Park Parade, provision for Boarders
being made by arrangements with the Head Master or Assistant
Masters, will effect a saving of £100

(C). By a rearrangement of the teaching staff as between the Day School
and Evening Classes your Committee are of opinion that further
economy could be effected of £100

TOTAL .. £520

The sanction of the Board of Education, which is indispensable, has been given to this arrangement solely and only upon condition that a Scheme for a permanent Day School for Boys is at once promulgated, and that permanent arrangements for Technical Instruction are also initiated. The letter from the Board of Education is set out at the end of this Report as Appendix " B."

Your Committee, therefore, make these recommendations with reference to the temporary carrying on.

In the next place your Committee have considered the question of permanent arrangements.

The suggestion that Abington Square should permanently house the Day School and Technical Institute has been fully considered. The question as to the inherent desirability of this plan can scarcely arise, for under the circumstances your Committee find it to be impossible.

The Grants from the Board of Education are essential if the Town and the County are not to be saddled with impossible expenditure, and the Board of Education are now, and have been for several years, absolutely opposed to the same buildings being used permanently for Day School and for Evening Technical Instruction. The Board of Education also insists upon an area for recreation which cannot be found on Abington Square, and your Committee, therefore, for these as for other reasons, unanimously recommend that Abington Square be reserved for a Pupil Teacher Centre, Evening Classes, and Technical Institute, while the Billing Road site should be devoted to the Boys' Secondary School.

> *It will be understood that your Committee, in mentioning the Billing Road site, have no objection whatever to the alternative site at Cliftonville which was discussed some years ago if that does not involve greater expenditure.*

The question of a site for a Girls' Secondary School is left for further consideration but must not be lost sight of.

Your Committee next recommend that the Institution upon Abington Square should be under the exclusive control of the Town Council, acting through its Education Committee, while the contribution from the County of £100 year would cease, and no representatives from the County Authority on the management of Abington Square Institution would be sought, and persons from the County would be admitted on payment of fees to be agreed between the Town and County Education Committees.

It is further recommended that the Boys' Secondary School should be on the Billing Road, where £2,500 have already been given for the purpose by Lord Spencer and Lady Wantage, and that the control and management of this School should be in the hands of a Joint Committee of the Town and County Councils, on which the representatives of the Town should be at least two-thirds. This Joint Committee is, of course, on the assumption that both Town and County Councils contribute adequately to the School, and such Committee would take the place of the existing Board of Governors.

In pursuance of these recommendations your Committee have carefully considered the cost of a School on the Billing Road, a scheme for which, it will be remembered, is the necessary condition for the temporarily carrying on of the various departments on Abington Square, and obtaining the assistance of the Board of Education.

Your Committee have visited Secondary Schools at Luton and Wolverton; they desire to record the gratuitous help they received from the Secretary to the Bedford Education Committee and the Head Master of the School at Luton, as also from the **Head Master** of the School at Wolverton.

They have procured from Mr. Herbert Norman plans for a School to accommodate 250 boys, which they now submit to the Governors ; these plans are estimated to cost £10,500 and the additional expense incidental to carrying out the same will be

Boundary Walls and laying out Ground	1000
Balance owing upon Ground	3300
Furnishing ..	1250
Architects Commission	750
Sundry Expenses ..	500
Overdraft ..	3500
	£20,800

It will be observed that this estimate indicates a great and substantial economy on the scheme of two years ago.

Your Committee recommend that the County be asked to waive any demand for building a Hostel, provided, of course. that boarding accommodation for County boys from a distance could be arranged with masters upon satisfactory terms.

They also recommend that no Head Master's House be built at the present time, but that he hire a house in the town ; there would be nothing to prevent either or both of these additions coming about in the future if the state of the Day School and the wishes of the Town and County Councils should make it desirable.

Accordingly with these curtailments of plan and the avoidance of all but absolutely necessary expenditure at once your Committee report that the sum of £20,000 is necessary.

They suggest that the Governors should ask the County to continue their annual sub-vension of £400 a year, and to make a grant of as much of the £6,000 earmarked for the larger scheme, as the present needs of the County as regards number of boys and other circumstances may be equitable, and that the remainder should be provided by the Town, which has up to now supplied two-thirds of the boys, and which has a far larger population to draw upon than those parts of the County of which the town is the centre.

Your Committee conceive it to be their duty to make a further recommendation with regard to finances. Abington Square and the buildings upon it are the property of the Governors, and they suggest that these should be sold to the Town Council, and the proceeds treated as part of the contribution of the Town towards the cost of the land and buildings on the Billing Road.

If the Governors adopt this Report and the Town and County Councils sanction the scheme, your Committee would be enabled to make a further recommendation with regard to the temporary carrying on of the Evening School, viz. :—

As has been stated before, they think that the rearrangement of staffing referred to between the Day School and the Evening Classes, while still being held on Abington Square, would promote economy, and in view of this and of their ultimate separation in accordance with this Report, they suggest that during this intermediate time the Evening Classes should be controlled by a Special Committee of the Governors, which would naturally consist as far as possible of those gentlemen on the Governing Body who are members of the Town Education Committee.

APPENDIX A: NORTHAMPTON COUNTY MODERN & TECHNICAL SCHOOL: STATEMENT SHEWING CAUSES OF INCREASE IN OVERDRAFT

CAPITAL EXPENDITURE ACCOUNT

		£	s.	d.			£	s.	d.	£	s.	d.
1895	Sale of Consols	863	2	8	* Purchase of 4 Cottages, Lower Mounts		918	3	2			
,,	Ditto Ditto	897	8	2	* Purchase of Playground		897	8	2			
1896	Withdrawn from Deposit	475	0	0	* Building New Front		792	19	5			
1897	Ditto Ditto	100	0	0								
1898	Ditto Ditto	96	0	0								
1900	Sale of Consols	1467	1	8	† Purchase of 2 Shops and Cottages,	£3539	10	0				
	Balance, being Advance from Northampton-				Lower Mounts By Mortgage	2070	0	0		1469	10	0
	shire Union Bank	179	8	3								
		£4078	0	9						£4078	0	9

* These Properties do not yield any income.

† These Properties yield £65 per annum, and there are annual charges for interest and repayment of principal amounting to £127, which leaves an annual deficit of £62 0 0

Loss of Income from Consols sold 40 10 0

Annual Loss £102 10 0

LOANS ACCOUNT

(Being Advances from the Northamptonshire Union Bank and forming part of the Bank Overdraft).

		£	s.	d.			£	s.	d.
Advance from Northamptonshire Union Bank		179	8	3	Balance of above Account		179	8	3
Ditto	ditto ditto	231	0	0	Erection of New Class Room		231	0	0
Ditto	ditto ditto	183	0	0	Ditto ditto ditto		183	0	0
Ditto	ditto ditto	331	0	0	Interest upon Billing Road Loan Account		331	0	0
		£924	8	3			£924	8	3

The total Deficiency amounted on the 31st March, 1906, to £3520 11s. 1d., which is made up as follows:—

	£	s.	d.
Overdraft at December 31st, 1895	571	2	8
Balance of Surplus and Deficits on School Account	1285	10	0
Loans Account	924	8	3
Liabilities *less* Credits	727	10	6
	£3508	11	5

This £1,285 has accumulated during a period of ten years, the actual surplus and deficits being as follows:

	SURPLUS	DEFICIT
1896	£250- 1-8	
1897		£ 33- 3 -7
1898		£ 94- 2 -6
1899		£266- 8 -6
1900	£ 18- 2- 6	
1901		£424- 6 -5
1902	£ 9-18- 0	
1903		£298- 10 -4
1904		£525- 15 -4
1905	£ 78-14- 6	

	£356-16- 8	£1642- 6 -8
		£356- 16 -8

£1,285-10 -0

Note: This is really better than it may at first sight appear, as it has been largely caused by depletion of income on account of Capital expended amounting to nearly £100 per annum and by payment of interest upon the increased Overdraft amounting last year to £163-2-0.

The original of this memorandum was attached to the copy of 'Appendix A: Northampton County Modern & Technical School: Statement shewing causes of Increase in Overdraft' in the possession of David Walmsley. It is handwritten and believed to be by Alfred Eamer, for many years the Clerk to the Governors, to whom the letter reproduced in Appendix B is addressed.

APPENDIX B

BOARD OF EDUCATION,
WHITEHALL, LONDON, S.W.,
27th March, 1907.

E. E. 02722.
NORTHAMPTON AND COUNTY MODERN AND TECHNICAL SCHOOL
SECONDARY SCHOOL. No. 8561
E. E. 2658/07

Sir,

With reference to the interview that took place on the 26th instant between the deputation representing the Governing Body and Officers of the Board, I am to state that after that consideration of the representations made by the deputation, it has been decided that the application for continued recognition under the Regulations for Secondary Schools of the above-named School during the present session, will be admitted on the following terms. Recognition will be given provisionally for the year ending 31st July, 1907. This provisional recognition will be confirmed only upon condition that the Board, before the close of the session, receive an assurance which they can accept as satisfactory that suitable accommodation will be provided for the School within a time that is reasonable in their opinion. No grant will be paid until this condition is fulfilled.

The Governors should now take the necessary steps to ascertain the cost of providing the buildings that are required, and to formulate their project for the conduct of the School in the future. Plans should be submitted to the Board in due course, together with full financial particulars, when the project is settled.

The Board will consent to the continuance of the School until next July by means of the overdraft on the account of the Foundation which is required to provide the necessary funds.

In their letter of the 15th December last, the Board sanctioned the increase of the overdraft existing at that time by £790, raising the total to £3456 16s 11d., and they now sanction such an additional increase as will bring the overdraft to a total amount not exceeding £4,000. According to your estimate submitted to them by Mr. Wells, this amount should suffice for the period. In order that there may be no misapprehension on the subject, I am to state that an overdraft is an alienation of capital *pro tanto*, and that the Governors would thus be personally liable in respect of an overdraft incurred without the sanction of the Board.

It has already been intimated that the Board will not sanction the School's being carried on at a loss beyond the end of the present session. It will be necessary then to consider the steps that will have to be taken to liquidate the large outstanding liability that the Foundation has incurred, and in any estimate as to the future, an allowance for the annual sum which will be required for this purpose should not be omitted. The Board will probably be able to treat the School of Art on the same footing as regard recognition as the Day School. A further communication will be addressed to the Governing Body of the School of Art on this subject.

I have the honour to be,
Sir,
Your obedient Servant,
R. E. MITCHESON

A. O. EAMER, ESQ.,
    NORTHAMPTON AND COUNTY
        MODERN AND TECHNICAL SCHOOL,
            NORTHAMPTON.

Extract from the Annual Handbook of the Education Committee of the County Borough of Northampton for the year 1929:

The Salary stated is subject to a deduction of 5% for Superannuation Contribution.

TECHNICAL COLLEGE.

Name of Teacher.	Annual Salary on 1st April, 1929.	Date of Increment.	Qualification.	Appointment to this School.	First Appointed
Principal—	£				
Mr. J. Blakeman ...	750	...	M.A., M.Sc.	1911	1911
Deputy-Principal—					
Mr. W. J. Chater...	528	Max.	B.Sc.	1915	1903
Head of Leather Dressing Dept.—					
Mr. D. Woodroffe...	550	Max.	M.Sc.	1920	1920
Assistants—					
Mr. O. F. Bailey ...	415		B.Sc.	1924	1901
,, W. R. Morgan	373		...	1918	1918
Miss G. P. Rumming	330		B.A., B.Com	1919	1919
,, K. L. Ritchie	306	Max.	Dip.	1920	1920
Instructors—					
Mr. W. J. Barnes	333	Max.	...	1919	1919
,, J. S. Matcham	333	Max.	...	1919	1919
,, F. M. Howes	333	Max.	...	1918	1918
,, R. F. Farey ...	333	Max.	...	1919	1919
Miss A. Self	180	Max.	...	1924	1924

BRANCH TECHNICAL SCHOOLS.
Head Teachers—

Kettering Road	... ...	Mr. A. Harrison (T.C.)
St. George's	... ...	,, J. S. Barton (T.C.)

HANDICRAFT INSTRUCTORS.

Name of Teacher.	Annual Salary on 1st April, 1929	Date of Increment	Qualification	Appointment to this School	First Appointed
	£				
Mr. A. T. Bliss......	366	Max.	C.	1922	1905
,, R. H. Sharman	366	Max.	T.C.	1921	1905
,, H. G. Hornsby	344		H'cft.	1921	1918
,, M. G. V. Smith	229		H'cft.	1928	1924

DOMESTIC SUBJECTS TEACHERS.

Name of Teacher.	Annual Salary	Date of Increment	Qualification	Appointment	First Appointed
Supervising Teacher,					
Miss S. E. Shillito	†68	Max.	Dip.	1919	1919
Assistants—					
Mrs. M. K. Heap	270		,,	1919	1919
,, D. M. Atkins	252		,,	1920	1920
Mrs. E. Abbott ...	188		,,	1924	1924
,, C.E.U.Merriman	162		,,	1928	1928
,, M. York-Jones	186		,.	1928	1928
,, R. E. B. Atkinson...	162		,,	1928	1928
,, *R.C.Ownsworth	97		,,	1928	1928

*Part-time Teacher. †Proportion.

SCHOOL OF ARTS AND CRAFTS

Name	Salary			Qualification	Appointment	First Appointed
Principal—						
Mr. L Duckett	581			A.R.C.A.	1926	1926
Assistant—						
Mr. T. W. Rutter ...	414			A.R.C.A.	1915	1915
Miss D. Thornton ...	174			A.R.C.A. Design Emb.	1928	1928

Extract from the Annual Handbook of the Education Committee of the County Borough of Northampton for the year 1940:

The Salary stated is subject to a deduction of 5% for Superannuation Contribution.

COLLEGE OF TECHNOLOGY.

Name of Teacher.	Annual Salary on 1st Jan., 1940.		Qualification.	Appointed to the College.	First Appointed
Principal :	£				
Mr. J. Blakeman ...	800	Max.	M.A. M.Sc.	1911	1911
Head of Leather and Boot and Shoe Departments :					
Mr. D. Woodroffe ...	650	Max.	M.Sc. A.I.C.	1920	1920
Head of Commerce Department :					
Miss G. P. Rumming	400	Max.	B.A. B.Com	1919	1919
Head of Junior Technical School (Industrial Section) and Electrical Engineering Department :					
Mr. O. F. Bailey ...	500	Max.	B.Sc.	1924	1901
Assistants :					
Mr. R. E. Coombs	362		B.Sc.	1933	1933
Miss L. Carter	174			1938	1938
Miss E. M. T. Hawkings	215		Dip.	1934	1934
Mr. J. E. Linnell ...	274		C.& G.	1936	1934
,, D. Plews	272		B.Sc.	1936	1936
,, L. Sabey	440		B.Sc.	1933	1911
,, P. E. Tompkins	480		B.Sc.	1932	1909
Miss M. C. Turner	275		Dip.	1929	1929
Mr. F. C. Wright ...	302		B.A.	1933	1928
Mr. W. Siddall	372		B.Sc. A.I.C.	1937	1937
Miss J. M. Soutar ...	188		Dip.	1938	1938
Mr. C. W. Johnson	411		B.Sc.	1938	1938
,, E. G. Bennett	294		B.A.	1940	1933

COLLEGE OF TECHNOLOGY—continued.

Name of Teacher.	Annual Salary on 1st Jan., 1940.	Qualification.	Appointed to the College.	First Appointed
Instructors :	£			
Mr. W. Bailey ...	184	C.	1938	1938
,, G. Burrows ...	190	A.B.S.I.	1938	1938
,, R. F. Farey ...	344	A.B.S.I.	1919	1919
,, J. Harris ...	185		1938	1938
,, J. S. Matcham	349	A.B.S.I.	1919	1919
,, F. N. Warner	225	* C.T.S.	1936	1936
Miss G. Prior ...	200	F.C T.S. (tac.)	1932	1932
,, L. G. Redley ...	165		1938	1938

Registrar :—Miss D. K. Phillips.

EVENING INSTITUTES.
Head Teachers :

Barry Road	...	...	Mrs. C. I. M. Coombes
Bective	...	...	Mr. H. J. Norton
Kettering Road	...	...	Mr. A. J. Smart
Rothersthorpe Road			Mr. B. Knight
St. George's	...	...	Mr. J. H. Barton
Spencer	...	...	Mr. C. J. Amos

SCHOOL OF ART.

	£			
Principal :				
Mr. F. E. Courtney	600	A.T.D.	1937	1937
Assistants :				
Mr. J. A. Spencer	234	A.R.C.A. A.T.D.	1938	1938
,, T. Wrigley ...	234	A.R.C.A. A.T.D.	1939	1939
Miss G. M. Burrows	223	A.R.C.A. A.T.D.	1939	1939
Mr. P. Revitt ...	50	Student Teacher	1938	1938

SAMUEL SMITH CAMPION

Samuel Campion was born in Horsemarket, Northampton, on 18th October 1846, but spent his early years at Little Brington, where his father, the Revd Joseph Campion, was a Baptist minister. At his father's death Frederick the 4th Earl Spencer, offered to send young Campion to Guilsborough Grammar School, but his mother wished him to remain at home, and thus they moved to Northampton. Mr Campion attended the British School and at the age of fourteen began his career as a teacher there. At fifteen he was the Honorary Secretary of the Northampton Temperance Society and Band of Hope. While still in his teens, Mr Campion was appointed assistant master of the British Schools.

However Mr Campion's ambitions lay in the direction of journalism, and an offer to join the staff of the *Northampton Herald* was eagerly accepted. When nine months later the position of chief reporter on the *Northampton Mercury* became vacant, Mr Campion, then nineteen was invited to fill it. Five years later the editor, Mr George de Wilde, became seriously ill, and Mr Campion performed the duties of editor for a period of eight months. When at de Wilde's death the editorship passed to another man, Mr Campion returned to the *Herald* as chief reporter. In 1876 he started publishing the *Northamptonshire Guardian* to champion the cause of radicalism. His second paper, the *Evening Mail*, was first published on 26th January 1880 and had the dual distinction of being Northampton's first evening paper and the first paper to sell for a half-penny. It was like the *Guardian*, a radical paper and gave enthusiastic support to Charles Bradlaugh and Mr Labouchere. In opposition the *Mercury* began printing the *Northampton Reporter* a fortnight later, and the *Herald* commenced publication of the *Chronicle* a week after that. Due to insufficient backing against these competitors, the *Evening Mail* ceased publication within a year. In May 1885 the *Guardian* was incorporated with the *Mercury* and Mr Campion became proprietor and editor of both papers as well as of the daily paper, the *Northampton Daily Reporter*. He remained editor until in 1904 the papers were sold to a local syndicate. In 1898 Mr Campion founded the *Football Echo*.

An active member of his profession Mr Campion was one of the original members of the Institute of Journalists of Great Britain and Ireland. His membership in this organisation extended over a period of fifty years and he was a fellow of the Institute for forty years. He served as Vice President from 1896 to 1901 and was elected President in 1908. He also held the office of honorary treasurer and later was Chairman of the Institute's Provident Fund for many years. As one of the representatives of the Institute he attended the International Congress of Journalists held at Bordeaux in 1895 and at Lisbon in 1898. He was one of the founders of the British International Association of Journalists and served as its

President from 1902 to 1906.

Politically Mr Campion was an enthusiastic and vociferous advocate of Liberalism. He began his political career in 1880 when he was an unsuccessful candidate for the South Ward. In 1883 he won a Council seat in the West Ward, beginning a period of service as a member of the Town Council for forty-seven years. For nine years he represented the East Ward, and then in 1898 became an alderman. However in 1900 he resigned his aldermanic seat to stand as a candidate for St Edmund's Ward. In the election of 1913 he was defeated by four votes but sat on the Council as an alderman, an office he retained until 1932. As a member of the Town Council he was active in many areas, being Chairman of the Finance Committee for many years and deputy chairman of the Education Committee from 1902 until his retirement in 1932. Keenly interested in education, he was a governor both of the Northampton Town and County School and the Northampton School for Girls. In 1931 he officiated at the stone-laying ceremony for Northampton's new College of Technology, and he was also a Trustee of the School of Art.

Another of Mr Campion's chief interests was the library. He pioneered the library extension scheme in the Jubilee year and was appointed head of a special committee to negotiate a Carnegie grant for a new library building. Although the plan called for a grant of £5,000 the Committee finally obtained £15,000 for the erection of the library in Abington Street. For over twenty years Mr Campion promoted the Saturday Evening Talks the primary intent of which was to stimulate the love of learning and interest in local history while also encouraging the use of the library. He was also the author of several articles and books on local history including one on the Northampton Town Hall and a guide to Northampton upon which later editions of the Official Guide were based. When he visited the St Louis Exposition in 1904, he attended and was a speaker representing Northampton at the bicentenary celebrations in Northampton, Massachusetts.

Born a Baptist Mr Campion was a scholar in the College Lane Church Sunday School and when eighteen years of age became a teacher in the Spring Lane Branch School. A few years later he began attending Commercial Street Congregational Church and following his marriage to Miss Kew, became a Congregationalist. In 1886 he was elected deacon. For over sixty years he was engaged in Sunday School work as a teacher and superintendent and in 1915 was presented with a gold watch to commemorate his fifty years service. He organised the Sunday Evening Popular Services in the Old Theatre, Marefair, in the 1880s.

Mr Campion was made a Justice of the Peace in 1896 and was appointed Deputy Lieutenant for the county in 1935. In a ceremony held on 24th October 1923 Mr Campion was presented with the Honorary Freedom of the Borough for his long and distinguished career of public service. In his last years he was senior magistrate of the town both in years and in length of service. He died on 20th September 1938 at the age of ninety-one.

Extract from the Booklet on the
Honorary Freemen of Northampton
published by the former County Borough of Northampton.

REMINISCENCES OF J. T. WILSON

J. T. Wilson was a student at the School of Art, Abington Street in 1888 and subsequently became a teacher-instructor under John Blakeman. The internal evidence suggests that the following notes were written in 1936. They were found amongst the papers of the late O. F. Bailey.

In Northampton, fifty years ago, that wide old thoroughfare called Abington Street and Abington Square was at one and the same time the Harley Street and the seat of academical education. The whole district was less sophisticated than it is today. There were still a few private dwellings in Abington Street as well as on the Square. The Bantam Cock was an old building with a thatched roof, and the Café had only just displaced a local doctor's house, whose garden projected into the square, where the Bradlaugh Monument now stands. Next to the Bantam stood the old Grammar School, with its pleasing circular tower, a typical gothic building of the late nineteenth century. A little further down on the other side of Abington Street stood a large private academy, presided over by the father of the well-known Kingston family. Opposite this school was the Notre Dame School for Girls.

In connection with the Grammar School evening classes in art and science were held. These classes constituted the chief educational facilities for the workers and others offered in the winter's evenings by the local authority. There were, of course, a few evening continuation classes held in some of the day schools, but these were confined to a little book-keeping and such like subjects, which were really to help a boy or girl to be a good clerk or counter 'jumper' (shop assistant) if they aspired to anything higher than factory life in the local industry.

It was considered, in those days, quite a privilege for a poor boy to attend such classes as those held at the Grammar School. It can then be imagined with what joy I was enabled to enrol as an art student one day in September 1888 and sat in the preliminary art room, along with a score or more similar 'young hopefuls'. The advanced art room was entered through the preliminary room and was only separated from it by a thick red curtain. Many times had I seen the outline of a hand in white, on the wall at the bottom of the old stone staircase, pointing to the Art School above, but before then had never ventured beyond the iron gate at the corner of the Mounts against Hunting's tobacco shop.

At the top of the staircase were three doors, one leading to a lavatory, one to the art room, and a third to the Headmaster's private room. It would, however, be nearer the truth to call this a cabin, for it was less than 6ft. wide and about 15ft. long. Together with a store room, it was a piece partitioned off the preliminary art room. This cabin-like room was increased in size about 8ft. up, where a shelf over the top of the adjacent store room, provided an admirable place for junk and lumber. It had one luxury in the form of an old-fashioned fireplace with a stone mantelpiece, but I never remember seeing a fire in it, and I should imagine it a dangerous kind of room for a fire, as it was usually well-furnished with paint, easels, and canvas frames with pictures in various unfinished stages, and more often than not, was unoccupied. There was always a very homely smell about the place, as the Head was an inveterate smoker.

Between the door of this room and the art room door, was a small hatchway, through which could be obtained paper, pencils, rubbers, etc., by the students of the geometry and building construction classes on the other parts of the premises.

Inside the preliminary art room was the store-room mentioned before, which had a door, the upper half of which could be opened separately, sometimes called a stable door, and occasionally we boys would give the storekeeper an appropriate name in consequence. The art room was heated by a gas-stove and the early arrivals took good care to get as near to it as possible, especially on the very cold evenings in the middle of winter. For the tardy ones, a position in the room on the draughty side, gave all sorts of pretexts for getting out for a short interval, which was invariably spent down the stoke hole in the playground below.

There were two teachers, the Head, a Mr Bradbury and his assistant the late Albert E. Bailey, one of Northampton's talented artists, a man who not only was, but looked every inch an artist. Both were somewhat Bohemian in their habits and tastes. The former spent most time with the beginners, whilst the latter looked after the advanced students. Looking back it is sad to think that both these excellent gentlemen became victims to the drink habit. Many times we boys were treated to the odour brought into the room, after one or the other had paid a hasty visit to the Bantam Cock to quench their thirst.

Mr Bradbury was a splendid teacher as most of his former students would testify, and we have much to thank him for, because of his then improved method of teaching model-drawing. His little book has been used by a good many of his old pupils during succeeding years. Of Mr Bailey, I am inclined to think that he was a much better executant than teacher. It was always a delight to see his super-sensitive fingers at the end of a long pencil, making corrections on the side on one's paper. Some of us never rubbed his marks off our papers, as we almost worshipped his wonderful skill in drawing. Had he been a little more stable he might have made a name for himself. As it was, he got a picture hung at the Royal Academy.

As most of the boys in the classes were preparing to earn a living, the pursuing of art for arts sake was not considered by our parents to be altogether desirable, so that sooner or later a move had to be made either into the Science Department or private study, as there were yet no Technological Departments.

At this time in the early 1890s, the science subjects were chemistry or 'stinks' as they were called then as now, mathematics, physics, building construction and geometry. This branch of education was presided over by the late Mr Beeby Thompson with a few assistants.

From the number of boot and shoe and buildings students attending these classes, it soon became evident that there was a demand for more practical or technological work. Classes were therefore formed which took the name 'technical' as distinct from the academical side of education.

Well do I remember the first night in September 1893, when with my late father I stood at the table, the first student to be enrolled on this new register. The class was one in carpentry and joinery and was in preparation for the City and Guilds of London Institute Examinations.

My father was the first teacher and the class numbered seventy-two, and was held in the physics laboratory, and we sat on the gallery packed like sardines, and by the end of the first two hours, were well nigh asphyxiated. This large class, as was expected, soon became reduced to reasonable numbers, several giving up on account of the homework, which was too great an effort for some ill-prepared students. Some expected to be taught the difficulties encountered in first-class joinery, after a lesson or two, and gave up in disgust in consequence. By the time of the New Year, a class of twenty-four real students settled down to complete a very successful first years attempt. Eight of these had the temerity to sit for the City and Guilds Examination, most of whom passed in the second class, and if I remember rightly there were two first class. Most of these students afterwards obtained leading positions with firms of builders, both locally and in other parts of the country.

About this time appear the names of a few men who afterwards made their mark in the technological world: E. J. Swaysland whose memory is kept green by the Diploma in Boot and Shoe which bears his name. Reuben Lines, an engineer who invented an improved mitre-cutting machine which was widely used in joinery works up and down the country for many years. This teacher was succeeded by one of his most successful students Mr W. R. Morgan who recently retired after a connection of over thirty years. Under these excellent teachers many outstanding students were helped to obtain situations in other centres where the staple industries were similar to our own.

It is here to be regretted that the late Mr Beeby Thompson was given the 'cold shoulder' in order to make room for the late Mr R. Elliott Steele. This change was heralded by a most unwieldy name: The Northampton & County Modern & Technical School. The reception at the inaugural of this new Head, was a swell affair. The caps and gowns quite overawed some of us poor students, as we were unable to afford to match them with a dress suit. We had a good time notwithstanding, the fun was fast and furious and all the rooms were used for one or another kind of game or experimental lecture.

The electricians had quite a nice game with the young people, who were asked to link hands, a proceeding very much to the liking of the fair sex, who were there in large numbers, then without any warning whatever, the end persons, being in the know, completed the circuit, which gave a fairly strong shock. The howls, squeals etc. which followed gave cause for laughter for the rest of the evening. Another popular feature, owing to the darkness which was considered necessary, was a flash-light photograph, which when developed disclosed the new Head looking very sheepishly at his fiancée; she afterwards became Mrs Elliott Steele.

It was under this Head in 1906 that I commenced my career as an evening technical school teacher, taking a class in practical maths. which was part of a course, a system just launched by the Board of Education, and one which has been highly developed by the present Principal, Mr J. Blakeman. During this time I came into personal contact with Mr Steele, and had good reason to thank him for his kindly consideration and advice.

After a few years this Head shared the same fate as his predecessor, and had to make room for a younger man. This new Head was to have a new secondary school on the outskirts of the town, as this would free him of the irksome duties entailed in the principalship of a technical school.

So much for past Heads and teachers, but what of the administrators? This is another story and since there are so few of them left I do not feel as though I ought to hold them up to ridicule. Some of those remaining would perhaps like to read what a boy of those far off days, thought of them. Very little was seen of committee men or any other officials, during class hours, but at prize distributions, then as now, we were bored stiff by the City Fathers, who tried to instil into us, that if we only did as they did, we should all become Mayor, or some other wonderful sort of person. Some there were who appeared to be quite pleased with themselves because they had had no 'Eddication at all. No! not nothin.'

My most vivid recollection of officials was during examination times, for there we were confronted by spectacled gentlemen who placed themselves like sentinels to prevent us from looking at one another's papers. One gentleman in particular whose jet-black hair and mutton-chop whiskers, with an extraordinarily stern and severe countenance, so upset me on my first encounter with him that I had my first attack of nerves. Whenever I looked up from my paper I caught his eagle eye. I do not remember trying to cheat but I do remember feeling as though I was cheating all the time, and at the call of time, I quite expected him to come up to and say, 'Now I've caught you,' but strange to say he did nothing of the sort, just a gruff, 'Your paper please,' and passed on to collect the other papers. That gentleman was the present Mayor, Alderman G. W. Beattie.

His elder brother, the late Mr Stewart Beattie, was usually stationed at the other end of the examination room, and although he was not quite such a stern-looking man, it was not at all pleasant to turn either to the right or to the left when they were both on duty. It must however be said of Stewart Beattie that when collecting papers he was very lenient to those students who were anxious to use up every minute, and as his vigilance had enabled him to note this type of student, he always gathered up those who had finished before asking for the others. Several of us at different times were grateful to him for this.

One other invigilator of similar type but with an even gruffer voice than either of the other two, was the late Mr F. Lea, who for many years kept a local information bureau. This gentleman would not allow a stroke to be done after he had called time. On one occasion he nearly prevented me from taking an examination owing to a difference in clock times, a very common occurrence in Northampton fifty years ago, when the 'old Café' clock rarely synchronised with the church clocks in the centre of the town.

These examinations were held in the Town Hall, the Lower Assembly room, and the Temperance Hall and sometimes, when the numbers were few, in the art rooms. The light in each of these places was very uncertain. The fading daylight in the evenings of April and May, when most of the examinations were held, and the inferior artificial light by gas at dusk, did not tend to produce the best kind of drawing whether freehand or mechanical. As bad as was this light, that provided in some of the rooms of the Old Grammar School was far worse, for with star brackets and fish-tail burners, there were as many shadows across the surface of the paper as there were lines in an intricate perspective drawing. Many were the complaints made by suffering students, not infrequently on the answer papers as a protest to the Higher Authority.

It is amazing what a lot of excellent work was done in these days. Some of us still have a few examples of our early efforts, and I question whether any of the following, who were students in those days, would be ashamed to give a display of their early work: Councillor Bassett-Lowke; Henry Cooper, the well-known photographer; Percy Cole, the lithographer; Mr Frank Gill, a well-known artist whose light and delicately coloured pictures have delighted so many visitors to the local Art Gallery, and Councillor W. A. B. Leach.

Other students of the old days include Arthur Tustin, the respected secretary of the local Artizans' and Labourers' Society; his gifted younger brother, the late Frank Tustin; Sir John Brown; Mr E. J. Leach, late headmaster of Kingsthorpe Grove School; Charles Kew, brother of the Town Clerk; Mr Christopher J. Day; Mr Henry Abbey; and Tom Melloes.

Amongst the City Fathers was a very benevolent looking old gentleman who took a very keen interest in all kinds of education, too keen some folks thought. One of his self-imposed tasks was to be out early visiting the Board Schools, and woe-betide the teacher or scholar who happened to stroll into school after 9 o'clock in the morning. Evening school teachers were also looked after, so that no student could complain of getting short measure for his or her fee. A cartoon in a well-known paper of the time pictured him standing outside an Elementary School just before 9 o'clock with his watch in his hand, waiting for late-comers. A tall well-set-up old gentleman with a very striking face and a long white beard, his smile rarely won the heart of the errant youth of our day, as they rather preferred his absence to his presence. He was the late Mr Thomas Wetherell.

Contemporary with him was the late Sir Henry Randall, who always added dignity to a prize distribution, and though he had a tendency to exceed the time limit, he was usually brought to heel by her Ladyship, who gave a gentle tug at his coat-tail.

At one of these functions we were honoured by the presence of the President of the Board of Education, the late Right Hon. A. J. Mundella, it was in the year 1890 as it was my privilege to have an encouraging pat on the head from him, when I went to receive my first prize, a Bible, a choice entirely my own. I often wonder how many prizes have taken that form since that day forty-six years ago. That Bible, though very much worn, is still in my possession today, and has the Board of Examination prize label stuck in the first (front) page.

It would take too long to enumerate the peculiarities of many others, so that I must come back to the old Technical School at which I had served three winter sessions. Encouraged by the Head I applied for and secured a position under Worcestershire Education Authority. This necessitated my leaving the carpenter's bench for the stool of the pedagogue. After two years I returned to a similar position under the local authority at the old Technical School and came in contact with the present Principal of the College, who had just commenced that career of which he has just celebrated his silver jubilee.

The room allotted to me was that self-same old art room which had been fitted up as a handicraft room. The partitions of the old store room, being used to make a corridor, leading from the stone staircase to the old advanced art room, which had been fitted up as a mechanics laboratory.

At that time the permanent staff consisted of the Principal, his secretary, the caretaker, and myself. I must add, however, that my daytime duties were controlled by the Elementary Education Committee whereas my evening school duties were directly under the Principal. It is interesting to note that the monthly salary bill then was only about £50 per month, I hardly dare write down the figure which adorns the salary sheet of today. This arrangement lasted for seven years until 1918 when the day-continuation school time-off scheme was inaugurated. So once more we were blessed with another omnibus name. At this change I was appointed with several others, on the permanent staff of the school. Soon after this came the demand for training men disabled in the Great War, and for various reasons, the Time-off Scheme was not quite the success it should have been. About this time the late Mr Stewart Beattie lay down his task and made room for a Director of Education, the advent of which brought into being the Intermediate Schools of Northampton. The opening of these schools was mainly responsible for finding places for the unwanted teachers at the Technical School, so that in 1921 I again severed my connection with the old Tech. In spite of this, however, my connection with it was and still is, kept up during the winter seasons, so that it is not far wrong to say that I have been connected with the College, with the exception of two years, ever since 1888.

The most outstanding man connected with local education, both as teacher and administrator, is undoubtedly the veteran Mr Samuel Smith Campion. Although his great age does not allow him to take such an active part as he did, he is still able to hold an audience on his favourite subjects. When the College was opened four years ago, he was the only remaining member of the Higher Education Committee, who was also there when the Technological classes were inaugurated in 1890. He must really have been a very lonely man on that day for all the teachers as well as students knew nothing of the early struggles he had experienced when technical education was not quite so popular as it is today.

My twenty-five years connection with the school under Mr Blakeman has been of the happiest, and I am pleased to have taken some small part in helping him to realise his dream of a quarter of a century ago. Quite a lot could be written of his struggles to put Northampton on the map as an educational centre for the boot and shoe industry, his many ingenious contrivances and his keen research into every ability to do it. When he came to Northampton, the study of boot and shoe was in the realm of art. Today, although it has never forsaken its early love, it is essentially a science, and no one can talk to J. B. for five minutes without discovering what an intimate knowledge he has of the many details connected with their manufacture. The question is often asked, 'Can a man of theory understand a practical problem thoroughly?' and the answer is 'that it all depends on the man of theory.' It certainly is in the case of Mr Blakeman, and his valuable contributions have been highly spoken of. His worth was recognised by the local manufacturers when he was secretary of the Boot and Shoe Research Association. Perhaps one of the proudest days of his life, was when the new College was formally opened by Royalty in 1932. He will be no less proud, however, when the completed building stands four square to that open space of ours, the racecourse.

There is now only one wish that I have in that connection, that I may have the privilege of being at the opening on that occasion. May the Committee, the Principal, and the Staff continue the good work, so that the youth of today will have something to write about fifty years hence.

NORTHAMPTON COUNTY BOROUGH EDUCATION COMMITTEE

COLLEGE OF TECHNOLOGY

Visit of Their Royal Highnesses the Duke and Duchess of York

TO OPEN

The Northampton College of Technology

17th November, 1932

MEMBERS OF THE EDUCATION COMMITTEE
1931.

ALDERMAN C. J. SCOTT, J.P. (*Mayor of Northampton*).

COUNCILLOR J. PEACH (*Chairman*).

ALDERMAN S. S. CAMPION, J.P., H.F. (*Deputy-Chairman*).

ALDERMAN A. J. CHOWN, J.P. (*Chairman of the Sites and Building Sub-Committee*).

ALDERMAN C. EARL, J.P.

ALDERMAN G. S. WHITING, J.P.

COUNCILLOR MRS. A. A. ADAMS, J.P.

COUNCILLOR S. C. ADNITT.

COUNCILLOR W. J. BASSETT-LOWKE.

COUNCILLOR W. E. COLDHAM.

COUNCILLOR J. DALTON.

COUNCILLOR H. FOX (*Chairman of the Finance Sub-Committee*).

COUNCILLOR A. W. LYNE, J.P. (*Chairman of the Technical College Sub-Committee*).

COUNCILLOR G. F. SKINNER.

COUNCILLOR RALPH A. SMITH.

COUNCILLOR G. F. E. WILKINSON.

Co-opted Members.

MISS M. E. BLAXLEY.

MR. B. V. BROWNE.

MRS. J. T. CHAMBERLAIN, B.A.

MRS. G. S. EUNSON, M.B.E.

MR. J. HILL.

NEW MEMBERS, 1932.

COUNCILLOR P. W. ADAMS.

COUNCILLOR C. H. J. BUTTERFIELD.

COUNCILLOR W. H. PERCIVAL.

MR. E. L. POULTON, O.B.E., J.P.

PROGRAMME.

1.—Their Royal Highnesses will arrive at the College buildings at 11.30 a.m.

Members of the O.T.C. of the Northampton Town and County School will line the approach to the College.

2.—Upon arrival, the following Presentations will be made by His Worship the Mayor, Councillor P. F. Hanafy, J.P. :—

The Recorder, C. B. MARRIOTT, ESQ., and MRS. MARRIOTT.

The High Sheriff, SIR THOMAS FERMOR HESKETH, and MISS FERMOR HESKETH.

The Member for the Borough, SIR MERVYN MANNINGHAM-BULLER, and LADY BULLER.

The Ex-Mayor, ALDERMAN C. J. SCOTT, J.P., and MRS. SCOTT, and the Ex-Mayoress, MRS. R. STONE.

The Chairman of the Education Committee, COUNCILLOR J. PEACH, and MRS. PEACH.

The Deputy-Chairman of the Education Committee, COUNCILLOR H. FOX.

The Chairman of the Sites and Building Sub-Committee, ALDERMAN A. J. CHOWN, J.P., and MRS. CHOWN.

The Chairman of the Technical College Sub-Committee, COUNCILLOR A. W. LYNE, J.P.

The Chairman of the Higher Education Sub-Committee, COUNCILLOR S. C. ADNITT.

The late Deputy-Chairman of the Education Committee, MR. S. S. CAMPION, H.F., J.P.

The Secretary for Education, MR. H. C. PERRIN.

The Principal of the College, MR. J. BLAKEMAN, M.A., M.Sc.

3.—Presentation of Bouquet to Her Royal Highness the Duchess of York, by the Mayoress.

4.—His Worship the Mayor will welcome Their Royal Highnesses and will invite His Royal Highness the Duke of York, formally to declare the College open.

5.—Presentation to His Royal Highness the Duke of York, of the Key of the College, by Councillor J. Peach (Chairman of the Education Committee).

6.—Formal Declaration of Opening by His Royal Highness the Duke of York, from the steps of the College.

7.—After His Royal Highness has opened the main door, the Duke and Duchess will be conducted to the College Library, where the Chairman of the Education Committee (Councillor J. Peach), will present the following :—

The Architect, MR. K. COBB, L.R.I.B.A.

A Representative of the Builders, MR. H. GLENN.

A Representative of the Workmen, MR. S. FARR.

The Deputy-Principal of the College, MR. W. J. CHATER, M.Sc.

The Head of the Leather Dressing Department, MR. D. WOODROFFE, M.Sc., A.I.C.

The Head of the Commerce Department, MISS G. P. RUMMING, B.A., B.COM.

The Senior Teacher of the Junior Technical School and Electrical Engineering Department, MR. O. F. BAILEY, B.Sc.

The Chief Teacher of Mechanical Engineering, MR. W. R. MORGAN.

8.—Their Royal Highnesses will be conducted through the building and on reaching the Boot and Shoe Department, the Chairman of the Education Committee (Councillor J. Peach) will present MR. C. G. B. ALLINSON, President of the Northampton Town Boot Manufacturers' Association, and MR. A. H. HOLLISTER, J.P., C.C., Vice-President Boot Manufacturers' Federation of Great Britain and Ireland, who will make a presentation of Footwear to Their Royal Highnesses ; Mr. W. J. PARKER (Chairman of the Boot and Shoe Advisory Committee) will also be presented.

9.—Their Royal Highnesses will leave by the West door on the bottom floor and the roadway to St. George's Avenue.

———————

Guests are asked to remain in their places until Their Royal Highnesses have left the College. The building will be open for inspection by the invited guests until 3 p.m., and after 3 p.m., by the general public.

Those arriving by car may park their cars in Trinity Avenue and when leaving, are asked to proceed down Trinity Avenue to Kingsthorpe Grove.

A marquee will be erected by the side of the entrance, and guests are asked to be in their seats by not later than 11.15 a.m.

THE SOUVENIR PROGRAMME OF 17 NOVEMBER 1932

Historical Notes

Evening Classes for the development of scientific and technical education in Northampton were started on a small scale in the year 1867 under the auspices of the Museum Committee when two classes were conducted, one in the large room of the Working Men's Institute in St Giles' Street, and the other in All Saints' School.

At that time Mr Jonathan Edwards Ryland was Keeper of the Museum, and Mr J. B. Hensman, who later was Clerk to the School Board, was appointed Hon. Secretary. During later years classes were held at the Corn Exchange.

In the year 1876 Science and Art Classes were commenced at the old Northampton Grammar School on Abington Square in preparation for South Kensington examinations. The late Rev. Dr Sanders was Head of the Grammar School and the late Mr Beeby Thompson was appointed Master-in-charge of the Science Classes. In 1885, the Museum Committee, mainly owing to the efforts of Mr S. S. Campion, agreed to the commencement of classes in Boot and Shoe Manufacture and Mr Beeby Thompson was appointed Manager of the classes. An inaugural meeting was held in the large hall of the Grammar School early in October 1885, Mr P. Manfield presiding. The first class in Tanning was commenced in 1887.

The Technical Instruction Act came into operation in 1889, and at a meeting of the Technical Committee held on the 6th October, 1890, Northampton adopted the Act on the proposition of Alderman H. E. Randall, seconded by Councillor S. S. Campion. In December, 1890, the first meeting of the Technical Instruction Act Committee was held and Councillor Campion was elected Chairman. The late Mr E. J. Swaysland commenced teaching practical Pattern Cutting at this time. In 1894 the Technical classes were placed under the control of the Governors of the Northampton Town and Country Modern and Technical School, the governing body consisting of twenty-one governors, fourteen appointed by the Borough Committee and seven by the County Council.

In 1911 the Northampton Education Committee became responsible for technical education. At this time the late Mr Rowland Hill, J.P., was Chairman of the Committee and of the Technical Education Sub-Committee, and the late Mr Stewart Beattie was Secretary. The only Members of this first Sub-Committee who are now Members of the Education Committee are Alderman Earl and Councillor Peach. The Town and County School was transferred to the new buildings on the Billing Road and the old buildings on Abington Square were transferred to the Education Committee and opened as the Technical School, Mr John Blakeman, M.A., M.Sc., being appointed Principal. At this time, the teaching consisted of isolated evening classes with no departmental grouped courses, and there was very little equipment of any kind either for the teaching of Science or Technology.

The policy pursued included the linking up of senior classes with classes for Juniors in Continuation Schools, the establishment of departmental grouped courses, the purchase of equipment on a very modest scale for the teaching of the various branches of Science and the erection of temporary buildings and equipment for the teaching of practical Boot and Shoe Manufacture, these latter being in accordance with a scheme submitted by Mr E. J. Swaysland who was head of the Boot and Shoe Department. It was realised that the arrangements were of a temporary character, and the Board of Education were promised that new buildings would be erected at an early date. The Principal was instructed to prepare sketch plans for a new Technical School on Abington Square. This was done, but the War intervened, and in 1915 it was decided to abandon the proposals for the time being. In November, 1914, Councillor C. W. Phipps was appointed Chairman of the Technical and Evening Schools Sub-Committee, a position he continued to hold until 1924. During his Chairmanship he exerted a great influence in urging the importance of scientific and technical education, securing the co-operation of employers, foremen and trades union representatives and in improving the facilities provided and raising the standard of the work.

In September 1915, the Northampton Boot Manufacturers' Association agreed to a time-off scheme in which boy and girl employees of 14–16 years of age were released from work earlier than the normal time in order to attend Evening Continuation Schools. In September, 1918, a day time-off scheme was established in which boys and girls were allowed four hours per week from work, without loss of wages, in order to attend day classes at the Technical School.

Up to this time the work of the Technical School had consisted entirely of evening classes and was conducted by part-time teachers, except that Mr W. J. Chater, M.Sc, the present Deputy Principal, had given full-time service to the School from September 1915. The establishment of the Day Continuation Classes enabled a full-time staff to be appointed. In the year 1918 full-time instruction was provided in the Tanning Department. In 1919 the Committee purchased a factory in St Michael's Road, immediately at the rear of the Boot and Shoe Department, for use as a tannery and to provide further accommodation for Boot and Shoe instruction.

The Advisory Committee for Boot and Shoe Manufacture, under the Chairmanship of the late Councillor Edward Lewis, was formed in 1914, and an Advisory Committee for Leather Manufacture under the Chairmanship of Mr W. P. Cross was formed in 1918.

In 1919 the Boot, Shoe and Allied Trades Research Association was established at the School with the Principal as Acting Director, the work being conducted under these arrangements until 1922 when it had extended sufficiently to become a national concern and was transferred as a separate organisation to London.

In 1920 the late Mr Alfred Caine Boyde, M.A., LLB, was appointed Director of Education; he always took a keen interest in the development ot technical education and pressed very strongly for the provision of adequate buildings and equipment.

During the period 1917 to 1921 a most important service was rendered by the School, in conjunction with the Ministry of Pensions and the Ministry of Labour, in the training of Ex-Service Men in Commerce, Hand Sewn Boot Making and Boot and Shoe Manufacture. At one time there were as many as two hundred men attending these full-time courses together.

In 1919 Advanced Full-Time Day Courses were established in Boot and Shoe Manufacture, and in 1927 the Board of Education informed the Authority that the School was recognised as a College under the Regulations for Further Education.

In 1924 Councillor James Peach was appointed Chairman of the Technical College Sub-Committee, and in 1930 on Councillor Peach becoming Chairman of the Education Committee, Councillor A. W. Lyne, J.P. became Chairman of the Technical College Sub-Committee.

Mr H. C. Perrin became Secretary for Education in 1930, and he has been the Administrative Officer of the Committee during the whole period of the building and equipping of the new College.

Building and Equipment

In a Memorandum prepared by Alderman S. S. Campion, JP, HF, in 1919, it was recommended that a College be built on a site adjoining the Northampton School for Girls, and on Mr Boyde becoming Director of Education he immediately realised that the provision of buildings for Technical education in Northampton was extremely urgent. In 1924 he issued a Memorandum raising the question of the desirability of placing the new College on the above-mentioned site rather than on the site of the old buildings on Abington Square. He was of opinion that the latter site was a very valuable one and should be used for other needs of the Borough, also that it was too small to provide for the future needs of technical education; particularly in view of the tendency of this type of education to become day work. With this view, the Education Committee of the time with Alderman Sykes as Chairman, Alderman S. S. Campion Deputy Chairman, and Councillor C. W. Phipps as Chairman of the Technical and Evening Schools Sub-Committee concurred and in that year the Committee secured a site of 39 acres in St George's Avenue at a cost of £7,000, about 9 acres of which have since been allocated to the Northampton School for Girls for Playing Fields in lieu of approximately 2½ acres of front land transferred to the College of Technology. This site allows for the provision of adequate recreational facilities and during the year 1931 approximately 20 acres of the site were levelled and laid out as football and hockey pitches, tennis courts, etc., by 'unemployed' labour. The College Site is situated almost exactly in the centre of the extended Borough of Northampton.

In 1926 the Committee began to formulate their plans for the new College. The Principal of the College submitted a scheme showing the rooms required, their sizes and the conditions that must be satisfied as to the linking up of the various rooms for departmental organisation.

The Committee also had the valuable advice and assistance of the Advisory Committees for Boot and Shoe and Leather Manufacture. Various Colleges were visited by Members of the Committee, the Director of Education, the Principal, the Architect and Members of the College Staff, and in 1928 the preliminary plans of the College were forwarded to the Board of Education for consideration.

In December, 1930, the Board finally approved of the plans and of the acceptance of Messrs. Glenn & Sons' tender amounting to £79,850 for the buildings and fixtures. The completed scheme for the new buildings includes:

(1) Boot and Shoe, Leather, Engineering, Building and Science Departments. (2) Domestic Department. (3) Commercial and Literary Departments and Administration. (4) School of Arts and Crafts.

The first sod was turned in February 1931 and on the 3rd of December 1931, foundation stones were laid by Councillor Peach, Chairman of the Education

Committee, Alderman S. S. Campion, J.P., H.F., Deputy Chairman of the Education Committee, and Councillor A. W. Lyne, J.P., Chairman of the Technical College Sub-Committee.

The portion at present in course of erection comprises the Workshops and Laboratories, and some provision for Domestic and Commercial subjects. In addition to the sum of £79,850 for the building and fixtures, the equipment and furniture will cost approximately £14,000, whilst there will be in the building further machinery and equipment on loan to the value of over £10,000.

* * *

It will be seen that at present only a very small portion of the frontage has been erected. The remaining portion of the frontage will include the Administration and Commerce block, main entrance and part of the School of Arts and Crafts. The estimated cost of the portion of the complete building to be devoted to the School of Arts and Crafts is £25,000. The Education Committee made application in November last for this portion to be proceeded with, but in view of the financial position the Borough Council were unable to give their sanction. They have, however, given their sanction to the erection of the Domestic Department of the College at a cost of £11,000, which, when erected, will enable the Education Committee to vacate the present premises on Abington Square, so that they may be handed over to the Improvements Committee of the Council who will pay the Education Committee the sum of £10,000 for the buildings and site, thus providing nearly sufficient capital for the provision of the Domestic Department.

The plans of the College have been prepared by the Committee's Architectural Assistant, Mr Keightley Cobb, L.R.I.B.A., under the supervision of the Borough Engineer, Mr Alfred Fidler, M.Inst.CE. The requirements set out by the Principal, and approved by the Committee, were embodied in detail in these plans. The Fittings and Equipment were fully specified by the Principal and members of the staff, and a great deal of work has been done in this connection by Mr W. J. Chater, M.Sc, for the Chemistry and General Science Laboratories; Mr D. Woodroffe, M.Sc, A.I.C., for the Department of Leather Manufature; Mr O. F. Bailey, B.Sc., for the Electrical Engineering, Physics and Boot and Shoe Science Departments; and Mr W. R. Morgan for the Engineering and Building Departments, whilst the British United Shoe Machinery Company have given extremely valuable service in settling details as to the lay-out and equipment of the Boot and Shoe Department. All the requirements set out have been provided in detail by Mr Cobb and the building and equipment are fitted in every way to meet the local needs as proved by the experience of the last twenty years.

* * *

Description of the Building

The main Facade of the College when completed will have a frontage of 360 feet to St George's Avenue and will consist of an imposing central feature carried out entirely in stone and embodying the main entrance giving direct access to the Great Hall with corridors extending right and left to the various departments of the College.

The buildings to the East of the central entrance will be occupied by the School of Arts and Crafts and on the West by the Administrative and Commercial sections of the College of Technology.

At the East and West ends of the front elevation two further entrances are provided, the one at the East end giving access to the School of Arts and Crafts.

The entrance at the West end gives access to the College of Technology and is the only portion of the front elevation at present erected. The architectural treatment is Classic in character, a dignified appearance being obtained by careful consideration of proportion and selection of materials rather than by elaboration of detail. The front is carried out in reconstructed Ketton stone with panels of dark red sand-faced bricks. The main entrance doors are of unpolished teak with a stone door-case flanked on either side by Ionic columns 28 feet high supporting a heavy stone entablature and cornice, the roof being covered with green slates.

From St George's Avenue a 20 feet wide concrete roadway leads down the side of the main buildings and along the back, advantage having been taken of the fall of the site to give access from the roadway to the various floors. The West elevation has a frontage of 264 feet and the North elevation a frontage of 234 feet to this roadway, and these elevations have been carried out with cream Cambridge brick piers and dark red sand-faced brick panels forming a pleasing and inexpensive treatment. To the left of the roadway a Caretaker's house, 12 lock-up garages and ample accommodation for cycles have been provided.

The building is a steel-framed structure cased in brickwork with reinforced concrete floors and flats throughout. The main portion is three stories in height and the rooms are arranged on either side of corridors 8 feet wide, which run the full length of the building, fireproof staircases being provided at the ends of each corridor. A subway is carried below the bottom corridor to take all gas, water, heating and vacuum cleaning pipes, also the electric lighting and power cables to all departments.

A feature of the College is the entrance vestibule, the walls of which are panelled out with adamant marble with green borders and cream panels, the floor being laid with Terazzo marble tiles.

The half-glass doors and screens are in unpolished teak with semi-circular fanlights over. The walls above the marble panelling are finished in plaster with a bold dentilled cornice at the ceiling level and a specially designed bronze electric light fitting forms a central feature to the ceiling.

Three small rooms adjoining this Vestibule will be used as office accommodation for the Principal and Clerical Staff until the remaining portion of the College is built.

*   *   *

Courses of Study and Future Development

The College offers at present a wide range of courses of further education in accordance with the following scheme:-

Junior Technical School. This is a full-time day school for boys and girls 13 to 15 years of age, providing a two-year course of specialised training for industrial or commercial life whilst at the same time continuing the general education. Separate courses are provided for Commerce, Trade and Homecraft, Boot and Shoe and Leather Manufacture, Engineering, Building and General Artisans.

Continuation Schools. There are six Evening Continuation Schools providing evening courses for boys and girls of 14 to 16 years of age, preparatory to the College courses, and students attending these are allowed to attend the College on one morning per week for instruction in practical subjects if they can get the necessary time off from the employer.

Senior Full-time Courses. These are specialised one-year full-time courses normally for post-Secondary students of 16 years of age. Separate courses are provided in Commerce for boys and girls, and in Housecraft for girls.

Advanced Day Courses: Full-time and Half-time. Separate two-year advanced courses are provided in Boot and Shoe Manufacture and in Leather Manufacture. A thorough training is given in technology including all branches of pratical work. The complete courses are designed for students who attend full-time for two years, but provision is made for half-time students who work in the factories each morning and attend the College each afternoon.

Senior and Advanced Evening Courses. These are normally for students over 16 years of age who have previously attended Secondary Schools or Junior Courses at the Evening Continuation Schools. In the Boot and Shoe and Leather Departments older students are encouraged to join the College for minor courses mainly of a practical character, irrespective of their previous education. The Evening Courses are conducted in the following Departments:- Commerce, Housecraft, Boot and Shoe Manufacture, Leather Manufacture, Electrical Engineering, Mechanical Engineering including Motor Car Body Work, Gas Fitting and Plumbing, Building, Science including Chemistry, Pharmacy and Materia Medica, Baking and Confectionery.

Senior Part-time Day Courses. These include the following: Pharmacists' Course: students prepare for the Preliminary Scientific Examination of the Pharmaceutical Society of Great Britain. Electrical Engineering. Housecraft Department: Afternoon classes are held in Cookery, Needlework, Dressmaking and Upholstery.

Under the adverse conditions that have prevailed up to the present Northampton students have done so well as to prove that they are worthy of better things. About 2,000 students per year attend the College and the preparatory Continuation Schools, and the work has been developed to a remarkably high standard.

In Commerce the students take advanced certificates in the examinations of the Royal Society of Arts and gain many group certificates. There are Ordinary Grade National Certificate schemes in operation in Mechanical Engineering, Electrical Engineering, Building and Chemistry, and a Higher Grade National Certificate scheme for the Chemistry of Leather Manufacture.

Very special attention is paid to the Departments of Boot and Shoe and Leather Manufacture as these industries are so important to Northampton. During the last ten years the College has gained an international reputation in these departments and has attracted students from almost every European country and from India.

The experience of the last few years has clearly defined the broad lines of future development. The Junior Technical School will become of increasing importance; the work done here will make its mark on the town as the students are absorbed into industry and commerce, and moreover a large number of students will be passed on from this School to the advanced College courses. There will probably be a marked development of part-time day courses, whilst the advanced day courses will become of increasing importance. National Certificate courses will be further developed and in particular there will probably be a very imporant National Certificate course in Commerce. Whilst in the past few years many students have qualified for the examinations of various professional bodies, the numbers doing this will increase considerably with the better facilities now offered. Almost immediately a number of students will prepare themselves for Intermediate Degree examinations of London University in Commerce and Science and in a few years it is confidently expected that the work will reach Degree standard. In particular it is intended to raise the standard of Scientific and Technological education in relation to the Boot and Shoe and Leather industries. The Education Committee are determined to establish a College which will be second to none so far as these industries are concerned. It is expected that the advanced courses in Boot and Shoe and Leather Manufacture will in time attain to such a standard that University Degrees will be possible in these subjects.

> Extracts from the Souvenir Programme
> published by the Northampton County
> Borough Education Committee on the
> occasion of the visit of their Royal
> Highnesses the Duke and Duchess of York
> to open the Northampton College of
> Technology on 17 November 1932

A REPORT OF THE ROYAL VISIT

Northampton has enjoyed the honour of many royal visits dating back to the earliest years of its history. Few, however, have transcended in potential importance that of Thursday, November 17th, when T.R.H. the Duke and Duchess of York came to open Northampton's new College of Technology, which has arisen on a site in St George's Avenue, and the John Greenwood Shipman Convalescent Home at Dallington. The new College is likely to win educational fame for Northampton extending to the four corners of the earth and may be the foundation of its becoming a university town.

These auspicious circumstances should have moved the elements to cast their benediction upon the occasion. As it was, an overcast sky and a slight drizzle of rain prevailed from early morning and continued right up to the time of the royal visitors' arrival.

They came by rail to Blisworth and thence by car, travelling from London in a special coach attached to the L.M.S. 'Royal Scot' train drawn by the mammoth engine, 'Goliath.' Immediately the coach came to a standstill the Duke and Duchess alighted, stepping out into the rain for, owing to a slight misunderstanding, their compartment had over-run the covered portion of the platform. Both were undaunted, however, the Duchess, while looking anxiously at the skies breaking into the sunny smile which has won all hearts wherever she has gone.

The Duke was wearing a grey suit with dark overcoat and bowler hat, and the Duchess was a figure of welcome brightness amid the gloomy conditions, attired in a delicate shade of sapphire blue velvet. Her long coat had a rich roll collar of fox, her velvet hat to match being up-turned at the left side and secured with a bow of the same material.

A Triumphal Progress

At once the official party from Northampton approached and exchanged cordial greetings. The Mayor of Northampton (Councillor P. F. Hanafy) and the Mayoress (Councillor Mrs Hanafy), who wore a dark green coat trimmed with black fur, where introduced to T.R.H. by the Town Clerk (Mr W. R. Kew). The Duke and Duchess shook hands with each and were then introduced to the Chief Constable (Mr John Williamson), who led the party throughout in the pilot car, and Mr H. W. Ede (District Goods and Passenger Manager of the L.M.S.). The Stationmaster (Mr J. Leal) was also introduced. Conversation at once turned to the weather and the Duchess expressed relief to learn that it was much brighter at Northampton.

Then began a triumphal progress through crowds of cheering villagers at Milton and further vast crowds at Northampton lining the route to the new College. At Far Cotton, on the steps of All Saints' Church, outside the Notre Dame High School in Abington Street and the Kettering-road Intermediate School, and beside the road of St George's Avenue opposite the Northampton Girls' Secondary School, thousands of schoolchildren were massed. As the royal party approached each section in turn, while they waved hundreds of flags, set up rounds of cheering which must have been heard all over the town.

Both the Duke and Duchess were obviously deeply appreciative of such a welcome and repeatedly bowed and smiled to right and left.

Students' Welcome

The College reached, the loud speakers, which had been amusing the waiting assembly with popular music, ceased to give way to a tumultous outbreak of cheers from hundreds of guests accommodated in a marquee opposite the entrance, more hundreds of college students on the lawn and leaning out of every upper window and from crowds of people massed on the Racecourse opposite. Again the Duchess smiled her response while the Duke raised his hat repeatedly.

At the entrance members of the Northampton Town and County School O.T.C. formed a guard of honour, and the party having passed through, the Mayor then made a number of presentations detailed in another column.

In each case both the Duke and Duchess extended a hearty greeting. An especial response, however, was reserved for Mr S. S. Campion, J.P., H.F., Northampton's only Honorary Freeman and pioneer of Technical Education, who, despite his advanced years, had cheerfully braved the cold breeze and drizzle.

This ceremony over, the royal pair mounted the steps of the College which had been covered with a decorated awning, although, happily, the rain had now ceased.

As they did so the Mayoress, with a graceful curtsey, presented an exquisite bouquet of mauve orchids and pink carnations to the Duchess. 'Oh! thank you,' exclaimed Her Royal Highness. 'How lovely!'

The Mayor's Address

His voice amplified by loud speakers directed to all parts of the assembly, the Mayor then delivered his address of welcome

'I am privileged,' said his worship, 'to offer to you, on behalf of the Borough Council and the citizens of Northampton, a very sincere and hearty welcome to our ancient borough. We are highly honoured and deeply gratified that you have been pleased to visit Northampton, and to signify by that visit your deep interest in and approval of the efforts which are being made to forward the interests of technical education in the borough.

The establishment of this College is the culmination of many years of anxious thought on the part of the Borough Council and the Education Committee, and your visit intimates your approval of the results of our efforts.

Royal Interest in Northampton
We are aware of the keen interest which you and other members of your Royal House have taken in the town of Northampton, and we are cognisant also of your sympathy with, and interest in, any efforts to improve and extend the industrial development of our country.

This College is established to improve the quality and technique of the productions which have for centuries been associated with Northampton. A fully-equipped and up-to-date factory for the instruction of students in the technique of boot and shoe manufacture has been provided in the College, as well as a complete tannery for the instruction of students in the manufacture of leather. Laboratories for chemistry and general science, and facilities for the instruction of students in commerce, housecraft, electrical and mechanical engineering, gas fitting and plumbing, building, pharmacy, baking and confectionery, and domestic subjects have also been provided.

Students From Overseas
Northampton has specialised in the provision of boots and shoes and the manufacture of leather, and during the past 10 years the College has, despite many handicaps, gained an international reputation in these departments, and has attracted students from almost every European country and from the British Colonies.

The College includes a junior technical school, available for students between 14 and 16 years of age, and it is anticipated that this will become of increasing importance as the students are absorbed into industry.

National certificate courses will be developed, and a number of students will shortly be preparing for the intermediate degree examinations of London University in commerce and science, and in a few years it is confidently expected that the work will reach the full degree standard.

The building represents only a portion of the complete structure intended to be raised by the authority. The domestic subjects portion, the school of arts and crafts, the large hall, and the administration block remain to be erected.

A College Second to None

The Education Committee aim at establishing a College which will be second to none so far as the making of boots and shoes and the manufacture of leather are concerned, and we hope that the advanced courses available in those subjects will in time attain a standard justifying the conferment of University degrees in those subjects, with the possibility of the establishment of a close link with a University, so that the Northampton College may become a constituent part of that University preparing students for internal degrees.

At the rear of the College there are extensive playing fields for the use of students, so that the recreational side of the work of the College has been amply provided for.

There has been generous and wholehearted co-operation by the Boot and Shoe Manufacturers' Association and the local leather manufacturers in this effort. The Northampton Town Boot Manufacturers have very generously presented the shelving and about 600 volumes for the College library.

May I again express to your Royal Highnesses the great pleasure it has given to the Borough Council and the whole of the inhabitants of the Borough of Northampton to have you present on this notable occasion, and it is with much pleasure that I ask the Chairman of the Education Committee (Councillor James Peach), who has worked unceasingly on its behalf for many years, to present to your Royal Highness a key with which we ask you to unlock the doors and declare open the Northampton College of Technology.

The Mayor's peroration was greeted with cheers and applause which were renewed when the Duke passed over to the microphone to reply.

The Duke's Speech

Speaking in clear, evenly modulated and deliberate tones he paid the following gratifying tribute to the occasion:-

On behalf of the Duchess of York and myself I thank you most sincerely for the welcome you have given us to-day, and I can assure you that it gives us very great pleasure to be with you.

I had occasion to visit Northampton at your wish two years ago and was then gratified to learn of the beneficent activities of the townspeople in philanthropic and social efforts, and on this occasion I am proud to take part in the inauguration of the College of Technology, which will show for all time that the Borough of Northampton, under the guidance of its local legislators and their staff, is alive to the importance of extending to the utmost the facilities for technical education and instruction, which are so vital to the progress and improvement of our national efforts.

Mr Mayor, you have in your speech referred to the fact that this building is the culmination of years of thought, and I am sure you and the members of the Council and the Education Committee feel a gratifying pride in to-days's ceremony. I have been privileged during past years to see a great deal of what is being done in the factories and works in our great industrial and manufacturing areas, and have also spent some time in witnessing similar developments in some of our Dominions.

Students' Opportunities

The opportunities that a building such as this College affords to students to obtain technical knowledge and to learn the rudiments and practice of arts and professions vital to our industrial developmemt are unbounded, and I congratulate those who have been responsible for this work for their foresight and enterprise.

You have informed me, Mr Mayor, that the Chairman and members of the Education Committee and its Sub-Committees have devoted much time and thought to the elaboration of this work. As these gentlemen have made their sacrifices of time and effort to provide the opportunity and to bring their scheme to fruition, may I voice the hope that the students who are privileged to enter this College may also seize the opportunities afforded them, and by their research and work bring credit to the College and to the town and our country by what they may learn here.

Value of Playing Fields

I am very much interested to note that you have deemed it desirable – may I say necessary – to provide for recreation facilities in the splendid playing fields attached to the College. As President of the National Playing Fields Association, I fully realise the great value of your action in this respect, and hope they will meet with general approval and appreciation.

I now have much pleasure in declaring open the Northampton College of Technology.

It affords the Duchess and myself the greatest gratification to be with you to-day, and we wish you prosperity in the efforts you have made and are making, and trust that these efforts may be successful in every possible direction.

Opening the Door

This address, redolent throughout of sincerity, captured the imagination of everyone present and was greeted with applause which lasted until the Duke took from Councillor James Peach (Chairman of the Education Committee) a key of the College with which he then turned and performed the most important, if the shortest, ceremony of the day – that of opening the College door.

The royal party then passed within and at once fell to admiring the design and appointment of the entrance hall. 'How delightful,' remarked the Duchess.

A Student Presented

Then further presentations followed, one of them being of a particularly pleasant character. This was the introduction to the Duke and Duchess of Miss Gertrude Cherry, elected by ballot to represent the students of the College.

Miss Cherry, who is the only daughter of Mr and Mrs C. E. W. Cherry, of 14, Cloutsham Street, Northampton, has been a student at the College for ten years. Educated at St Mary's School, she first attended the College for a commercial course, her chief interest now being English. She is on the staff of Mr H. W. Whitton, the Northampton land agent.

Royal Visitors' Comments

The royal tour of the building then began. At every turn were floral decorations and the whole of the departments with their equipment in meticulous order and neatly attired students standing by were a revelation of order and method.

Throughout the tour both the Duke and Duchess plied their guides with a succession of interested queries.

* * *

The Duchess was, naturally, keenly interested in the domestic science section, asking numerous questions as to the average age of the girls, whether they remained at work while at the College, and so on.

There were several further presentations on arrival at the boot and shoe department which were followed by the presentation by Mr C. G. B. Allinson, on behalf of the Northampton Town Boot Manufacturers' Association, of shoes made for Their Royal Highnesses and Princess Elizabeth.

The Presentation Shoes

There were two pairs for the Duchess. One was a pair of Sahara evening sandals made of gold kid and piped, laced and thonged with silver kid. The straps were fastened with silver slip buckles, set with brilliants, and the 2¼ inch Spanish heels were covered with gold kid. As fancy shoes they are magnificent work, and they reflect the utmost credit upon their makers, Messrs Padmore and Barnes, Ltd.

The second pair was of salmon pink glace kid turnshoes, with a contrasting band and bow of dark glace, and high Spanish heels. These were the product of Allison and Co., and in their quieter way are equally beautiful.

The Duke's gift consisted of a pair of black brogue shooting shoes with Uskide

(Canadian) soles, made by Messrs F. Cook and Co., Ltd., of Long Buckby.

Some months ago, when the Duke was invited to accept a gift of shoes he gave an intimation that if it could be arranged he would prefer them to be made by Cook and Co., who have previously made his footwear. A gratifying testimonial indeed!

Extracts from the *Northampton and County Independent,*
26 November 1932

'OUR HOPES AND ASPIRATIONS AT THE NEW COLLEGE:
BLAZING THE TRAIL TO INTERNATIONAL FAME'

Like one who has climbed a mountain peak, and, pausing, reflects on the rigours and hardships of his journey, so does Northampton to-day reach the summit of fulfilment in regard to technical education and look back on the difficulties and struggles of past years.

But there is another side to the picture. The climber reflects not only on by-gone toils; he sees before and around him the illimitable prospects which was at once his goal and his spur. Memories of the past are dim in comparison with the feeling of triumph and mastery which floods his mind.

So it is with those in Northampton who have striven for the new era in technical education. The past – and it has not been without its successes – fades before the dawn of better and greater prospects. The future is opening, rosy with the promise of magnificent achievements.

Finest in the Country

The culmination of years of work has arrived in the erection of the new college buildings in St George's Avenue. It is no exaggeration to describe them as the most up-to-date and the finest equipped of their kind in any town of similar size in Great Britain.

Architectural skill has blended with mechanical genius to produce a college adapted for the teaching of craftsmanship as demanded by modern standards; and we who have lived and worked in Northampton know that the human material which that college will fashion and develop is second to none in this country, if not the world.

Science and the Future

Let there be no mistake. The new College of Technology could not have reached completion at a more opportune time. When we look at other industries and at the whole tendency of science and production, we have every right to be certain that the changes which will take place in the boot and shoe industry will be far greater than any which have yet occurred.

Those changes will be closely linked with the development of science. Their nature no man can foresee; but is it not a fair assumption that in the developments ahead the growth of the new college is bound to play an important part?

The teaching of craftsmanship is, of course, not the sole function of the college. It has work to perform in connection with almost every branch of human activity; it will endeavour to fit boys and girls, men and women, for the demands of the high-pressure civilisation in which it is their lot to live.

But craftsmanship, especially in a town of the character of Northampton, is of vital importance. The people of America and of continental countries have perhaps been quicker than we in Britain to realise that. They have made it their business to teach craftsmanship to people likely to remain workers, and I am quoting the opinion of one of the foremost technical experts in Britain when I state that unless we follow suit, the British workman will not remain the best in the world.

What are our aims at Northampton? It is our proud boast that all over the world the town is noted for the production of the best boots and shoes; it must become similarly well-known everywhere that Northampton has the best technical education for that industry.

We are out to develop in Northampton an international college for the boot and shoe industry. During the past few years we have had students from almost every country in the world; we want to attract more students until the fame of Northampton's educational facilities has spread over every quarter of the globe.

Brains in our Industries

It is sometimes said, I know, 'Why should we teach foreigners our business?' To that criticism there is an obvious and adequate reply. We can afford to teach everybody all we are doing, and if we don't teach them they will find out.

The condition of progress in a vital industry is that, while these bands of people are going back and putting into operation what they have learned, the progressing country has marched ten years ahead.

What we cannot afford to do is to give away our brains. It is my hope that brains will be fostered in the boot and shoe industry, and that they will be given an opportunity in this locality as far as possible.

A University College?

In its provision for technical education, Northampton up to the present has been sadly behind the progressive towns. Now, with the new college, it is quite ten years in front, and it is my opinion that we are on the threshold of a greater educational advance than the town has yet known.

We intend to develop far more advanced work in connection with the boot and shoe industry than has been possible in the past. The equipment we shall possess will be absolutely the best obtainable; in some particulars we shall be in advance of any factory.

It is our dream that the college may one day become a University College. Its facilities and opportunities for expansion are sufficient to justify its aspiration to that status.

One possibility certainly exists within the realm of practical politics. That is the granting of university degrees in boot and shoe manufacture. I am certain it can be done, and I shall not be content unless I see it in my time. You can get degrees in engineering and leather manufacture; why not in boot and shoe manufacture?

Whilst the requirements of the boot and shoe and leather industries must be kept steadily to the fore in Northampton, the College caters for every branch of commerce, science and industry, and the equipment and courses of study up to degree standard in commerce, chemistry, physics, mechanical and electrical engineering, building and allied industries, whilst there is a most important and successful domestic department.

Let the future hold what it may, we stand ready to seize all that it offers. Northampton has forged to the forefront of technical education and that position it will not readily surrender.

Article by Mr John Blakeman, MA, MSc,
Principal of Northampton College of Technology,
published in the *Northampton
and County Independent,*
26 November 1932

3 The School of Art

Derek Brooks

From their inception in Northampton in 1867 science and art classes were inextricably linked together for the next forty years. Art was not treated as an entirely separate institution although there was always a separate master in charge. The first one, in 1867, was Mr Abram S. Taylor, who was keeper of the Museum in the town as well as a certificated art teacher. It was significant that at least one of the founders of these early classes was an artist of national repute, Sir Henry L. Dryden, Bt. Perhaps only he, of all the founders, thought more in terms of art than technology; certainly from the beginning the art side of the partnership seemed very much a junior partner. Thirty-five pupils were in the original class with an age range of 13–32 years.

One of the students in the early years was Beeby Thompson who in 1869 took art studies and passed in two papers in the science and art examinations and two in the Society of Arts examinations. When Beeby Thompson was appointed master of the new Science School, attached to the Grammar School in 1876, he found that the art classes were already in residence at the Grammar School under the headmastership of Mr Henry Hill. They moved into the new Science School, in a large upstairs room over the laboratory. Mr Hill remained head of the classes until 1885 when he resigned and Mr A. A. Bradbury was appointed. He came at a rather unfortunate time since the first five years were fraught with economic hardship. It was not until the 'whisky money' became available after 1890 that the town could really adopt the Technical Instruction Act. So big an improvement was this, that in 1891 the head of the art classes found himself in receipt of a salary of £150 per annum plus a proportion of the grant earned without being responsible for any of the expenses.

There was an abortive attempt in 1892 to merge art, science and technology within the framework of the Grammar School. In 1894 this was accomplished and the art classes became part of the Northampton and County Modern and Technical School under the headship of Mr R.

GOVERNMENT
SCHOOL OF ART,

Abington Square, Northampton,

In connection with the Science and Art Department of the Committee of Council on Education,

Chairman of the Committee—LORD A. COMPTON.

HEAD MASTER—MR. HENRY HILL.

COURSES OF INSTRUCTION.

I.—ELEMENTARY: including *Freehand, Model Drawing, Chalk Shading* from the Round and from Flat examples.

II.—ADVANCED: *Drawing* and *Shading* from the Round in Water Colour. Drawing and Painting Flowers, Still Life and Landscape from Copies; the Principles of Ornamental Design, Illuminations, &c., Artistic Anatomy; the Analysis of Plants for deriving New Ornamental Forms; Designing Lace and other Art Manufactures, &c.

III.—PAINTING: Painting the Human Figure from Copies and Casts; Painting Flowers, Still Life and Groups as Composition in Colour from Nature.

IV.—TECHNICAL: Orthographic Projection, Machine Drawing, Building, Construction and the Principles of Architectural Design; Modelling in Clay and Wax.

LECTURES on Perspective and Practical Geometry are given during the Winter Months, and *Free* to all Students.

HOURS OF STUDY AND FEES.

CLASSES.	FEES.			DAYS.	HOURS.
	LADIES' AND GENTLEMEN'S.			AFTERNOON CLASSES.	
Ladies' and Gentlemen.	Elementary. Advanced. Painting.		21/- per Term	Mondays & Thursdays.	2.30 to 4.30
Ladies' and Gentlemen.	Elementary. Advanced. Painting.		10/6 per Term	Thursday.	2.30 to 4.30

LADIES' AND GENTLEMEN'S EVENING CLASSES.

Ladies'.	Elementary. Advanced.	7/6 per Term	Mondays, Thursdays, and Fridays.	6 to 7.30
Gentlemen.	Elementary. Advanced.	7/6 per Term	Mondays, Tuesdays, Thursdays & Fridays.	7.30 to 9.30

ARTIZAN EVENING CLASSES.

Ladies'.	Elementary. Advanced.	4/- per Term	Mondays, Thursdays, and Fridays.	6 to 7.30
Gentlemen.	Elementary. Advanced.	5/- per Term	Mondays, Tuesdays, Thursdays & Fridays.	7.30 to 9.30

ALL FEES MUST BE PAID IN ADVANCE. NO ENTRANCE FEES.

The working year is divided into Four Terms, which commence as follows: 1st Term, August 7th; 2nd Term, Oct. 16th; 3rd Term, January 8th; 4th Term, March 19th. The Half-Terms commence Sept. 11th, Nov. 27th, Feb. 11th, and April 23rd.

All Students are eligible for the Prizes awarded by the Science and Art Department, London, including Scholarships of the annual value of £11 and £25, and Free Studentships for Twelve Months, which may be renewed annually; also for the Bronze Medal, and Local Prizes, which are given for excellence in the above-mentioned subjects.

Further information may be obtained from the Head Master.

J. B. HENSMAN,

HON. SECRETARY.

Stanton & Son, Printers, Northampton.

Elliot Steele, MA. Art was one of the four departments in the school and students worked for the South Kensington examinations. Results were good, numbers on the roll increased, and the number of classes expanded to include needlework and embroidery, dressmaking and wood carving. The room above the science laboratory was by this time most inadequate. Notwithstanding repeated threats and entreaties by the Education Inspectors little or nothing was done. The only real change was in 1907 when Elliot Steele left the school, and the combined art and technical classes carried on alone, in the Grammar School, but not of it. It reorganised itself in that year as the Northampton and County Technical and Art School.

At last, towards the end of 1907, the situation was recognised by the Authority as being in need of improvement and premises were rented at 100a Abington Street. These were to be the new home of the art classes. They moved in, under the guidance of the art master, George C. Duxbury, ARCA, who came from London. From that moment they were to all intents and purposes an Art School, although for official purposes they were linked with the Technical School.

In 1908, the head of the art classes, George Duxbury, initiated a scheme for liaison between the Art School and the elementary schools for art teaching, which was to last for many years. It was coupled with lectures, by him, on the teaching of art, and was to culminate in an exhibition of art work from schools within the scheme.

Change was afoot however. The upheaval caused by the removal of the Grammar School from the Abington Square premises in 1911, and the change of that building to a Municipal Technical School, caused ripples which upset the administration, but not the executive aspect of the Art School. The control of the School passed from the central government department, the Board of Education, to the Local Education Authority. For the first time the Art School was to have a headmaster. The post was advertised, it was stipulated that whoever was offered the position should be an Associate of the Royal College of Art or a qualified art master with a first-class certificate and a Mr Thomas J. Nelson from London was appointed. Mr Nelson came from the London County Council Norwood Technical Institute, where he had been head of the Art Department. He was a man of wide experience having taught at seven art schools and six pupil teacher centres since his debut in teaching at the age of 15 years. He became qualified at the age of 23 years following four years at the Royal College of Art. He did not believe that art was purely a gift, but that it could be inculcated, and he thought that there was great scope for art in elementary schools, and that it could be used in other subjects.

Amid a blaze of publicity this 'new' Northampton School of Art began its work giving instruction in the 'Fine Arts and Decorative Arts and Crafts'. The staff of the school consisted of the headmaster (later known

as principal), two full-time assistants and an art pupil-teacher. Accommodation comprised six rooms for all drawing and craft work, which was to
be provided for both day and evening students, with special provision for
elementary teachers on Saturday mornings. Fees payable for the day
classes were eight shillings per term, or one pound per session for one
class per week, or one pound per term for three classes. Evening class fees
were five shillings per term or ten shillings per session and students had a
choice of general art, life drawing or craft classes. To help with the paper
work a full-time lady clerk was seconded from the Education Office at a
salary of £80 per annum. The first year culminated in an official visit
from His Majesty's Inspectors, who approved all they saw, and suggested
that the Art School should extend its scope to include both painting and
decorating and also to co-operate with local architects to provide
architectural drawing.

By 1912 Thomas Nelson, the head of the Art School, had really
established himself, and proposed (no doubt aided and abetted by his
Technical School counterpart) that he should be responsible for the
establishment of a continuous scheme of Art throughout the elementary
and evening continuation schools which would lead to certificate
qualification. However, this authority was denied him, as it would have
meant undermining the position of the headteachers of the elementary
schools. Nelson did gain a point with the institution of Art Scholarships
for elementary school pupils and evening continuation students, to study
at the Art School. Also in 1912 the classes for painting and decorating
were commenced and a further assistant teacher was appointed.

For three years the scene was untroubled. New subjects were added to
the curriculum such as etching, and the examination system continued as
before. In 1915, the anomalous position of having a school in rented
premises was revealed. The owners of the building, who owned the
printing business next door, required the basement premises for litho
printing, and said that if this could not be arranged they would have to
ask the authority to quit the entire premises. This demand caused a storm
in the Higher Education Committee. Plans were formulated for new Art
School buildings, alternative accommodation was considered, and much
correspondence was exchanged. The result was capitulation by the
authority and the resignation of Mr Nelson, who went to be the principal
of the Municipal School of Art, Portsmouth. Mr Oswald Crompton,
ARCA, was appointed to the vacant position. The basement was
surrendered and the school stayed on in the premises. The war may well
have influenced the decision. It did not appear to deter the Art School.
Junior classes were instituted which met between 6 and 7 pm, and for
which the fees were two shillings and sixpence per session. Lace-making
and millinery were added to the senior subjects, and many additions were
made to teachers' art and craft subjects.

By 1916 the war was beginning to make itself felt. There were classes for disabled servicemen, and the possibility arose of Mr Crompton being conscripted into the Army. However he was exempted, and pressed on with his work. The junior classes proved an immense success, and as a token of this, the school issued its own certificate award. In 1916 printing assumed greater importance in the Art School, and photographers' apprentices first attended day classes. This seems to be the earliest example of day-release within the authority.

The school was redesignated the Northampton School of Arts and Crafts in 1917, and the headmaster became officially the Principal of the school. The growth statistics of the school at this time indicate the popularity with which it was viewed (see the table).

Enrolments at the Northampton Art School/School of Arts and Crafts

Year	Total – all sessions		Industrial students	
1912	84		15	
1913	86		17	
1914	89		21	
1915	108	) 32	28	) 24
1916	233	) joined	29	) joined
1917	245	) army	55	) army
1918	282		–	

Some two-thirds of those totals were eligible for Board of Education grants in that they completed a minimum of fourteen hours attendance per session. In 1917 the first advisory committee to the Art School was set up, that for typography, and membership was drawn from the Master Printers' Association in the town. A design course was instituted at the request of local manufacturers and a new assistant appointed, Miss Rebecca Soar, who held a City and Guilds' full technological certificate in needlework. This appointment was a great success, for the following year the school achieved 100 per cent success in the City and Guilds' needlework examinations and led to the first scholarship for needlework to be awarded to girls from elementary schools.

A proposed innovation in 1918 too, was for pre-apprentice courses combining both art and technical subjects. Unfortunately this came to nothing, as a decision was deferred in view of the impending Education Act. A course that was run with success, however, was one for convalescent army officers from the local hospital, but even this small addition strained the accommodation, and an appeal was made for more spacious premises.

This plea was underlined in an official report by the Board's Inspectors the following year. The response was simply to house the overflow, mainly demobilised soldiers on refresher courses, in two rooms in the nearby St Giles' School, Boys' Department. The staff of the Art School at this time was the Principal, three full-time assistants, seven visiting teachers and two pupil art-teachers.

The failure of the Local Authority to solve the problem of accommodation led to a double blow in 1920. The Principal, Mr Crompton, resigned, and when he left he took his needlework genius Miss Soar, who had recently become his wife. No wonder he had repeatedly extolled her virtues to the Higher Education Committee! The new principal appointed was Mr Walter Travis, MC, ARCA. True to form the Local Authority attempted to smooth the path of their new principal by removing his main obstacle – lack of space. They authorised extension – but only to the extent of renting former café premises on Abington Square. The following year this theme of expansion was pursued by the Higher Education Committee, and it was proposed to rehouse the Art School in a house and hut in St Giles' Street. This plan never materialised, as by this time there was some hope of clinging to the skirt of the Technical School and getting in on the St George's Avenue site. The immediate problem of accommodation was still unsolved. Problem it certainly was since, in addition to recreational classes, there were by 1921 pre-apprentice classes in printing, painting and decorating and cabinet making. In addition the School was working for the Board of Education Art Examinations for the first time. The situation worsened the following year when the lease of the studio at 100a Abington Street was terminated. By way of redress the School once more obtained the use of their own basement rooms. In these restricted quarters some lace exhibits from the Victoria and Albert Museum were housed – from the sublime to the ridiculous.

In 1924 there were two highlights – the first when the guest speaker at the Prizegiving held at the Carnegie Hall was no less a person than Professor Rothenstein; the second when the Local Authority inaugurated a travelling art scholarship valued at £10 to be spent in Paris. These two highlights could not eliminate the constant struggle the school had to maintain decent standards caused by the lack of facilities. In 1925 the Principal, Mr Travis resigned his post upon appointment to the inspectorate. His successor was Mr Lewis Duckett, MC, ARCA, who was also to be principal designate of the new Art College when it was built in the near future. The new principal got off to a flying start. He extended the scope of the classes and the school now worked for examinations conducted by the East Midlands Education Union, City and Guilds, National Society of Art Masters and the Board of Education in Art and Industrial Design. In addition the art students found time to decorate the heraldic panels formerly in the Reference Library in the town. In 1926 a new 'high' was reached when the work of a former student was hung in the Royal Academy. The innovation of a junior full-time day course of two years duration which included general education also occurred in 1926. Pupils entered from elementary schools at 13 + years, and worked at subjects with a vocational bias. Expansion continued under Lewis Duckett in the years that followed. New subjects were added – window dressing, art, metalwork and architectural design – existing classes expanded, the printing class grew to 32 strong by 1929 and new honours were claimed, including two scholarships to the Royal College of Art in 1929 and three more in 1931.

In 1932 the Borough boundary was extended and the New Technical College was opened, but the Art School stayed where it was. Its proposed extensions were cut off by the wielding of the 'Geddes' Axe'. Disappointing as this must have been to Mr Duckett, he continued his efforts. His Junior Technical (Art) School was an undoubted success with ten fee-paying day students and eleven scholarship children, recruited from the Intermediate and Senior Schools. A student was awarded an open scholarship in architecture, and classes in etching were started. The building in Abington Street was once more bulging at the seams, whereas a mile away in St Georges' Avenue the new Technical College was nine-tenths empty during the day. A year later classes for unemployed printers were organised, to keep them in touch with their trade and by 1934 the numbers on roll for the Art School were 30 full-time day students, 64 juniors and 245 evening students. In view of the numbers, and the high standard of work, an attempt was made to have the status of 'Central College of Art' conferred upon the school, but this failed.

In 1935 the plans for the new Art building received the approval of the Board of Education, and the new era promised in 1926 seemed within grasp, whilst the old Art School still promoted new classes and expanded. Book-binding and theatre art appeared in the syllabus and Eric Gill, the sculptor, was the speaker at speech day.

In March 1937 Lewis Duckett resigned from the post of principal of the School of Art, and principal designate of the new building then nearing completion. He went to be Principal of Plymouth Art School. Mr Frederick B. Courtney, ATD, from Mansfield was appointed in his place, and it was he who took over the new building when it was opened officially on 17 September 1937, by Professor Jowett, ARWS, ARCA, Principal of the Royal College of Art. Messrs Glenn and Sons had again been the builders, at a cost of £14,645.

The new session in the new building in St George's Avenue (the twin to the College of Technology) opened with 327 students on roll. The palatial accommodation comprised: six fairly large studios, an exhibition room, a small craft room and three basement rooms. Photographic classes were an early success, and with new printing machinery installed in 1938 the printing classes thrived and included classes for teachers. Then came the war.

Northampton was designated a reception area for evacuees from London, and to the Northampton School of Art came the LCC School of Art, the Camberwell Art School and the Willesden Art School. The first two mentioned schools shared the accommodation and the Willesden Art School amalgamated with Northampton. The dressmaking section of the Paddington Trade School also came, to add to the discomfort. Teachers, both full and part-time, were conscripted to the armed forces, air-raid shelters were built in the grounds, blackout precautions frustrated many artists, but still the work went on in shifts, and in converted basements. An early innovation which proved popular was pottery classes. In 1941 a craft therapy course was introduced, followed in 1942 by a course in architecture and town planning. As the war situation improved the evacuees returned to their homes and overcrowding was considerably relieved. By 1944 Mr Courtney and his staff were able once more to think of new courses rather than just keeping classes going. The early craft therapy course developed in conjunction with St Andrew's Hospital, into a two-year occupational therapy course. The army was catered for by courses in painting and decorating, and refresher courses were planned for returning ex-servicemen in various printing trades. This year too brought recognition of the Art School (coupled with the boot and shoe department of the College of Technology) as the Regional College for Leather Design. Full status as a Regional College of Art eluded the School however, and with the publication of the Education Act of 1944, it was realised that the School was in fact understaffed and could not even implement the provisions of the Act. One of the big changes which the 1944 Act brought to the Art School was the translation of the junior Technical (Art) School scholars into Technical High School pupils. When this occurred in 1945 they passed from the Art School and became a separate school with their own headmaster and staff. This was in a sense a clearing of the decks for the post-war era.

The demobilisation scheme was in full swing by 1946, and the Art School found itself with a increasing number of full-time scholars as a result of the Further Education and Training Scheme organised by the government. Classes worked for the National Diploma in Design for the first time that year, and the first post-war teachers' course drew ninety-five applicants. Mr Courtney, having seen the school through ten most difficult years, resigned in 1946 and went to be principal of Bournemouth College of Art. He was succeeded by Mr Howard Buckley, ARCA, ATD.

Mr Buckley inherited a thriving school with some 345 students on roll. There were eighty-one in the painting and decorating department alone, and 1947 saw the considerable growth in the part-time day-release system. The printing trade adopted the scheme that year and the School became the centre for Northamptonshire, North Buckinghamshire and Bedfordshire. FETS students were still flocking in, and, three of the first group gained places at the royal College of Art. By 1948 the numbers on roll at the Art School had reached 623 students, an all-time high. There were twenty-six part-time teachers on the staff in addition to the full-time members, and the school seemed poised for greater things. Yet in midst of this expansion Buckley resigned his post as Principal after only two years. He was succeeded by Mr A. H. Beavan, ARCA, ATD the last Principal of the School of Art, who also became the longest serving principal the school had. Under his guidance work expanded in all departments, but particularly in the printing and the painting and decorating sections, both of which were almost hybrid in their combination of art and technology.

By 1952 the school had emerged from its post-war overcrowding, the last ex-serviceman had left and work had resumed on more conventional lines. Perhaps the most important classes were the day-release courses. Those for the printing and the painting and decorating trades were quickly off the mark. A day-release class for architectural students was inaugurated that year. Some of these students went on to achieve full ARIBA status. Part-time day-release student members that year rose to 185, apportioned as follows: printing, 68; painting and decorating 41; architectural, 16; photographic, 6; dressmaking, 6; commercial art, 5; general education, (with College of Technology, 43).

Full and part-time courses for the National Diploma in Design became paramount in the work of the school, and many successes were recorded. This was matched by work of an equally high standard in the printing department, which was growing rapidly. In spite of this success, the School of Art failed to achieve recognition as a regional college, being overshadowed by the College at Leicester; it also failed to gain recognition in 1966 as a full College of Art because of a lack of facilities on the fine arts side. Some evidence of the growth of the school could be seen from its staff which consisted of the Principal and fifteen full-time teachers, plus a list of about thirty visiting lecturers.

Compared with its technical counterpart, the Art School had seen many changes of principal. What sort of men were these principals? They certainly had much in common. The first head, Mr Nelson, although coming from a London school, was a Yorkshireman, tall, keen and businesslike. He was a very ambitious young man, a fine artist, painter and draughtsman. He remained long enough to make an impression and then moved on to a better position as Principal at Portsmouth. Mr Oswald Crompton, the second principal, though a different personality, achieved definite results. He was a quiet scholarly type of man, with a great fund of academic knowledge, a good organiser although not a brilliant teacher; he was reserved and professional in his approach. In work he was a fine figure painter, and specialised in imaginative interpretations of literary ideas, which were often quite mediaeval in style. He was greatly respected and admired, and it was a great surprise when his marriage to the brilliant needlework teacher, Miss Soar, was announced, as she was apparently the complete 'modern miss' of the period.

Walter Travis was another north-countryman, from the 'red rose' county this time. He was an ex-army officer who had been decorated on active service in the Middle East; he was also an ex-Lancashire League cricketer. He was a fine teacher and strict disciplinarian, who was much admired both for his organising ability and his artistic draughtsmanship. He had the disturbing effect on people of making them think. He left the school to become one of His Majesty's Inspectors for Art Education.

Lewis Duckett, who succeeded Travis, came from Bridgnorth to Northampton. He had won his MC as a captain in the Army in the 1914–18 war. As an artist, teacher and lecturer he was in great demand, and gave excellent lectures on the history of art to the whole Art School. A much admired and very friendly man he was an inspiration to his students. Although he painted portraits, and his portrait of Mr Blakeman, Principal of the Technical College, hangs in the college, it was as a landscape painter that he excelled, Welsh landscapes in particular. His appointment to Plymouth School of Art and his engagement to a Welsh girl were announced simultaneously in the Northampton papers. Lewis Duckett was a prominent citizen during the eleven years he spent in the town. He was president of the Northampton Town and County Art Society and chairman of the Design and Industrial Association of Northampton.

Frederick Courtney, ATD, successor to Duckett, came to Northampton from Mansfield, but had originated in the Leeds district and had been on the staff of the Leeds College of Art. He was very similar in manner and approach to his predecessor, and was also a fine draughtsman although his speciality was woodcuts and engraving. He handled the difficult years of wartime, with its problems of overcrowding and rival principals, extremely well, and it was no great surprise when he was appointed to the 'plum' art post on the south coast – Principal of Bournemouth College of Art. He certainly contributed to the life of Northampton while living in the town. The Town and County Art Society was among his interests, he founded the Visual Arts Committee and was a commander in the Home Guard.

William Howard Buckley, an ex-RAF Flight Lieutenant, was the next principal. Although coming to Northampton from Shipley School of Art, Yorkshire, he was Croydon-educated, plus the Royal College of Art of course. His speciality was engraving and he had exhibited at the Royal Academy. He did not stay long, however, and after two years was appointed to a similar post at Derby.

Mr A. H. Beavan was then appointed. He hailed from Yorkshire and specialised in lithography at the Royal College of Art, where he could have become a member of staff as his work was of such a high standard. A quiet, determined man, he saw many changes in Art Education after becoming principal. Under his leadership the School of Art expanded to become nationally known.

Of course it was not merely principals who made the school, especially when some were using the post as a stepping-stone to higher things. Under such circumstances there is usually a 'Mr Chips' helping continuity. The Northampton Art School had such a character who spent most of his career there. He was Thomas W. Rutter, known to his students as 'Uncle Tom', who was chief assistant for nineteen years until his retirement in 1934. A native of Swaledale, Yorkshire, educated in Lancashire and RCA, London, he was a teacher at Burnley School of Art before coming to Northampton in 1915. He was Hon. Sec. of the Northampton Town and County Art Society for many years and succeeded Lewis Duckett as president. He taught painting, publicity and design, but was really a landscape painter, specialising in landscapes of his native Yorkshire, and Newlyn in Cornwall. He was 'hung' in the Royal Academy, where he had four acceptances altogether. He lived in Northampton after his retirement.

Quite a number of well-known personalities in the art world have been connected with the Northampton School of Art. One who has received international recognition is Mrs Constance Parker (née Howard), who is renowned for her work in embroidery. Mr Frank Taylor, who became principal of Dagenham School of Art, was a student too. Among contemporary artists who were former students were, Henry Bird, G. B. H. Holland, Peter Berrisford, Christopher Fiddes and Peter Newcombe. Renowned internationally in a slightly different sphere was Osborne Robinson, the theatrical designer.

In retrospect one can say of the Northampton School of Art that it was one which never quite made the grade for obvious reasons, but principally because the town as a whole only wanted art as applied to industry. Undoubtedly, the old Abington Street premises, crowded and uncomfortable though they may have been, had atmosphere – something that the new building never attained. However, it was a generating station of personalities and creative ideas, even though the reference library did only consist of three shelves of standard works, whilst the nature study section held merely a stuffed peacock and a stuffed white Pomeranian dog on a red cushion (which until recently survived as a 'prop' in store at the Royal Theatre). The School Sketch Club held monthly exhibitions as well as an annual show. The Travelling Scholarship to Paris (on £10) was a much sought-after prize, and the source of many amusing stories among the students. A big annual occasion was the Art School Revel, which always featured 'The Stunt'. This was a skit on some local affair and was often near libellous. Work was of a high standard and scholarships to the Royal College of Art were regular events.

The School suffered from being in the shadow of the Technical College. It was frequently thought of as being part of it and yet it never was; the students rarely mixed. This overshadowing was made worse when the School moved to become the twin of the Technical College in St George's Avenue in 1937. So far as one can trace, the opening of the building did not receive a paragraph in the local papers, though criticism of the building certainly did. Apart from a scathing leading article on the building, a senior art student said that the school's design was lacking in imagination. It was suggested that no one could suppose for a moment that art was to be taught there, for the building was uninspired in every way and redolent of petty provincialism. Mr Osborne Robinson said, in the same issue, 'If the building had been designed for use as a reformatory, a Poor Law institution or a barracks, it could hardly have been rendered more crudely remote from its present purpose'.

Nevertheless the building served the cause of art in Northampton and still serves Further and Higher Education today. The 'two-wing' building of the original design balances and although the central frontage block is to a different design this blends in with the original building to produce a very pleasant effect worthy of the purpose to which the whole is put.

4 Developments Affecting the College of Technology, 1956 to 1973

David Walmsley

Oliver Bailey retired in 1956 and was succeeded as Principal by Eric Jewitt, BSc(Eng), MIEE, in 1957. It was a case of one electrical engineer succeeding another to continue the tradition of the work of the College of Technology in this field.

Since 28 June 1954 the College had enjoyed its own Governing Body which reported to the Further Education Sub-Committee of the Education Committee instead of coming directly under the direction of that Committee. Jewitt worked with five Chairmen of Governors, namely: Councillor C. H. Edwards; Councillor Philip McShane; Councillor (later Alderman) T. H. Dockrell; Councillor David Walmsley; and Councillor (later Alderman) Harold Cockerill. Shortly after his appointment Councillor Edwards left the County Borough Council on taking up a post in the town as Secretary of the Boot and Shoe Manufacturers Association. David Walmsley (the Chairman of the Education Committee) acted as Chairman of Govenors briefly in the period when the plans for the extension (opened in 1970) were under discussion. Philip McShane, who was a builder in the St James area, did not retain his seat on the Council, so that the two Chairmen with whom Jewitt was particularly involved were Hayes Dockrell (an orthopaedic surgeon) and Harold Cockerill (the engineer to a local brewery company who lived in St George's Avenue close to the College and who consequently was able to spend much time on the premises).

Blakeman had been supported by a Deputy Principal in the person of W. J. Chater until 1940 but after Oliver Bailey became Acting Principal in 1941 the role of Deputy Principal was not filled and remained unfilled until Hugh Johnson was appointed in the late 1960s. However (in addition to Hugh Johnson) Jewitt was well supported by some formidable heads of department in the persons of: Alex Parthenis (engineering); John Sharphouse (leather manufacture); Dr Walter Siddall (science); and John Thornton (boot and shoe). Johnson went on to become Principal of the Nuneaton College of Further Education. From there he transferred to the post of Principal of the Wharfedale and Airedale College of Further Education. On his retirement Johnson joined the staff of Bradford Cathedral.

Arthur Angus succeeded Johnson as Deputy Principal in 1970. He was a chemist and an Ulsterman. Originally he had worked for ICI before moving into the field of education. Angus was gifted academically and was a fine teacher but he had a reserved personality. He died of a heart attack whilst still in office.

RONALD GEORGE GARNETT, BA, MSc(Econ), PhD

Dr Garnett was born in Liverpool in 1924. He obtained an honours degree in economics and politics at Manchester University, went on to take an MSc (Econ) externally at London University in 1958, and was awarded a PhD in 1970. He is married and has two sons.

Dr Garnett was first a lecturer and then Head of Department before being appointed Vice-Principal of the Manchester College of Commerce. He became Principal of the Hendon College of Technology in 1970

Dr Garnett was closely associated with assessing national and regional examinations for the Department of Education and Science, one of the GCE boards and the Regional Union of the Lancashire and Cheshire Institutes. He was a founder-member of the economics board of the Council for National Academic Awards and became a member of the CNAA Committee of Arts and Social Studies in 1969. In 1967 he was a visiting associate professor at the University of Alabama Graduate School of Business. At the time of his appointment to Northampton in 1973 he was an Assistant Director of Middlesex Polytechnic. Garnett was an extrovert whose main interests were in developing the ideas of business management which had their beginnings in the College at this time. He had written a text-book on the subject of 'Administration' as well as books on the Co-operative movement and on Owenite Socialism. His concern was that his students should be able to translate their specialised technical skills into profitable business ventures. In his previous position Dr Garnett had suffered a considerable disappointment in that he had served as a successful Principal of the Hendon College of Technology but following College amalgamations his then local Authority (with three ex principals claiming top jobs) had only offerred him an Assistant Director's post (at Middlesex Polytechnic) in 1973. He was unfortunate that the same thing happened to him in Northampton. Having succeeded Mr Jewitt as Principal of the College of Technology Dr Garnett was not offered the Director's post when the College of Education, the College of Technology and the (by then) College of Art were amalgamated to form Nene College in 1975. Shortly after the amalgamation Dr Garnett resigned to take up a position as Principal of a highly regarded College of Further Education in Western Australia.

These staffing and structural matters however run ahead of developments at St George's Avenue during Eric Jewitt's time. He inherited buildings which were inadequate for the student numbers and consequently his first task was to seek an expansion of the premises. The fact that the 'frontage' block had remained unfinished since 1932 was a reproach to the town notwithstanding the intervention of the war which had caused plans to be postponed. Although the completion of the frontage was needed, in fact the more urgent requirement was for additional workshop accommodation. In 1957 plans were brought before the Education Committee for a two-phased building programme, namely a workshop block to the rear of the existing buildings and instead of the two-storey frontage in a classical style of architecture intended by Keighley Cobb in his original designs a four-storey frontage block, that is a semi-basement and three storeys on top to accommodate a main hall, administrative offices and a library. The design was prepared by Brian Bunch (the County Borough Architect) and was accepted by the Committee and the Governors. To aid the financing the work was to be spread over three years – the workshop block in 1958/59 and the frontage in 1959/60. The contract for the workshop block was let to Messrs A. Glenn & Son Ltd. The contract for the frontage was let to Bernard Sunley Ltd.

The official opening ceremony for the two projects took place on 26 January 1961 and the guest on that occasion was Jack Longland, the Director of Education for Derbyshire, a well-known radio and TV personality. Not all those who attended the ceremony were aware of Mr Longland's links with the town which were not reported in the local press though the event was otherwise covered succinctly. Jack Longland's parents were in fact married in St Matthews Church and he was baptised there. In his boyhood Northampton was very much a second 'home' to him in that both his grandfathers were Northampton men. Mr John Longland had been a teacher at the then Northampton Grammar School. Mr James (later Sir James) Crockett was one of the founders of the well-known local boot and shoe firm, Crockett and Jones. Sir James, who was a leading Liberal, lived for a time at 6 Spencer Parade, Northampton, next door to his 'Conservative' rival Harvey-Reeves at 7 Spencer Parade. The local links extended to Jack Longland's aunt, Miss May Longland, who despite her considerable age was present to greet her nephew. Miss Longland had been the Headmistress of the Wellington Place Special School (later renamed Northgate and later still moved out to a site adjacent to Thornton Park, Kingsthorpe). The opening was a particularly happy occasion for Alderman Arthur Chown (the Chairman of the Education Committee), who had led the agitation for the completion of the frontage. Some wondered as to the views of Harold Skerrett (the Chief

Education Officer for the County Borough). For many years a pencil sketch of Keighley Cobb's original design for the frontage hung on his office wall at the County Borough Education Committee's offices at 'Springfield', Cliftonville, Northampton. Harold Skerrett was discreet and said nothing.

The new accommodation enabled Jewitt to organise the College (which at that stage went under the title of the Central College of Further Education) into nine departments each with its own Head of Department, namely: (1) boot and shoe manufacture; (2) leather manufacture; (3) building; (4) commerce; (5) domestic subjects, catering and bakery; (6) engineering; (7) general studies; (8) mathematics; and (9) science. As well as courses planned to deal with specific industries and professions the 'Tech' (the old name stuck) offered a range of non-vocational classes including languages, which today would be called DIY instruction and, of course, sport.

Miss G. P. Rumming was the Head of Commerce and her department offered a variety of courses including a very popular one-year course of office training. In his early days of association with the College, David Walmsley, in his capacity as Chairman of the Education Committee in succession to Arthur Chown, was called on to present the prizes to this group at the annual ceremony. He felt it appropriate to enter into conversation with the attractive 'star' pupil as he handed her the prize she had won. 'For whom do you work?' he asked, 'For you, Sir,' she replied. And so she did, but in a different section of the office and in a different building! She worked for Mr Walmsley's firm for many years thereafter.

The Head of Domestic Subjects was Miss M. C. Turner, who was troubled by a lady HMI who came to inspect the department from time to time. This good lady always had a fresh concern on each visit: 'would a silicone covering in a frying pan damage your health?' 'Was Vitamin C really "good" for you?' Eventually Miss Turner entered into an arrangement with Dr Siddall, who as Head of Science would intercept the lady and lend a sympathetic ear to her latest worry. Time flew by and the' inspection would be over before the Inspector got down to detail in the Department.

Two of the lecturers in domestic subjects were Mollie Hawkins, who came from a Bedfordshire farming family, and Audrey Baillion, a member of the well-known local brewing family. On one occasion Earl Spencer (that is, the father of the present Earl) expressed a desire to see what work was being done in the department. David Walmsley invited the Earl to come round to see for himself and to have a lunch cooked by the students. The Earl came and charmed everyone but the lunch was a disaster. Something went wrong in the kitchens and the distinguished visitor had to be given a scratch meal out of a tin. This experience did not put Earl Spencer off – he came again and, indeed, visited other educational establishments from time to time 'to keep in touch'. These unofficial off-the-record tours and visits were much appreciated.

Facilities for students included the Students' Association which had its own club and common rooms – and was responsible for sharing in the organisation of physical recreation as well as acting as a liaison with the staff.

In 1960 Mr V. A. Hatley was appointed as Librarian and Mr B. A. Bailey came as his Assistant. Mr Hatley is a well-known local historian and has very kindly read this manuscript to check the same for unnecessary historical errors. If any errors remain then these are the fault of the contributors! Mr Bailey still works for the Northamptonshire County Council in a senior post. Before 1960 the so-called College Library consisted of a limited number of books scattered through the building chiefly in cupboards or on shelves (where they accummulated dust) in the rooms used by the individual heads of department. Within half-a-dozen years of 1960 the library had expanded to around 15,000 volumes and thereafter continued to expand steadily. Mr Hatley was also the custodian (on behalf of the School of Art) of the quite remarkable and nationally known treasure of the Osborne Robinson collection of posters.

There was also now on site a large refectory supervised by Mrs Gardiner and in the administrative offices, Alan Riley (who has helped with the Appendices to this book in his capacity as the present Chief Administrative Officer of Nene College) was appointed as the first College Registrar.

Accommodation was still strained. It was Jewitt's policy (endorsed by the Governing Body) to foster as much community involvement in the College as possible. The main hall with its fully equipped facilities (at least fully equipped for those days) was available for both College and non-College functions. It was heavily used.

The special interests of Hayes Dockerell led to the erection on site of a sports hall, one of the first of its kind to be attached to a College of Further Education (as distinct from a gymnasium). If this now appears a somewhat functional building nevertheless in its time this was a pioneering move and the unimpeded space under the curved roof comes in useful for a variety of uses such as counting votes at election times – the lack of heating damping down over enthusiastic party political spirits in the early hours of the morning. This sports hall was opened in 1968 and was followed by another major expansion to the rear of the original buildings.

Again designed by Brian Bunch and built by Messrs A. Glenn & Sons Ltd at a cost of £176,557 these extensions provided three storeys of teaching accommodation. On the ground floor there was a coffee bar, a motor vehicle workshop and a leather dyeing room with a drum store and hide and skin store. The first floor was mainly taken up by boot and shoe facilities but included also an electrical installation work-room. The top floor served general science and a lecture room for the building department. There were corridor links at first and second-floor level to the existing building.

Mr Gerald Fowler MP, the Minister of State at the Department of Education and Science, opened these extensions on 24 March 1970. It was appropriate to invite him to do so, since not only was he a 'local boy' (having been born at Long Buckby and educated at the Northampton School for Boys) but he was the central government Minister with responsibility for Further Education.

Whilst the new buildings were going up (and indeed afterwards) accommodation problems still persisted and were a constant anxiety to both Mr Jewitt and his staff and also to David Walmsley (Chairman of the Education Committee) and Harold Cockerill (by then the Chairman of Governors). Some temporary relief was secured by sharing the use of an empty house in St George's Avenue known as 'Calderfield' with the Northampton School for Girls for teaching purposes and by moving some of the engineering work to the John Clare School Buildings in Kettering Road, Northampton. This is not the last time the John Clare Buildings will be mentioned in connection with the story of Nene College. These buildings were originally part of the local response to the 1870 Education Act. Some day a history of the school will be written and will reflect the changes in educational patterns from 1870 onwards. By the 1970s however the 'School' had departed to become the Cliftonville Seconday Modern School (now the Cliftonville Middle School) and the buildings themselves stood in the way of a projected Inner Town Ring Road (colloquially known as the 'Expressway'). Consequently these buildings were put to a variety of 'temporary purposes' one of which was for the overflow of the College Engineering Department and another was as an outpost of the Scraptoft Teacher Training College, Leicester (in the form of its Northampton Annexe). When both of these temporary uses ceased then the Northamptonshire Music School moved in and is still there. That temporary use seems to have become the permanent use since the Inner Town Ring Road was never built.

The accommodation problem at St George's Avenue was finally resolved by the building of a brand new College of Further Education in Booth Lane, Northampton, which premises were opened in 1973. Booth Lane, however, represented something more than just simply a solution to the problems of space. It also represented new thinking on the local approach to Higher Education. It was realised that the opportunities to expand the facilities for Higher Education in Northampton would not develop unless there was a separation of Further Education from Higher Education. The difficulty of trying to do everything in one place had held back and in the end defeated the hopes of Blakeman and Bailey. Now it was holding Jewitt back in turn. Room to expand Higher Education work at St George's Avenue had to be created if a way forward was to be found.

At Education Committee level David Walmsley, Harold Cockerill and Carol Trusler (the Labour Group's spokeswoman on education matters) were urging their colleagues that separate premises should be build to provide accommodation for the very important bread-and-butter local craft courses. The suggestion was that two new colleges were required, one on the eastern side of the town and one on the southern. The Booth Lane College materialised on the eastern side of the town but the southern side college (which would have been built if it had proceeded on the land at Hardingstone on which the replacement for the Northampton High School for Girls, Derngate, is currently being erected) did not. Interestingly the suggestion of a second college was revived in County Council days in the mid-1970s. The proposal then was that the second college might be sited at Daventry to serve the western part of the county as well as parts of Northampton. This idea was not pursued either in the end.

The desire to develop Higher Education facilities out of Further or Technical Education is the nub of the story so far as Northampton and Northamptonshire is concerned. Added impetus to do so was created by the expansion of the town under the general provision of central government policies to build 'New Towns'. Town development brought new demands. It also created increased demands for more advanced work and more advanced training to be provided locally.

In addition the staple industry of Northampton and county towns such as Kettering, Wellingborough and Rushden was in decline numerically. The 'craft' emphasis òn boots and shoes (and on leather technology) was a diminishing demand so far as the local Colleges of Further Education throughout the county were concerned. At one stage it was reported that the County and County Borough together were providing something like 1,000 places for training and only some 80 or so students were coming forward. But if 'quantity' was no longer required 'quality' was. This was emphasised by the new needs for boot and shoe manufacture and also in the needs of the tanning industry. Basically the process of changing hides into leather has never altered but the methods of securing this process became more sophisticated. Consequently, training fewer students to a much more advanced level was what was needed.

At the same time the local importance of engineering training increased. Some major firms had moved to the area to escape the bombing of cities and conurbations elsewhere. After the war many of these firms remained in Northampton and such slack as there was in the boot and shoe department at the Tech was rapidly taken up in the engineering department. This shift in emphasis was another problem that Jewitt had to ride.

In 1946 the then Ministry of Education approved the engineering department as a Grade I Department which resulted in the appointment of Mr H. M. Marklow as Head of Department as from January 1947. Mr Marklow was assisted by five full-time members of staff. At that time there were 150 part-time day students and about 300 evening only students. By the early 1950s a very considerable increase in student numbers was evident due to the growth of British Timken. An Engineering Advisory Committee was set up and British Timken were invited to appoint a representative to serve on this Committee. In this way Mr E. R. Knapp, who eventually became Managing Director of Timken Europe, began his long association with the work of the College. Mr H. M. Marklow left the Department in 1953 and was succeeded by Mr J. Metcalfe. By 1957 the part-time day enrolments exceeded 750 and the Department began to experience difficulty with accommodation. Mr J. Metcalfe left the Department in 1961 and was succeeded by Mr A. Parthenis.

With the advent of the 1961 White Paper, 'Better Opportunities in Technical Education', which recommended that craft, technician and professional courses should be developed, considerable changes were needed in the course structure of the department. This included the introduction in September 1961 of a number of new courses, the general course in engineering, the mechanical engineering technicians course, the electrical engineering technicians course and a revised Ordinary National Certificate in Engineering with stricter entry conditions. These changes created an even greater need for workshop space. The 1961–2 session saw the introduction of block release courses in the College. Starting with fourteen students, this number increased each year to a maximum of about 250 students.

The 1966–7 session saw the introduction of a new Higher National Certificate in Engineering, and with the growth of civil engineering courses, approval was sought to run a Higher National Certificate in Civil Engineering. The session also saw the introduction of the 48-week college year for the training of students in accordance with the recommendation of the Engineering Industry Training Board. The 1968–9 session saw the start of the Higher National Certificate in Civil Engineering. The number of students enrolled in the department then exeeded 1,600 compared with only fifty part-time day students in 1944.

It was perhaps a weakness in the department that engineering was taught in only one department. In many other similar colleges there would have been three departments – electrical engineering, mechanical engineering and production engineering. In Northampton they all came together but the satisfactory results achieved meant that changes were not proposed.

New courses were constantly being introduced: (a) in calculation and computers; (b) in business management for accountants, bankers and legal executives; and (c) advanced level machine printing (in the School of Art). All this activity led to a certain amount of liaison with the regional authority. The Regional Advisory Council for Advanced and Further Education in the East Midlands (RACAFEEM) had its base in Nottingham. The Council had oversight of all courses in the region. It was set up to prevent overlapping courses being provided. In principle this was a sensible idea but in practice it led to strained relations, especially with Leicester Polytechnic.

The East Midlands comprised five counties, Derbyshire, Leicestershire, Lincolnshire, Northamptonshire and Nottinghamshire. The main centres of population were Derbyshire and Nottinghamshire, with Leicestershire coming third. The principal existing colleges were at Derby, Leicester and Nottingham. The problem with Northampton was that although it was the fastest growing town in Europe at that time the other colleges did not want to shed courses to oblige a potential competitor.

Northampton was constantly being invited to allow its students to join existing courses elsewhere rather than set up new (and so far as the existing colleges were concerned, competing) courses in the East Midlands area. This was a problem shared with Further Education colleges throughout the county. It was also a matter of practical difficulty since joining existing courses meant long travelling distances for students and additional costs as a result. In fact the LEAs (i.e. the County and the County Borough) came to object vigorously to sustaining higher-level work elsewhere at the expense of not allowing facilities to develop naturally 'at home'. Usually after a struggle Northampton (and Northamptonshire) got most of what it wanted because the 'travel' argument worked both ways. When RACAFEEM said 'travel', this contention could be shown to be unreasonable both in terms of 'time' and in terms of 'cost'.

Furthermore, Northampton was very much an outpost of empire so far as RACEFEEM was concerned and many of the courses the College wanted to provide attracted students from places to the west and south such as Rugby, Stony Stratford and Wolverton. Strictly speaking these were outside the East Midlands area but they had to be served by Northampton. In particular there were some aspects of technical training in the Rugby area for Advanced Higher Education work which were affected by the fact that Coventry was seeking to develop university work at Lanchester. The College always had concerned friends outside its own area as a result.

Another aspect of this was the introduction of Advisory Committees. This began under Bailey but was taken up and developed by Jewitt. Each of the departments had its own Advisory Committee. This was no sinecure. Members of such Committees were encouraged to involve themselves in the work of the College. The Governing Body took the unusual step of inviting the Advisory Committee to oversee expenditure and to submit budget proposals to the Governors for onward transmission to the Education Committee. In addition, there was an annual meeting between the Chairman and Vice-Chairman of each Advisory Committee on the one hand and the Governors on the other. Some of these meetings were not easy when finance was limited but the free and frank discussions which ensued were helpful all round. Furthermore, since there was a real job of work to be done on an Advisory Committee and they were not just 'talking-shops', the College was able to attract to its Advisory Committees many of the leading businessmen of the town. Mr E. R. Knapp of British Timken has been mentioned but there were others: Mr V. H. C. Amberg of Express Lifts, Miss Barbara Adams of Adams Bakeries, Mr Philip Chown and Mr Herbert Glenn. These are just some names that come to mind but there were many more. Together they were more than simple 'friends of the College', they formed a powerful pressure group especially when the Local Authority was considering matters such as the annual level of rates.

Against the background of this support it is surprising that the scheme for Training Boards towards the end of the 1960s just did not get off the ground. Support was poor. The smaller firms were not wholly co-operative over releasing young employees and these firms resented the training levy imposed on them. The larger firms felt that they were being called on to help to pay for the training of young employees in the employ of their competitors. They also felt that as larger employers they could do the job better on their own. British Timken, for instance, developed for a time their own 'Apprentice School' which offered in-service engineering training of a very high quality. They even took on a girl from the Northampton School for Girls to train as an engineer. In local circumstances at the time this was regarded as a great breakthrough but when the young lady was asked what she was called by her instructors and fellow students, she replied 'Fred'!

The interests of members of the Advisory Committees spilled over into acts of great generosity so far as the College was concerned. The College acquired its first computer as a gift from British Timken who replaced the original computer with a second similar gift in 1975.

The three Timken brothers started up in the roller-bearing business in America and subsequently they established factories in England and in France. Each year they set aside a proportion of their profits from each of their factories for the benefit of the communities in which their employees lived. Thus in each of the three countries concerned the Timken brothers set up a committee to advise them on suitable bodies or causes to be supported financially in the local area. The British body was known as the 'Nene Foundation'. Whilst the trustees were independent people they always took advice as widely as possible and usually their recommendations were endorsed by the Timken brothers. Many good causes in Northamptonshire benefited in this way – not least the College of Technology – and the generosity of the Timken family has continued so far as Nene College itself is concerned.

Other local firms in the 1950s and 1960s which generously donated equipment (either by way of gift or by way of permanent loan) included: A. H. Allen & Company; Blackwood Hodge Limited; Brown Bros Limited; Express Lifts; Painton & Company Limited; and Pianoforte Supplies Limited (Roade). These gifts established another tradition of local support from which Nene College later on also benefited.

There was one other matter close to the heart of Mr Jewitt and that was the promotion of international friendship. Nowadays many educational institutions are interested in this since overseas students help to balance the budget. In the late 1950s and early 1960s the Northampton College of Technology was something of a pioneer in promoting such developments. Jewitt was criticised because it was said that (a) ratepayers money should be used to educate ratepayers' offspring not 'foreigners'; and (b) it was training 'our' rivals who would then take away our foreign markets. Jewitt did not see things in that light. He wanted to hold out the hand of friendship and if it was 'bread upon the waters' then so much the better. In any event all five of his Chairmen of Governors gave him strong support so that despite some grumbling away from the College the matter never came to a head.

In leather technology the declining national requirement for training led to a growth of international links which has stood Nene College well especially in connection with the development of the Leathersellers' Centre in later days. In other areas the same was true. In science, Dr Siddell established early links with China through the proprietor of the old 'Sunlight Laundry' in Grafton Street which was run by a leading ex-patriate Chinaman. There were regular student recruits from Iraq through contacts with a Mr Barnes at the Embassy. In those days it was not unknown for devout members of the Islamic faith to retire to the back of a laboratory to observe their proper prayer rituals during the course of a day's instruction. This was allowed for by appropriate timings in their lectures and in their practical training. Students came from Greece, from Nigeria and other parts of Africa. Students came in numbers from Thailand but the total of overseas students was not allowed to exceed 25 per cent of the whole student body.

In science, immediately after the war, Dr Siddall ran a course (tied in with an external degree from London University) for returning soldiers. This was offered for limited numbers, perhaps twelve at a time. One of these students obtained first-class honours and many obtained good second-class honours even after starting at the bottom of the ladder with the need to obtain Higher School Certificates. This venture died away after a while as university places became more readily available following the post-war flood of students seeking to catch up on their 'lost years'. However the fact that this particular service was offered by the College at the time does make two points. First, the degree of flexibility there was within the College and, second, the way in which the College was at all times reaching out from the base of good sound courses in Technical Education towards the goal of establishing Northampton as a base for Higher Education. There was always that desire to go further even allowing for the fact that initially numbers were not great.

The proposal to establish a College of Education in Northampton was welcomed by the College of Technology (who took the College of Art along with them in this respect). The proposal was seen as a way of enlarging the base for higher education work in the town and also as a means of strengthening the claims of the town to aspire in due course to either polytechnic or university status.

Samuel Smith Campion had dreamt of this in his day. He had embraced the Nonconformist philosophy common to his generation that education was the way forward to liberate the 'common man', which was one of the fundamental beliefs of the old Liberal party (especially prior to the First World War). His successors were perhaps a little more hard-nosed. They wanted to see a polytechnic or a university blossom in Northampton but they knew that the reality of the situation was that only hard work to establish the right conditions locally would bring the dream to fruition. For them the ultimate realisation of Campion's dream would mean a gain to the town in terms of the quality of life and in terms of new opportunities rather than simply a matter of 'status'.

ERIC JEWITT, BSc(ENG), MIEE

Eric Jewitt was born in 1911 in Bradford. He was educated at Bradford Technical College and took his BSc. (Eng.) as an External Degree with first-class Honours at London University. He was apprenticed to a firm of electrical engineers in Bradford and soon started to lecture at his old school – the Bradford Technical College. This led him to decide that his future lay in education and he went to the Derby Technical College in 1935 as a Lecturer. He was appointed Head of Department at Derby in 1941 and Vice Principal in 1947. A year later in 1948 he became the Principal of the Walsall Technical College and Headmaster of the Technical and Commercial Secondary School. He spent seven full and happy years in Walsall before succeeding Oliver Bailey as the Principal of the Northampton College of Technology in 1955. The remainder of Eric Jewitt's career was spent in Northampton up to his retirement in 1973 where, out of College, he was associated with the International Friendship League and with Rotary. During his time student numbers rose from around 2,000 in 1954 to between 5,000/6,000 in 1972–3. Mr Jewitt saw the Technical High School remove from the St George's Avenue premises to their own building; he saw the extension to the premises; and he carried through the hiving off from the Avenue of much of the Further Education work to Booth Lane. In this he not only gave a firm lead but exercised considerable tact and diplomacy. His wife, Margaret, died at the age of 56 on 30 March 1968 after some years of ill-health. She had not only supported her husband in his work but had been very much associated with St Alban's Church of England and particularly with the work of the Mothers Union. In retirement Mr Jewitt continues to live in Northampton keeping in contact with the affairs of the College and with his three grown-up children, enjoying his hobbies of watching cricket and listening to music.

ALEXANDER PARTHENIS, BScEng, AIMEE, FIM, MInstW, MInstMet, AMBIM

Alex Parthenis was born on 28 November 1918. He gained an upper-second class degree in engineering at Liverpool University. In 1944 he went to the research and experimental department of the English Electric Co. Ltd at Rugby, as a research assistant, rising to become deputy head of the research department before moving in 1955 to Rugby College as senior lecturer in engineering technology. In September 1961 he was appointed head of department of engineering at Northampton College of Technology, and became Dean of the School of Technology at Nene College in September 1975. He retired in August 1984.

Alex Parthenis was a pivotal figure both at the College of Technology and later at Nene College. To the Principals and Director of both these colleges he offered loyalty and reliability. To his colleagues in the engineering department and in the School of Technology he offered leadership and support. To his students he offered the qualities to be seen in himself, namely a sound practical knowledge of the techniques of engineering. As a result he attracted great affection and respect. Alex would never claim to be an academic engineer, his great strengths were as a teacher and as an organiser. In his early days at the College of Technology he had to deal with the problems of 'quantity' control as his department expanded in all directions. In his later days at Nene College he had to deal with the problems of 'quality' control as Nene moved over from a Further Education base to a Higher Education base. Despite all the stresses and tensions of the time, it is doubtful whether anyone ever saw Alex ruffled. He was a big man in more ways than one, who had a cheerful outlook on life and went out of his way to be helpful. For instance, in his early days at St George's Avenue – which did not have the improved facilities for drama provided by the apparatus at the Park Campus site – if the students appealed to him for help with lighting effects when putting on a dramatic production, he would not only design and make whatever piece of equipment was required but also at the time of the production he would be sitting back-stage working it. He loved the 'Ward models'; he loved old cars.

For many years he was a bachelor living with his mother, and he married late in life. He and his wife live locally in retirement. They attend many College functions and Alex's penetrating chuckle continues to be heard in the corridors of power which he graced in the 1960s and 1970s when he was a member of the formidable team (with Ronnie Knapp as Chairman of the Engineering Advisory group) running what became numerically the largest department of the old 'Tech'.

JOHN H. SHARPHOUSE, BSc, CGIA, PSLTC

John Sharphouse was a Yorkshireman who was educated at the City of Leeds School and studied chemistry and leather chemistry at Leeds University, graduating with first-class honours in 1939.

In the Second World War he was drafted to the Ministry of Aircraft Production and worked at British Celanese, Spondon, Derby, on cellulose derivatives for aircraft windscreens and later on gas-proof clothing based on vinyl polymers. After the war he joined ICI Ltd in Manchester as a leather technologist. In 1949 he became technical director of Messrs G. W. Russell of Hitchin (a large sheepskin tannery). During this period John Sharphouse was Chairman of the London Society of Leather Chemists (SLTC) and a director of the British Leather Manufacturers' Research Association (BLMRA). For a few years he was a director of Henry Beakbane and Son of Stourport, and then worked on technical development with the Badische Anilin und Soda Fabrik (BASF) in West Germany and contributed to *Einfuhrung in Leder Technologie*, the standard German textbook on this subject.

In 1959 John Sharphouse was appointed head of the department of leather technology at the College of Further Education (as it then was) in Northampton. Courses were updated and expanded, notably Block Release Courses on leather for 'out-of town' students (significant for a small, scattered industry). Overseas students were attracted to Northampton and two standard textbooks on leather manufacture were written which are still in use internationally, and indeed are still the recommended texts in the United States and in India.

Whilst at the College of Technology John Sharphouse continued his research work, which led to his presenting about a dozen papers at meetings of leather chemists. In 1980 he was invited to give the prestigious J. A. Wilson Memorial Lecture to the American Leather Chemists' Association at Wisconsin. He was much in demand as a consultant.

In 1972 he had six months sabbatical leave to act as a consultant to the Sudan Leather Industries in Khartoum on behalf of the United Nations Industrial Development Organisation (UNIDO). In 1973 the United Nations approached him again and appointed him to establish, on behalf of the Food and Agriculture Organisation (FAO), the Turkish Leather Research and Training Institute at Istanbul. This appointment led to John Sharphouse resigning his post with the College. He spent the following four years abroad in Istanbul and visiting Botswana.

In 1984 he was given the senior award of the London City and Guilds Institute – the Insignia Award – for a treatise on chamois leather manufacture. Recently as technical consultant to the Turkish Tanner's Association (of which he was made an honorary member), John Sharphouse has been concerned with the establishment of a new tanning industry estate in Ankara. One of the problems encountered in Istanbul had been the control and disposal of effluent, avoiding the centuries old practice of putting it straight into the Bosphorus.

In retirement John Sharphouse lives at Grange-over-Sands, Cumbria, where he can contemplate the hills and local pot-holes, which once provided his principal source of recreation. His influence lives on from his days as a tanner with a national and international reputation, and survives through the many leading figures in the industry whom he has trained.

DR WALTER SIDDALL, MBE, BSc, PhD, MRSC, CChem

Walter Siddall was born in Halifax, Yorkshire, on 25 February 1906. He trained at the City of Leeds Training College, where he obtained a Board of Education Teacher's Certificate with distinction in chemistry and advanced mathematics in 1926. Between 1926 and 1937 he taught in various schools in Bradford and from 1934 to 1937 was a part-time lecturer in chemistry at Bradford Technical College. While doing this he studied for a BSc in chemistry from London University, which he obtained with upper second-class honours in 1934. In 1938 he was appointed as a teacher in science subjects at the Northampton College of Technology. In 1941 he became both Head of Science and a Member of the Royal Society of Chemistry (MRSC). He gained a doctorate at London University for his work on unsaturated ketones and their derivatives in 1944. In 1968 he was awarded the MBE for work in Technical Education.

He was Examiner and Moderator for all science subjects in the East Midlands Educational Union (EMEU) and Chairman of their Science Panel. He was also Chairman of the General Course in Science for the City and Guilds of London. During the Second World War and afterwards he was frequently used as a consultant by many local and national industries. Dr Siddall was the main Civil Defence Officer for Northampton (and later Northamptonshire) up to 1980. He retired from the Northampton College of Technology in 1971. His wife (Mrs Jessie Siddall) was for many years a leading member of the Northampton Magistracy.

THE WARD MODELS

For over thirty years certain models have been on display at the St George's Avenue Campus. These models now consist of: Quadruple Expansion Marine Engine; Craven Railway Service Crane; Rocket Locomotive and Tender; LNWR Railway Locomotive 'Cornwall'; LMS Railway Locomotive 'Royal Engineer'; LMS Railway Locomotive 'Duchess of Buccleuch'; Fosters Showman's Road Locomotive.

History

Sidney James Ward, who died in 1952, was a Northampton engineer and an amateur model maker of great distinction. His models, made in the workshop at the bottom of the garden at his home on Victoria Promenade, Northampton, won national prizes, cups and medals. Such was his merit that the Road Locomotive was on exhibition at Kensington Science Museum from 1923 to 1967. Other models, prior to the outbreak of war in 1939, were exhibited at the Great Hall at Euston Station, in recognition of which Mr Ward was granted by the railway company the signal honour of a footplate pass. The Euston models were removed to St George's Avenue for safe custody in 1939, where they were joined, first in 1952 by the Rocket Locomotive, and then in 1967 by the Road Locomotive.

On Mr Ward's death the ownership of the models passed to his wife. She, because the models were made in Northampton by a Northampton man who had been Chairman of the Highways Committee of Northampton County Borough Council, was anxious that the models remained in Northampton and for that reason refused repeated requests from the Science Museum that the models be exhibited in London. At one time negotiations took place for the models to be donated to the County Borough Council but these negotiations broke down. On the death of Mrs Ward ownership of the models passed to Mr Thomas Taylor, a former County Borough Engineer. In his Will Mr Taylor has bequeathed ownership of the models to his three children. However, Mr Taylor and his children are anxious that the models remain in Northampton on public display and to be used in the teaching of engineering students. In view of his age, Mr Taylor is anxious that all uncertainties over the models be removed in the near future and the following proposals represent the arrangement which best reflects the interests of all parties and ensures that the models remain in Northampton for the foreseeable future.

Proposals

(a) Mr Taylor and his children, being the beneficiaries under his Will, agree that the seven models should remain on indefinite loan to the County Council, to be on public exhibition at the School of Technology of Nene College (at present being located at the St George's Avenue Campus), so that the models may be used for the purpose of instructing engineering students. It would not be possible without prior consent (which is unlikely to be given) to exhibit the models other than as part of the School of Technology. Mr Taylor is adamant on this point.

(b) Mr Taylor and his beneficiaries reserve the right to remove the models at any time for whatever reason on two months' notice.

(c) The County Council will, whilst they have custody of the models, maintain them in good condition and insure them on an all-risks policy in the sum of £20,000; this figure has been agreed with Mr Taylor and may not reflect the actual value of the models, the level of insurance to be the subject of annual review. This clause may require amendment in the light of the review of the County Council's insurance arrangements.

(d) The County Council will whilst they have custody of the models meet any Capital Transfer Tax (or its equivalent) that the models might attract on Mr Taylor's death. Mr Taylor is anxious that if the models remain in Northampton, they should not be a burden to his estate. The risk of the County Council having to make a payment under this head is slight, since the models are classed by the Capital Transfer Tax Office as being of 'national, scientific, historic or artistic interest' and only a change in the legislation would render the models liable to tax. Mr Taylor and his children are willing to give appropriate undertakings to the Treasury required under the Finance Act for this purpose.

(e) Mr Taylor and his children wish to offer on loan, on similar terms, the cups, medals, photographs, plans and documents associated with the models, which Mr Taylor has in his possession.

(f) The County Council will pay Mr Taylor's legal expenses in preparing an agreement.

(g) Mr Taylor or his successors are to be given prior notice of any removal arrangements for the models, which might be necessary if, for example, the School of Technology were to be relocated.

Advice

The Governors of Nene College considered these loan arrangements at their meeting on the 13th February and recommended their acceptance.

Report of the County Secretary (Mr John Fursey) to the
Further and Higher Education Sub-Committee of the
Northamptonshire County Council dated 27 February 1980

'AIM OF EDUCATION SYSTEM IS GRADUALLY SHIFTING':
CHANGE FROM MERELY LITERATE TO EDUCATED COMMUNITY

[A report of Jack Longland opening the extension to the college in 1961]

The aim of education in this country was imperceptibly shifting, Mr Jack Longland, Director of Education for Derbyshire, said in Northampton yesterday. No longer was the goal merely a literate population. They were trying to create for the first time anywhere a largely educated community.

Mr Longland, a regular broadcaster and TV personality, was opening the new £365,000 extensions to Northampton College of Technology and he went on to speak of the part the college could play in helping to fulfil the aim. Mr Longland said the programme prepared for the event contained more than the story of the college. It showed a very important thing: that the history of the college in Northampton was a genuine and honourable microcosm of the whole history of English education. And, as the programme pointed out, the lovely new building was not the final coping stone being put on the edifice. It should be looked upon as one admirable milestone in the still continuing process of the growth of education.

Tide coming in

Mr Longland, commenting on how new the vision of an educated community really was, said his father was born in 1869, a year before the first great Education Act came into law. At that time, the nation set itself for the first time the goal of achieving a literate population. This was because a 19th century industrial nation could not possibly get by with anything less than a literate population.

But they had to put up for long years with a very minimum system of education – education for the children of the labouring poor with a staff of grossly underpaid teachers. Yet during this short period of history, those with enough brains and detachment to look and observe, truly had watched the tide of education coming in. As with the tides of the seas there had been checks and set-backs, and some times there seemed to be no measurable advance at all. There had also been sudden floods, and the tide was still coming in. As the tide advanced, so the aim and goal of English education was imperceptibly shifting as well. No longer did we want only a literate population, but we were on the next lap already.

This was an infinitely more difficult lap to cover. The aim was to bring to birth for the first time, not only in this country but elsewhere, a largely educated community, and it was no good our flattering ourselves that we had got that yet.

Future lives

Mr Longland said that an education system conditioned the future lives that we wanted our children to lead. There was no other service in this country about which that could be said.

He went on to refer to the changing nature of the speeches that nowadays were being made by ministers of the Crown and to statements in election manifestos. It stood out a mile – education had been promoted from the third or fourth division to somewhere near the top of the league stakes. That had happened in a short time.

In local government, education was now recognised as by far the biggest service the most important and the most expensive as well. Education provided the strongest of arguments for preserving local government, for it was the most intensely personal of all social services.

It would lose its virtue if governed and administered from Whitehall. As one professor had put it: 'Education is chaps.'

Hungry millions

Mr Longland said that science and technology were today tremendously important. They had to make the most economical and efficient use of our main power, brainpower and horse power. Britain had nothing left to export but its brains. They had to use the skills of more efficient industry, greater productivity and more exports. Without these we could never reach or maintain the standard of living which all classes of the community now expected. More important still we could not bring more tolerable living standards to those uncounted hungry millions all around the curve of the world who were a standing reproach to our comparative prosperity.

The importance of the college and all it could and would do should not be measured only in terms of more refrigerators, more TV sets and more washing machines. There was a double purpose of better work and better living.

In the forefront

Affluence in itself was not enough, and leisure was meaningless unless education had developed the native resources we possessed and unless technology had been properly used for civilised human purposes.

Earlier, Alderman Arthur Chown, chairman of Northampton Borough Education Committee, in introducing Mr Longland, said that with the extensions they were well equipped to undertake technical education in Northampton.

This was a thing which was most necessary as appeared from a recent White Paper and he was sorry that some of his colleagues apparently thought that 'technical' was a dirty word.

Alderman Chown said that Northampton could claim to be in the forefront of technical education, which was most necessary if Britain was to maintain her place in the industry of the world.

Mr Bernard Sunley, whose firm built the frontage block, said it was absolutely wonderful that Northampton should be in the lead again with this 'fantastic college.' It must do everyone connected with industry a tremendous amount of good.

Amid laughter, especially from Mr R. T. Paget, M.P. for Northampton, who was on the platform, he commented: 'I put it down to the Social and Liberal touch of the town.'

Mr Sunley also said: 'We have not made any profit out of this contract. I am quite sure that we shall get repaid many times over, through the staff and personnel we hope to get out of this great building.'

A proud day

A vote of thanks was proposed by the Mayor (Councillor Mrs E. F. Wilkinson), who said it was a proud day, and seconded by Councillor T. H. Dockrell, chairman of the college governors who mentioned gifts of books and equipment to the building.

Councillor Dockrell said they had a fine library, and he hoped students would take advantage of the excellent facilities provided.

The new buildings were dedicated by Canon D. F. Andrews, vicar of Kingsthorpe and Rural Dean.

After the ceremony the visitors toured the building.

> Report from the *Chronicle & Echo*,
> 27 January 1961, following the official
> opening ceremony on 26 January 1961

MINISTER OPENS NEW £167,000 COLLEGE EXTENSION

Mr Gerald Fowler, Minister of State at the Department of Education and Science, today opened the £167,000 extension to Northampton College of Technology.

The three-storey building provides facilities for the traditional Northampton leather and footwear trade. Accommodation is also provided for science, general studies and engineering.

Welcoming the Minister, Councillor David Walmsley, chairman of Northampton Education Committee, pointed out that the college cost more than half a million pounds to maintain each year – one seventh of the total spent on education by the borough.

He hoped that the college in St George's Avenue would be able to concentrate on more advanced work after the building of a new college of further education on a 30-acre site at Booth Lane.

Work would start on the first instalment of the college in the next financial year. This would eventually house the departments of catering, commerce, engineering, general studies and science.

He went on:

> The new college of further education will meet many of the needs of the first 35,000 people we are expecting to move to Northampton in the new town development in the next five years, as well as offering bigger and better opportunities in the further education field to the present citizens of Northampton.
>
> The Booth Lane college was expected to enrol over 4,000 full-time and part-time students.
>
> 'In addition there is little doubt that there will be a need for a third

college on the southern or western sides of the town sometimes in the next 10 to 20 years.'

Councillor Walmsley thanked the staff at the Borough Education and Architect's Department for their work in the design and provision of the new extensions.

Earlier, Mr Fowler, who lived at Long Buckby and was educated at Northampton Grammar School, lunched with staff and students at the college.

He was taken on a tour of the extension which is between the sports hall and the workshops behind the main building.

An entrance from the car park leads into a coffee bar area and most of the ground floor is taken up by a motor vehicle workshop and a leather dyeing and shoe store.

Work on the extension started in August 1987 and was completed last September. Since then improvements have been made to accommodation in the main building which Mr Fowler also toured.

Report from the *Chronicle & Echo*,
24 March 1974

5 Higher Education Facilities Return to the Town and County

The relationship of Cambridge University with Northamptonshire, through the medium of University Extension Lectures, covers nearly half a century. To the county town falls the title of pioneer. Northampton had its first course of University Extension Lectures in 1885. Never far behind (and sometimes a little ahead) Kettering began in 1888, and Wellingborough followed the lead in 1893. But these three towns do not complete the list.

Four other centres in the county have had Extension Courses through Cambridge University. Who, not knowing the answer, would guess them right first time? They are Finedon (1893), Desborough (1904 and 1919), Raunds (1925) and Rushden (1932).

A glance at the tabulated records for the county town (the remainder of this article is confined to Northampton) reveals a number of interesting items. There have been 59 Extension Courses in Northampton, each Course consisting usually of twelve lectures.

The first Course, way back 'in the Michaelmas Term of 1885', was entitled 'Masterpieces', and the lecturer was R. G. Moulton, a Cambridge graduate, afterwards Professor of Literary Theory and Interpretation in the University of Chicago. Northamptonians of those days had apparently taken to heart the dictum of 'mens sana in corpore sano.' For the second Course, 'Lent Term, 1886,' was on 'Body and Health,' the lecturer being Dr. D. W. Samways, of Cambridge, London and Paris Universities.

Happily a record of the attendances at the Lectures has been kept. The audiences were not an exclusive coterie. At Professor Moulton's lectures the average attendance was 500 according to the record. It is a big figure, and suspiciously round, but it can be safely accepted. For Dr Samway's lectures, each of which was given twice over, afternoon and evening, attracted an even larger number. The average attendance was 100 in the afternoon and 432 in the evening.

Encouraged by this response, the local committee organised six more Courses in quick succession. These Courses (1886 to 1889) were on the Roman Empire, the French Revolution, Elizabethan Literature, Astronomy, Victorian Poetry and the Forces of Nature. The first two of these were given by A. J. Grant, later Professor of History in the University of Leeds. Judging by the sizes of the audiences,

Northampton wasn't interested in the Roman Empire (the average audience was only 51), but very keen about the French Revolution (average audience of 339). This discrimination is understandable, bearing in mind that it was the period of Bradlaugh and Labouchere. Very successful, too, was the Course on Astronomy, given by the late Sir J. D. McLure, who on average had 303 people to listen to him.

For some reason, perhaps the dwindling audiences after McLure's lectures, the Courses were abruptly terminated in 1889. Not a single Course was held throughout the eighteen nineties, 'the decadent decade.' But revival came with the turn of the century.

From 1904 to 1914 there were no fewer than 23 courses, most winters, two, one before and the other after Christmas. At these lectures the audiences ranged between 100 and 250. Variety was the keynote of the subject-matter of the Courses, but a fairly equal balance was maintained between Art and Science. Among the lecturers the most frequent was the Rev. J. H. B. Masterman, afterwards Professor of History in Birmingham University, and later Bishop of Plymouth.

Not even the War stopped activities, though naturally it affected the size of the audiences, which were, however, surprisingly large. There were nine Courses between 1914 and 1918. Some of the titles will come as a shock to those who remember the period in terms of war-time psychology. Dr E. Markham Lee lectured on 'Makers of Modern Music' and 'Music of Modern Russia': Mr. J. E. Pythiam on 'Outlines of the History of Painting,' and the Rev. J. L. Harkway on 'Literature and Life.' There was a courageous sanity about this selection.

After the War the Committee continued to arrange two Courses each winter until 1928, but the expectation of an increase in the audience to the pre-war size was not fulfilled. Out of these 19 courses only three attracted an average audience of over 150, whilst after 1924 the average audience was consistently below 100. Apparently the lectures and the times were temporarily out of joint, and in 1928 the Committee suspended activities indefinitely.

Oddly enough, the poorest attended Course in the entire series was on the subject of 'The USA and its Relations with Great Britain'. That course was given in 1927 – five years too soon. The two other courses, with titles which are specially interesting when considered retrospectively, suffered also from small attendances. They are 'Transformation of the World,' the last completed course before the outbreak of the War, and a course, which was in progress when the Armistice was signed, entitled 'Some Economic Problems of War and Reconstruction.' It seems that the chief problem about Mr H. G. Wells' recent proposal for 'Professors of Foresight' may be the difficulty of getting people to listen to them! By the time these lines appear, Northampton will be starting its Sixtieth Extension Course, six lectures on 'Britain's Economic Problems since the War,' in the Lecture Hall of the Public Library. The lecturer is Mr Frank Lee, B.A., B.Sc. (Econ.). The Mayor (Councillor P. F. Hanafy), Councillor William Barratt, Malcolm Nash, Esq., Councillor James Peach, J.P., Hector Marlow, Esq., and W. J. Bassett-Lowke, Esq., are the chairmen for the six lectures. Mr Frank Lee, who lives at Wollaston, was appointed at the end of 1931 by the University of Cambridge to supervise the development of the work of the Board of Extra-Mural Studies in Northamptonshire. These will be his first public lectures in the county town.

This Sixtieth Extension Course, besides being a kind of jubilee, is intended to initiate a permanent revival in Northampton of the Cambridge University Extension Lectures Movement. With this objective in view, it is proposed to form in Northampton a University Extension Society. The chief function of the Society will be to arrange, in conjunction with the Board of Extra-Mural Studies of Cambridge University, courses of University Lectures in the Arts and Sciences. Mr A. H. Jackson, the well-known son of Councillor James Jackson, is the provisional Hon. Secretary of the Society, membership of which will be open to all who are interested in its objects.

In the past, through the medium of University Extension Courses, Northampton has had some of the finest lecturers in the country. The new University Extension Society will aim at the maintenance of this high standard, which will assuredly be attained if adequate public support is forthcoming.

Extract from an article by Frank Lee for the
Northampton County Magazine,
Vol. 6, 1933, pp. 33–4.

ALDERMAN FRANK LEE, BA, BSC

The late alderman Frank Lee was born in 1899 at Blackburn in Lancashire, his father being a clerk on the railway and his mother a weaver. He started work in a cotton weaving factory at the age of twelve, later working on the railway at Huddersfield as a booking clerk until he was twenty-one. He served in the Army for a few months after the end of the 1914–1918 war, but did not go overseas. By diligent attendance at evening classes at the Technical College at Huddersfield, he won a Trade Union scholarship at the London Labour College in 1921, and proceeded by scholarships to Ruskin College at Oxford in 1923, where he took economics, and to Balliol College, Oxford, in 1925. He became a lecturer in economics for London University, of which he was a graduate, and in 1931 settled in Northampton as an extra-mural lecturer for Cambridge University. He soon started to pull his weight in local politics and public affairs, became Leader of the Labour Party on the Town Council and was Mayor in 1951–52. His other activities included membership of the East Midlands Gas Board and of the Nene River Board of which he became Chairman.

Though Lee was a keen politician and threw himself with zest into party strife, he found his greatest joy in the study of Northampton's history from the earliest times, to which he had been led by his interest in town-planning – an example of the value of a knowledge of history in making sensible present-day decisions. His studies soon brought him into contact with the Record Society when its headquarters were in the County Hall. After the war he continued his researches at Lamport Hall, where he transcribed or made copious notes from the medieval records relating to the Borough. He was, of course, a member of the Society, and when the time was ripe for handing over the custody of the MS/collections to a joint committee of the Local Authorities, Frank Lee gave the Society his unqualified support and played a major part in bringing the scheme to fruition. When it came into being (1st January, 1952), he declared that he had much rather be a 'consumer', but was persuaded to become the first chairman of the Northamptonshire Archives Committee. He strove untiringly for the next three years to secure Delapre Abbey as an ideal home for the Northamptonshire Record Office. His health had been rapidly failing for some months before the end, but he attended an Archives Sub-Committee Meeting the day before he went into Brompton Hospital, where he died three weeks later on Whitsunday, May 29th 1956.

Lee was a masterly lecturer – the most lucid I have ever listened to. He had an extraordinary grasp of his material and a phenomenal memory, using hardly any notes. This was in some ways a pity, for he wrote down and printed little and so much that he had unravelled about the history of the town from the 12th to the present century died with him. He did, however, leave two important articles in print:— *'Leges Ville Norht, or The Laws of the Town of Northampton, originally drawn up by the 40 Old Wise Men circa* 1189 *A.D.'* and *'A New Theory of the Origins and Early Growth of Northampton'*, the last being given as a paper to the Royal Archaeological Institute at their summer meeting at Northampton in1953. (Offprints of this can be obtained from the Record Society.)

A man of considerable ability and charm with a very good speaking voice. Lee was an excellent Chairman. It fell to him as Mayor of Northampton to proclaim on the Market Square Queen Elizabeth II's accession to the throne, and no-one who witnessed the ceremony will easily forget the dignity and grace with which he invested the occasion.

He married in 1926 Olive Mary Spouge, who shared all his political and civic interests to the full and who survives him with two sons.

Had he been spared Frank Lee would undoubtedly have written an important history of our County Town. As it is, in the midst of a busy life, he had already earned for himself an honourable place in the succession of our local historians. For the cause of history generally through his work for the archives he accomplished much, of which future students will reap the benefit. He is greatly missed by his friends and fellow-labourers in these fields.

Northampton Past and Present
Vol. II, No. 2, p.44

UNIVERSITY OF LEICESTER

UNIVERSITY CENTRE
NORTHAMPTON

OPENING OF THE CENTRE

Thursday 21 September 1967

ORDER OF PROCEEDINGS

The Chancellors's Procession will enter the Hall at 3-15 p.m.

(The audience is requested to stand until the Chancellor has taken his seat)

THE VICE-CHANCELLOR

(MR T. A. F. NOBLE, M.B.E, M.A.)

will invite the Chancellor to open the Centre

THE CHANCELLOR

(THE RT. HON. THE LORD ADRIAN, O.M, F.R.S.)

will declare open the New Centre

THE MAYOR OF NORTHAMPTON

(ALDERMAN T. H. DOCKRELL, F.R.C.S.I., J.P..)

will propose a vote of thanks to the Chancellor

THE CHAIRMAN OF THE NORTHAMPTONSHIRE
EDUCATION COMMITTEE

(ALDERMAN W. J. PENN)

will second the vote of thanks

The Chancellor's Procession will leave the Hall

(The audience is requested to stand until the Procession has left the Hall)

———————

Tea will be served after the Ceremony in the
Centre's two Common Rooms

Guests are invited to inspect the Centre after tea

The University Centre

For more than ninety years the County and Borough of Northampton were provided with University Extension Courses and Tutorial and Sessional Classes by the University of Cambridge, but in 1962 responsibility for making this provision was transferred to the University of Leicester. Already, however, Leicester had started providing courses for practising teachers in the area. Since 1962 both types of provision – the one made by the Department of Adult Education, the other by the School of Education – have greatly increased. This growth in the work encouraged the University to seek to establish a Centre equipped to suit the educational and social needs of its students in Northampton and the surrounding county districts.

After a long search a building suitable for conversion was found – the former Nazareth House situated in Barrack Road. Built in 1878 in Northamptonshire stone and in a style reminiscent of the Renaissance, it has made a handsome, spacious and efficient structure for the various functions it is intended to serve, which include not only the housing of classes and courses provided mostly in the evenings for adults by the Department of Adult Education and the School of Education, but also a graduate teacher training unit of thirty full-time students specialising in primary education.

The new Centre provides a joint Lecture Hall for the Department of Adult Education and the School of Education, separate libraries and common rooms, eight workrooms for the Department and five for the School, as well as staff rooms and offices. The Warden of the Centre, who is a member of the staff of the Department, is Mr Ronald L. Greenall, and the Tutor-in-charge of the work of the School is Mr John Doe; Mr D. J. Ratcliffe is the Secretary of the Centre. Plans made for the year 1967–68 are for the provision of sixty classes and courses by the Department and thirty by the School, in addition to the courses for full-time students.

Conversions of the building were made under the direction of Mr F. G. Sutton, the Bursar of the University, assisted by Mr W. L. Lower, the Buildings Officer, and the main contractors were R. E. Lewis Ltd, of Northampton.

Extracts from leaflet produced for the Opening of the University Centre,
21 September 1967.

REFLECTIONS

Ron Greenall

In towns undergoing the pains and pleasures of redevelopment (like Northampton) when people say 'That fine old building should be preserved' a relevant question to ask is 'And what can it be used for afterwards?'

One answer is, 'Turn it into an Adult Education Centre'! This is what Leicester University did when it bought the old Nazareth House in Barrack Road in 1966.

The University Centre (UCN to its friends) is now celebrating its tenth anniversary. [*Compiler's Note:* this contribution was written in 1977.]

Mind you, before the conversion of some old buildings starts you need faith. The first time I saw Nazareth House my heart sank into my shoes. Outside, this erstwhile orphanage and old folks home, built about a century ago, was not too bad. Indeed, built to look like a Tudor mansion it has a certain dignity. What is more, it does not look in the least like a school, and adult education centres are better that way.

But inside it was terrible. A Victorian institution gone to ruin, all black and brown paint, and wards with derelict curtain rails, it had been empty for several years, and the day I first entered it was damp and very cold. And there was the Professor, eyes twinkling, saying 'This will be the bar and common room . . . That will be your office . . . Ah, and this is perfect for the library.' My nerve nearly failed me. Had I given up my nice Grammar School job for this? If the place had possibilities, as far as I could see I had only his word for it.

In due course the bursar and buildings officer arrived from the University. Around this place they marched, dictating notes to a secretary who took them down at the trot . . . a hatchway here, a new door there, remove that wall, new floorboards here. Electricians, carpenters and painters all came and went, and the place at length was filled with furniture. No desks, the place is for adults! Done in the standard Leicester University conversion decor of dark blue doors, silver grey walls and sisal carpeting in every room, the place was ready for use by Easter 1967.

We started with a summer term programme that year. The Professor was right, the place had possibilities. The fabric was good and it is amazing what light paintwork and fluorescent lighting can do for an old building. And let no one denigrate Victorian design: with its thick walls, on a hot summer day, UCN is the coolest place in Northampton: on a cold winter evening it retains its heat very well. And with its high windows no one whose attention wanders can find distraction by gazing at the world outside.

Well, what was UCN brought into use for, and what has it contributed to the educational and intellectual life of Northampton these ten years? The reason for its opening was because, a few years before, the new University of Leicester took over from Cambridge the responsibility for providing university adult education courses in Northamptonshire. The success of Vaughan College, the University's centre in Leicester, persuaded it to look for a building to fulfil the same purpose here in Northampton. That is, to be a friendly, adult-centred building in which people can take part in informal education in their own leisure time.

To the discerning eye of Professor John Allaway, Nazareth House, first suggested by the Local Education Authority, seemed just the place. However, being on the large size for adult education purposes alone, another department of the University, the School of Education, agreed to share in the venture. Professor Tibble had two uses for it: the training of young graduates for the teaching profession, and the promotion of in-service courses for teachers in the schools of Northampton and district.

When it first opened about thirty adult education courses a year were being put on. Nowadays the figure is double that. Over the last ten years the people of Northampton have had about five hundred different courses to choose from. Universities put on a wider range of adult education than people generally realise. Of course, the vast majority are still in the format of weekly evening classes. The most popular subjects at UCN are literature, art, history, archaeology, sociology, psychology, geology and natural history. In Northampton local students – particularly in history, archaeology and geology – find ready takers. Basically the purpose of these courses is to bring specialists, many of them from the University, others local people, to take courses in which above all they want to communicate their enthusiasm and feeling for their subject to ordinary members of the public. Learning for its own sake if often a cliché these days, but it exists more often in adult education than in any other branch of education.

Besides evening classes for the general public a range of courses for specialist groups are promoted at UCN. Three day-release courses a week are running at present (in association with the Workers' Educational Association and the TUC) for shop stewards in industry. There are courses for people in management, and the social services and one day conferences for professional bodies.

Wherever possible we arrange field trips and theatre visits for people in our classes, and we hire coaches by the score for these outings each year. We tie in our courses with local events – the Northampton Festival and productions at the Royal Theatre, for instance. And over the years we have brought distinguished composers such as Edmund Rubbra, actors such as Brenda Bruce, as well as academics as well-known as W. G. Hoskins or Kenneth Mellanby to perform or give lectures.

Over the years the academic staff based at UCN has grown. Richard Foulkes came as deputy-warden in 1973. Trevor Hold, the organising tutor for North-amptonshire, a musician and composer, uses the Centre as his base, and Phyllis Annis, Pat Ashton and Colin Richards have all been added to the personnel of the School of Education of which John Doe is tutor-in-charge. Particularly pleasing is that some of part-time lecturers who gave courses in the early years still work for us.

Whether many of us who work there will be still around to see UCN's twenty-first birthday I cannot say, but one thing is sure. UCN will almost certainly be providing courses for the education and intellectual stimulation of Northampton people.

THE UNIVERSITY CENTRE, NORTHAMPTON

Richard Foulkes

From the beginnings of the university extension movement towards the end of the nineteenth century, the universities of Oxford, Cambridge and London deployed panels of lecturers across the country. A particularly vivid account of this way of life is to be found in the autobiography of John Cowper Powys whose weekly itinerary encompassed five or six towns from Liverpool to the home counties. As the new universities were founded – some of them directly from the extension movement – the old universities progressively ceded territory. Cambridge University continued to provide extension courses in Northamptonshire until the autumn of 1961 when the University of Leicester took over responsibility for the county.

In 1961-2 nineteen students attended one class and though the programme developed it was the opening of the University Centre in 1967 that signalled a major increase in activity. In taking over university extension provision in Northamptonshire the University of Leicester was under no obligation to establish its own premises and that it did so was largely thanks to the imagination and determination of John Allaway, Vaughan Professor of Education. A Yorkshireman of diminutive stature but imbued with forceful determination, Allaway was strongly committed to the establishment of centres for adult education, on the pattern of Vaughan College in Leicester.

In his aspirations for Northamptonshire Allaway found a formidable ally in Professor J. Tibble, of the university's School of Education. He appreciated the lack of professional provision for teachers in the county and saw the scope for a postgraduate certificate course as well as advanced courses for all members of the profession. The Allaway-Tibble alliance was crucial in persuading the university, the local authorities, the University Grants Committee and the Department of Education and Science of the viability of a self-contained outpost for the university in Northamptonshire.

As the university was considering possible sites in Northampton, the Roman Catholic diocese was coincidentally disposing of Nazareth House, an imposing mid-Victorian stone building in the Cathedral complex on Barrack Road. It had been used as an orphanage and old people's home, but was no longer really suitable to their needs in the mid-twentieth century. Negotiations between the university and the diocese progressed to a satisfactory conclusion, with assurances from the purchaser to the vendor about the new use for the building.

The site was purchased for £6,500 funded by a special grant from the University Grants Committee; the university paid a further £5,000 for the building. However a great deal of work was required to make the building's 1,600 square feet suitable for its new function. A further £30,000 was spent on conversion and nearly £20,000 on furnishings and equipment to provide a lecture hall, eleven classrooms, two tutorial rooms, two Common rooms, two libraries and accommodation for academic and clerical staff.

By 21 September 1967 all was ready for the official opening. The university's Chancellor (Lord Adrian) and the Vice-Chancellor (Mr – later Sir – Fraser Noble) addressed the assembled gathering of 'town-and-gown', as did the Mayor of Northampton (Alderman T. H. Dockrell, JP) and the Chairman of the Northamptonshire Education Committee (Alderman W. J. Penn). The staff of the new Centre comprised Mr R. L. Greenall as Warden(Adult Education) and Mr J. Doe as Tutor-in-Charge

(School of Education), plus their respective secretaries (Miss Pat Perkins and Mrs Pat Clarke – both of whom are still at the Centre) and a range of ancillary support.

One curiosity concerning the opening has recently come to light in the papers of the late Professor Allaway. Although the university had expended £60,000 on the building, the Vice-Chancellor declined Allaway's request for a commemorative plaque. This was eventually paid for by members of staff, who contributed 'a shilling or so' each!

With the advantages of its own premises the University of Leicester quickly consolidated and expanded its activities in Northamptonshire, which then had no other institution of higher education. Within a couple of years the adult education programme increased to sixty courses with over one thousand students and the School of Education's professional courses for teachers and its postgraduate certificate (under the direction of Miss Phyllis Annis) found an enthusiastic response, to which the large number of University Centre trained teachers still working in this county bears testimony.

In the early 1970s the university acquired two further adjacent buildings: the Queen Alexander Nursing Institute and White Lodge, both of which were converted for their new role. Staffing at the Centre increased, with the appointments of an Organising Tutor for North-amptonshire and a Deputy-Warden. John Allaway was still to be seen at the Centre teaching courses in Group Dynamics and Transactional Analysis, but he had been succeeded as Vaughan Professor by Henry Arthur Jones, another strong advocate of educational centres. On Professor Jones's appointment as Pro-Vice-Chancellor of the university in 1978 Mr Greenall transferred to Leicester and Richard Foulkes took over as Warden.

The School of Education's activities changed significantly in the mid-1980s with the discontinuation of the postgraduate certificate, but, with the appointment of Dr Mark Lofthouse as Tutor-in-Charge, initiatives with the local authority resulted in closer liaison over INSET provision and the location of advisory staff and the Early Childhood Centre in the Queen's Building.

The adult education programme has expanded to the extent that in 1987–88 145 courses took place at the Centre with 2,747 enrolments and a further 54 courses, with 1,026 enrolments, elsewhere in the county. That the university can generate such a high level of activity (unmatched by any other university away from its main site) is thanks to the existence of the University Centre as an identifiable institution devoted to the particular needs of adults.

In 1984 the Friends of the University Centre came into being as a support group for social and fund-raising activities. In the intervening years the Friends' input has included extensive refurbishing of the

Centre, most notably the attractively furnished Clare Room opened in 1987. The University Centre is the Open University Study Centre for the town. It also acts as a favoured meeting place for many local societies – historical, archaeological, political and literary.

For a non-university county the residents of Northamptonshire have access to a unique range of educational provision. A glance at the Centre's Visitors' Book illustrates how many leading scholars, writers and public figures have contributed to the programmes over the years. Like all institutions the University Centre has responded to social and education change, but, with the expansion of the town and county and the increased emphasis on retraining and leisure activities, the Centre is and will continue to be central to the educational and cultural life of Northamptonshire.

THE SCRAPTOFT INFLUENCE

Phyllis Annis, Trevor Scholey, George Kitson and John Wilson

Scraptoft Hall was built in or about 1723 overlooking a village of the same name on the outskirts of Leicester. The town grew, became a city and in 1945, at the request of the then Ministry of Education, the City of Leicester Education Committee took a lease on the premises in order to open the first post-war, two-year teacher training college in the country. Students were admitted from January 1946 and the property was purchased by the City Council in 1954. The early academic association of the College was with Birmingham University. However, in 1954 when Teacher Education was reorganized under Area Training Organizations, the College began its association with the then newly chartered University of Leicester. The rapid expansion of student numbers led to the establishment of two 'outposts' – the Corby Annexe and the Northampton Annexe.

NORTHAMPTON AND CORBY OUTPOSTS *(Trevor Scholey)*

Having read about the Northampton Annexe in the particulars that came when I applied for my post, I was interested to make contact, as my previous work had been in a college of education during the expansion in teacher training in the 1960s. Colleges were undergoing changes which were not always seen to be a better preparation for future teachers. In the move to gain academic acceptability many colleges had squeezed out 'method', practical application, preparation and work with children in order to ensure that students were well prepared for the examinations which would ensure a degree qualification validated by a university.

What I saw at Northampton and later at Corby was very pleasing. Practical mathematics, environmental science, language work, making music, literature and art were all focused on children's learning. The discussions which I was invited to join were of a very high order. The students were keen to hear about what was happening in schools and how they could best prepare themselves for their contact with children.

The tutors I saw were obviously good practitioners and were intent on giving the students a rich experience which would serve them well in their teaching. The relationships between the tutors and students were born through mutual trust and there appeared to be a very strong bond of friendship as well as professionalism. George Kitson and John Wilson were appointed as tutors-in-charge at Northampton and Corby respectively and were justifiably proud of what they achieved, through the tutors they appointed and the students they trained.

THE NORTHAMPTON ANNEXE *(George Kitson)*

It is now more than twenty years since teacher training first became established in Northampton – the result of continuing teacher shortages throughout the 1960s. Even with the massive injection of new teachers through the highly regarded Emergency Training scheme in the late 1940s, the teaching force had not recovered from its depleted state after the Second World War. Schools were increasingly forced to appoint un-qualified staff as the colleges were unable to satisfy the demand for trained teachers to cope with a major population surge. Finally, in the mid-1960s, after the publication of the Crowther and Plowden Reports the DES was persuaded to seek some solution to what had become a considerable problem for the schools, for in some areas as many as 20 per cent of their staff were unqualified.

Economic stringencies at the time would not permit the substantial capital expenditure required for the building of new colleges, so a number of possibilities were discussed which would enable existing colleges to expand and involve minimal financial outlay. Of these, two possibilities were considered by the then Leicester College of Education, i.e. Box and Cox – a plan which made much more intensive use of the existing buildings or the setting up of outposts in areas where mature students were available and not too far distant from the parent college. Leicester decided on the 'outpost' solution and in 1966 it was agreed that two Annexes should be established; one at Corby and the other in Northampton town.

Accommodation
The Crowther and Plowden Reports had profound implications for

teacher training in that they recommended a three-year training course, instead of the then current two, and that teacher training colleges should be brought more centrally into the field of Higher Education, with closer relationships with the universities. In 1966 the Leicester University Institute of Education was planning a centre in Northampton to cope with the greatly increased amount of in-service work with local teachers and so, in line with the Crowther recommendations, a plan to bring the two projects together in a single building was considered. However, it soon became evident that the Convent building, adjacent to the Catholic Cathedral on Barrack Road, Northampton, which the University had just acquired, was insufficient to house both operations, and so the North-ampton LEA was approached for alternative accommodation.

Fortunately the John Clare School in Kettering Road, although partially occupied by the Technical College had some spare accommo-dation available and although not regarded as completely suited for the work, six large classrooms and a hall were allocated for use by the Leicester Annexe.

In 1966 I was appointed as tutor-in-charge with a remit to prepare the building and make plans to receive the first intake of some 50 students. The building was old and had been neglected for some years, yet one recognised its richness in Victorian school architecture with beautiful Gothic touches, mullioned windows, high ceilings and stone stairways. The hall was quite a gem of the period, several of the classrooms were still stepped, the walls green and brown and the lavatories outside in the yard reminded one of School Board days. In January 1967 I was given an assistant – an experienced head teacher from Leicester with wide experience and boundless energy and together, with quite admirable assistance from the Education Officer and his staff in Northampton, we set about the transformation of the building. The introduction of bright colours in the decoration and furnishings and carpets and the choice of non-institutional furniture all combined to create an environment that was pleasant and stimulating to work in.

However, we did not completely meet the deadline, for I well remember the workmen still adding the finishing touches on the first day of term, when a few uncertain staff met some sixty quite bewildered students face-to-face for the first time. Until a kitchen was installed at the end of the first year, students organised the making of coffee and tea and wheeled it on a trolley into the Common Room at breaks. Dining-room facilities were non-existent so the majority of students went home for lunch, or took sandwiches in the library or common-room or went to the University Centre at Barrack Road, which boasted a well-stocked buttery. The ancient heating system – unaccustomed to such heavy demands – frequently collapsed during the first winter and I well remember seeing students, huddled round a small heater, discussing a profound educational topic with a frozen tutor. Facilities were pretty minimal, but I feel sure that those early hardships and deficiencies fostered a strong sense of fellowship and community which pervaded the Annexe – under the stern, almost tyrannical, supervision of a Mrs Barnes – as were four hutted classrooms in the yard, new toilets and studies for tutors. We continued to make use of the University Centre and as numbers increased, extended our territory to the Barry Road Teacher's Centre.

Students
The students mainly lived in Northampton or the surrounding villages. The average age of the initial intake was around thirty (though several were in their forties) and mainly women, many of whom had brought up families and had had earlier careers. A number had worked in Northampton schools as unqualified teachers and were experienced in practical terms. Some were academically well-qualified, others had few or no qualifications in the accepted sense, but had wide experience in industry, commerce or other professions. All had at interview to show a capacity for study and some experience of working with children or youth. Nurses, physio-therapists, secretaries, executives, engineers, a photographer, several policemen, an ex-fighter pilot in the RAF and an ex-Mayor of Northampton were amongst those who applied. All were committed to a career in teaching and eager to be trained. In the first year we accepted a county cricketer, designing his course around the cricket seasons over a four-year period so that he could continue to play for his county. Unfortunately, it wasn't Northamptonshire.

Selection was based on two separate 'in-depth' interviews although certain candidates would be asked to produce work, particularly if they had elected to follow main studies in art or English. Our selection procedures were often criticised, but it is interesting to note that of the first intake, only one student failed to complete the course and she left at the end of the first year.

The main courses offered were necessarily restricted in number to English, art and environmental studies because of the lack of facilities and staff, but there was an extensive range of curriculum studies including music, art/craft, science, music, movement, English, history and story-telling which were mainly taught by visiting staff from the parent college in Leicester. The link with the main College was achieved through a weekly visit when the students spent a day in Leicester to make use of the facilities there, particularly the library.

Relationships with schools
Although a great deal of work had been done in preparing schools in Northamptonshire for the opening of the Annexe a few heads and teachers continued to regard the whole operation with suspicion and not

only had difficulty in accepting the basis of our selection of students but also felt concerned about staff/student relationships within the Annexe: standards would be eroded; people were being brought into the profession through the back door, and with few, or in some cases no, qualifications, how could professional attitudes be maintained if both staff and students were on Christian name terms? We listened and explained and as the Annexe became established we gained in confidence, and encouraged the involvement of both heads and teachers in the work. But it was, I feel sure, the students who contributed most to the Annexe becoming more fully accepted. During teaching practices and visits, it soon became apparent to the schools that these students were not mere apprentices, but equal members of staff, capable of accepting considerable responsibility. Of course, there were weaknesses and difficulties with some, but on the whole the students of the Annexe became highly respected throughout the educational community for their maturity and dependability.

Philosophy of training

I have often been asked about the philosophy behind the work of the Annexe. As far as I can remember, no particular philosophy was ever discussed or formulated. The Staff group as it came together and developed, was appointed on the basis of certain principles in education. Their combined attitudes were bound to create a distinctive ethos, which ultimately became the learning context to which students were exposed. Beliefs, attitudes, approaches to learning and teaching emanated from these principles. Thus there was a certain harmony of teaching throughout the Annexe and the way these principles were communicated to the students.

One basic tenet might be this – an acceptance that learning was most effective if experienced within the context of freedom, where students were able and encouraged to develop responsibility and an inspired sense of direction. Skills such as these should be the stock-in-trade of all teachers, but unless given the opportunity to be discovered and developed can regrettably remain dormant. Sir Alec Clegg expressed this rather well in his little book *Children in Distress* when he wrote: 'The object of teaching is not to convey knowledge, but to create a determination in the child to acquire it for himself.' This is no less important for adults.

The skills of teaching are essentially practical and at the Annexe we set out to provide students with opportunities to learn from experience, not only in the practical aspects of the work, but also in the social sense. We tried to create the kind of learning environment in which students could grow and change. Change invariably produces insecurity and a degree of vulnerability, particularly in adults, therefore a friendly, supportive background was an essential ingredient in the process. This we provided through small tutorial groups and as much individual counselling as was necessary.

Freedom undoubtedly released enormous resources of energy, creativity and imagination, which not only found their way into the academic work of the students but also into all their other activities. Drama, poetry-reading, music, folk-dancing, sailing and climbing clubs – all activities initiated and sustained by the students themselves. That splendid hall must still echo the gaiety of many fantastic evenings of enjoyment – such as the John Clare nights to celebrate the poet with broth, beer and Northamptonshire folk-songs played on a concertina by blind Harry. Diana Rigg, in her first year out of drama school, playing excerpts from Shakespeare, and which student can ever forget *Oh What a Lovely War*, a truly co-operative effort, dressed in the Joan Littlewood costumes from Stratford East – a cast of both students and staff, responding magnifi-cently to the inspired direction of a much loved member of the education staff. Those end-of-term celebrations in a local pub with dear Freda prancing on the boards to the strains of 'The Galloping Major'.

One also recalls the Annexe Magazine, *Nucleus* – a production of the highest quality, remarkable for such a small establishment. I have occasionally wondered if those students who passed through the Annexe were ever aware of its influence on their future careers. Then I came across a copy of *Nucleus* dated June 1970, and an article in it written by a student just about to leave, could be a partial answer to my query:

Gone – John Clare's neurotic and leisurely life. With me sixty other people are to leave this fantastic Victorian building. Three years have gone since the day we entered the College with quite a few preconceived ideas. How much have these prejudices been altered and how many have been removed? Consider the people who have taught before. They certainly have had their whole outlook on teaching transformed. But this is only in a way a technical detail for if one is going to be a worthwhile teacher, it is not enough to know about Piaget, Jackson and others. What really matters is to be a resourceful person, a rich personality. These three years have given people the opportunity to broaden their horizons and discover new interests. This was a golden opportunity to become 'educated' in the full sense of the word.

In its short life-time, the Annexe in Northampton trained (or should I say 'educated') some 300 teachers, many of whom are still working in the town and county and have, no doubt, made a considerable impression on the schools. Some have become head teachers and a number will have played a major role in determining the educational direction for the area. That the Annexe played a seminal role in the history of teacher education in Northampton is for others to decide. At least it established a sound platform for future developments.

'We have done this State some service, and they know't'.
Othello, Act V, Sc. ii.

THE CORBY ANNEXE *(John Wilson)*

In the early 1960s, the DES responded to the shortage of teachers by encouraging colleges to open 'outposts', away from the main campuses, to train mature students who normally could not take up residence. Thus, in 1966, the City of Leicester College of Education opened what became known as the Corby Annexe. This was a joint venture supported by the Leicester and Northamptonshire LEAs.

Originally the Annexe opened in a few rooms in Corby Technical College with about sixty students, ten of whom were residential in flats in Corby. Their age ranged from 18 to 54. Most of these students were to follow the full three-year certificate course; some, however, especially those who had been teaching unqualified and/or had exceptional qualifications, were allowed to complete the course in two years – not always a satisfactory scheme for mature students.

Students and staff
Staffing originally consisted of a tutor-in-charge and one other permanent lecturer along with itinerant staff from Leicester and some support from Technical College Staff.

Initially, there were doubts as to whether sufficient qualified students could be found to fill an intake of approximately fifty students a year. In fact, the difficulty became one of selection and the Annexe maintained a student roll of over 150 students of average age 30–35 (about 75 per cent of whom were women). With this roll the Annexe had to move to well-adapted and equipped premises in Rockingham Road in September 1967.

Originally it was envisaged that students would travel to the Leicester College for parts of their course. Though this did occur in specific subjects, geography and the expense dictated that the Annexe should build up its own permanent staff of ten. With many visiting lecturers from Leicester, a full range of subjects was provided. There was also considerable help and co-operation from teachers in the area.

The result was that the Annexe became what was virtually a small college on its own, with its own collegiate identity, ethos, professional outlook and traditions. It also became a centre for professional stimulus in the area, a buzzing community with committed staff and students from a wide variety of backgrounds, vocations and experience.

Philosophy
In the end, the flexibility the small college gave and the total involvement of staff and students meant that the Annexe produced many excellent teachers. But, what is more, it provided opportunities for students to develop their latent potentials to the full and the smaller college environment, with its logistical flexibility and easy relationships and no

top-heavy, time-consuming committee structures, aided this.

For those who were there, the Annexe was an exciting, warm and remarkable place to be in during those years. Its success or failure will have been judged by the performance of its teachers in schools. But it was always evident and rewarding to see the personal development and changing attitudes of students, which, even without any professional qualifications to be gained would have made it worthwhile.

*   *   *

Scraptoft is now part of Leicester Polytechnic and no longer enjoys an independent existence.

6 A College of Education in Northampton

David Walmsley

The developments previously described happened to coincide with the designation of Northampton as a 'New Town'. A group of young Councillors (both Conservative and Labour) had been elected to the County Borough Council. On the Conservative side these included Councillors John Barnes, Cyril Benton, Bert Bullard, Jack Corrin, Jill Knight, Jim Lewis, George Pollard, Mary Taunton (Mary Finch), and David Walmsley. On the Labour side these included Ron Dilleigh, Richard Gregson, Ruth Perkins and Carol Trusler. Amongst these a consensus emerged that positive steps needed to be taken to avoid Northampton suffering the fate of Buckingham a hundred years before with respect to Aylesbury, when that county town had been overtaken in its own county as the major population centre. The older and more experienced members of the Council did not resist change – indeed they had sought to lay the foundation for expansion over the preceeding twenty years* and they encouraged the younger group to develop their plans and ideas. Out of these members, Jack Corrin 'emerged' as the Leader of the Council following the death of Alderman J. V. Collier (who in his day had been known as the 'Mr. Northampton' of the 1950s) and David Walmsley emerged as Chairman of the County Borough Education Committee. He was supported by the major personalities on the Council at the time, virtually all of whom elected to serve on this Committee (and its Sub-Committees). Being a very much younger Chairman than would be normal, David Walmsley was given an 'anchorman' in his support. First of these was the previous Chairman of Education, Alderman Arthur Chown. Instead of resenting a younger man Arthur Chown went out of his way to support the new developments and to advocate the same to his generation. Unfortunately, he was going blind and so, after a short

---

* For details of these moves see *Expanding Northampton* by Hugh Barty-King (1985).

period, the 'anchorman' became Councillor (later Alderman) T. H. Cockerill. Harold Cockerill was for many years the 'father' of the Council and an ex-Mayor. He was a blunt and outspoken member of the County Borough Council, who could (and did) at times upset people. However, so far as David Walmsley was concerned, he came to adopt a 'protective' attitude. His shrewd advice was immensely helpful in enabling the young Chairman to pursue his ideas. However, none of these ideas would have come to fruition without the active support of Jack Corrin as Leader of the Council and Jim Lewis as the Deputy Leader. Perhaps it is also significant to record that for much of the period under review David Walmsley served as the Conservative Group's Party Whip.

Harold Skerrett OBE, BA, FRHistS, was the Chief Education Officer providing the professional advice (with first Frank Stuart, MA, who became Chief Education Officer for Lincoln, and then Jack Coventon, MA, as his Deputy). The Town Clerk was C. E. Vivian Rowe, LLB (London), and his Deputy (and ultimate successor) was Alan Parkhouse, MA. Mr Parkhouse provided the legal back-up for the various Education Committee initiatives.

The pressures at this time were very great. Selective secondary education revolved around what was intended to be a grading exercise called the 11-plus. This selection exercise however came to be regarded as a competitive examination which primary school pupils either 'passed' or 'failed'. Eventually the 11-plus became politically unsustainable but the merits (or de-merits) of its replacement, namely a non-selective secondary education system (comprehensive education), were also party-political matters.

In Northampton there was in fact very little choice. Although the County Borough Council usually had a 'Conservative' majority, central government at this time was Labour controlled and decreed that all new building should fit into a 'comprehensive' pattern. Despite very strong feelings over the future of the Northampton Town and County School (the old Northampton Grammar School), its status could not be changed since it had become a joint local authority school in 1911. An appeal to central government for special treatment for the school was rejected and the County Borough Council had to live with the consequences of the 1911 decisions in the 1970s. After extensive consulations (particularly with the teacher organisations), the decision was taken to re-organise in Northampton on a three-tier basis of lower, middle and upper schools. The funds made available by central government were used to adapt existing primary schools to become lower schools; existing secondary modern schools to become middle schools; and, the three existing grammar schools (the School for Boys, the School for Girls and Trinity Technical School) to become the core of eight planned upper schools. In effect the major part of the finance available to the County Borough was to be used to build purpose-designed and purpose-built upper schools on the 'frontiers' between the existing town residential areas and the new town residential areas to be fed from both and thus to build up as quickly as possible a one-town community. These hopes were not wholly fulfilled but certainly the new buildings gave the LEA an advantage over some other areas. Whilst the building programme was in the first instance triggered off by the need to provide educational facilities for the children of families moving to Northampton all this activity in turn generated the need for 'local' teacher training facilities.

The Leicester Education Committee had a Teacher Training College at Scraptoft, which had an annexe at Corby in Northamptonshire. A second annexe to Scraptoft was opened in Northampton in the John Clare buildings, Kettering Road, Northampton, when these buildings were vacated on the closure of the John Clare Secondary Modern School. The two Annexes were helpful so far as both the County and County Borough was concerned but essentially they were in the nature of 'stop-gaps'. When central government called for re-assessment of teacher training numbers, Scraptoft found it useful to meet central government requirements by 'reducing' its numbers through the transfer of its Corby annexe and its Northampton annexe to the Northamptonshire and Northampton LEAs respectively.

It was about this time the Ministry of Education (as it then was) announced that central government intended to build one further Teacher Training College in England and Wales before regarding that programme nationally as complete. A deputation from Northampton comprising David Walmsley and Harold Skerrett travelled to London to see a Mr Hugh Harding in the appropriate department of the Ministry (housed in Queen Victoria Street, London – not in the main building in Curzon Street) to press the case for this last College of Education to be built in Northampton. Mr Harding said that he was impressed by the arguments presented and indeed subsequently he became very much a friend at Court so far as Northampton was concerned. At the time Mr Harding was a fourth or fifth-tier officer in the Ministry but he was promoted from time to time and later on became a 'power-in-the-land' in the Department of Education and Science. Locally, the LEA often felt indebted to him for his interest and support.

The deputation came back to Northampton with the understanding that the Ministry had a short-list of three places for which permission to build might be given. Northampton was on the short-list and it was up to the three LEAs concerned to produce a practical scheme as quickly as possible. Without it actually being said, the deputation came back to Northampton with the clear impression that the first of the LEAs to produce viable plans would get the allocation.

It was at this point that Mr Skerrett retired as Chief Education Officer and Mr Michael Henley (then the Deputy Chief Education Officer at Southend-on-Sea) was appointed in his place. Mr Henley, during his career, had previously held a senior post with the Bedfordshire LEA at the time that County had built a Teacher Training College at Bedford. Mr Henley had in effect been the man on the spot in so far as the planning for educational needs of the Bedford College had been concerned. It also transpired that he had worked alongside a young architect (who had been on the staff of the Architect to the Bedfordshire Authority but was by this time in private practice in Northampton), Tony Stimpson. In the normal way the County Borough Architect, Mr Leonard Howarth, would have undertaken the architectural services for the design of a College in Northampton but he and his staff were snowed under with the School Building Programme. The Borough Architect 'knew' Tony Stimpson and indeed before Mr Stimpson moved to Bedfordshire he had employed him. With very considerable generosity the Borough Architect agreed that whilst he would be available in a consultative capacity the design of this prestigious project could be placed with COPA whose partner in charge of the project would be Tony Stimpson.

The next question was 'where to build'. The first thoughts of Mr Walmsley, Mr Skerrett and Mr Henley were to persuade the County Borough Council to release 50–60 acres of Delapre Park, Far Cotton, Northampton, as a site for the College, adjacent to the Eleanor Cross and with an entrance from Hardingstone Lane. This approach however was turned down by the full Borough Council who pointed out that Delapre Park had been acquired by the local authority for the general benefit of all the people of Northampton for leisure and recreational purposes and not for any specific purpose such as a College of Education. This was a severe blow at the time.

However, David Walmsley was a solicitor in private practice and it came to his knowledge that St Andrew's Hospital, Northampton, was desirous of building a new wing to their hospital. In that connection the Property Committee of the hospital, under the chairmanship of Sir Hereward Wake, Bt, of Courteenhall, Northamptonshire, was contemplating the sale of its Home Farm at Moulton Park to raise funds. Mr Walmsley's partner Charles Mumby, acted for the hospital; and, out of the bargain struck subsequently through Mr Alan Parkhouse the hospital got the funds for its extension and the local authority got a historic and prestigious site for its College of Education. It was 'historic' in the sense that along part of the road frontage ran a medieval boundary wall and it was 'prestigious' in that wonderful open views across the town to the Duston Hills and the Nene Uplands were opened up. With draft plans and an available site the local authority were able to go back to the Ministry (and to Mr Harding). If there was a race then Northampton won it and the necessary authority to proceed was given.

In its instruction to the architect the local authority indicated that: (a) it wanted the buildings to express the traditions of a 'college' by the creation of 'quads'; and (b) it would welcome the sympathetic use of wood in the decorative features of the interior of the public rooms. At one stage it was hoped that the old farm buildings (Home Farm) could be saved and used but unhappily a survey revealed extensive wet rot and dry rot to such an extent that the buildings would have to be demolished. A decision to demolish was in consequence inevitable. The cedars of Lebanon planted on the site by the hospital however were sound and were preserved. The planned new buildings were designed around them.

It was at this stage that the post of Principal was advertised. This attracted a good deal of interest but eventually David Walmsley and Michael Henley produced a long short-list which was reduced by a Committee representing both the Governors and the Borough and County authorities to a short short-list. Out of this (following interviews), a final choice between two candidates emerged. This final selection was a most interesting experience for those concerned. The first candidate had paced himself for a half-hour interview and wilted when the Committee gave him the benefit of one-and-a-half hours. The second candidate started nervously but as the interview progressed went on from strength to strength. In this way Dr Eric Ogilvie came to Northampton from the Weymouth Teacher-Training College and was involved in the final planning stages of the Northampton College.

At the same time another element in the whole development emerged at the direction of Mr Harding. The Ministry of Education had become the Department of Education and Science with a Secretary of State in charge instead of a Minister. Cornwall, Northamptonshire and Shropshire were the three geographical counties in England at that time without a teacher training college within their boundaries. Locally, it had been the view of the LEA that this factor had a lot to do with Northampton being given the go-ahead by central government anyway. In other words the desire of central government to 'spread' teacher training facilities coincided with the local need generated by the expansion of local school provision as a result of the New Town Programme. This belief as to the attitude of central government was reinforced by the news that Mr Harding felt it would be helpful if an existing teacher training college was closed and amalgamated with the new College. The suggestion was made that the Northampton LEA might discuss a 'merger' with another college in an area where it was deemed that there was an over-provision of teacher training colleges. Initially discussions were opened with the College of St Mark and St John, London, but these were not pursued and that College eventually moved to Plymouth.

The Director of Education in Liverpool was Mr C.P. R. Clarke, BLitt,

MA, who many years before had worked with the retired Chief Education Officer for Northampton, Harold Skerrett. Out of this link David Walmsley and Michael Henley were invited to visit the Kirkby Fields College of Education, Liverpool, and to explore the possibility of a transfer of that College from Liverpool to Northampton. A brief note about Kirkby Fields is included later in this chapter but in the story of the Northampton College of Education this was a very significant move. Thus the Northampton College was to be drawn from: (a) the Northampton Annexe of Scraptoft; (b) the Corby Annexe of Scraptoft; (c) Kirkby Fields, Liverpool; and (d) new recruitment.

Just down the road from Moulton Park was the College of Agriculture in Moulton founded and run by the 'old' County Council prior to the 1974 reorganisation of local authorities. At one stage consideration was given as to whether or not this institution should come into the proposed new College. However with the emphasis on 'teacher training' in the one place and on 'training for practical work on farms to a non-degree level' in the other place, the aims of the two establishments appeared to be so different that a common approach between the two could have been difficult to establish. Moulton consequently kept its independence, as it did when the issue was re-considered after the merger of the County Borough and County in 1974. However, when Moulton Park acquired on loan a modern art statue by Barbara Hepworth entitled 'Four Figures Waiting', the students at Moulton sent over a raiding party to 'borrow' the statue, which was then called back by the Hepworth Trustees.

Establishing a new College from 'cold' could have produced a difficult situation before a team spirit was generated and an *esprit de corps* built up. Bringing in a 'team' from outside, on the other hand, could have led to tension and problems of personal relationships. The fact that by and large the whole exercise went through without massive traumas was due to the rapid early rapport achieved by all those involved.

Michael Henley and his colleagues got on with their opposite numbers at Liverpool. Dr Ogilvie and members of staff at Liverpool quickly established friendships – and so did Leslie Skelton who had been appointed Clerk to the Governors and Chief Administrative Officer for the new College. The Chairman of Governors at Kirkby Fields was Councillor John Hamilton (who later achieved national fame/notoriety as the Leader of the Liverpool City Council at the time of the Derek Hatton confrontation with the policies of Central Government). John Hamilton usually appeared in an old grey hat, a blue suit and a knitted pull-over under his jacket. He was an old-time Quaker Christian Socialist. However in the Northampton/Liverpool situation John Hamilton offered nothing but kindness and consideration to the Northampton representatives (David Walmsley, Harold Cockerill and Carol Trusler), whom he invited to sit in on the Governors' meetings at Kirkby. This extended over a period of two years or so spanning the closure of Kirkby Fields and the opening of Northampton. Indeed, in this period John Hamilton virtually treated David Walmsley as an extra Vice-Chairman of Governors at Kirkby Fields, notwithstanding their different party-political stances. With such leadership extended in Liverpool the problems of transfer were greatly eased. Nevertheless, one of the particular difficulties was the future of Miss Bridget Danielli (the distinguished Principal of Kirkby Fields). Miss Danielli was a senior member of those who had been appointed College Principals and one of the few who had domestic science qualifications to have achieved such an appointment. Retirement (although not imminent) was only a few years ahead for her and Liverpool (which could have made this Northampton's problem) found a way for her to take early retirement honourably. In practical terms, from the Northampton point of view although Miss Danielli was 'senior' in terms of service to Dr Ogilvie, the Northampton Governors did not want to appoint a principal to the new College who could have retired within a few short years after the College opened.

Individual decisions had to be taken at the Liverpool end where existing staff had their roots. None of these had contemplated a move to Northampton and for all it was a leap into the dark to a brand new establishment without traditions or past experience. For some the move was not a possibility anyway for family and other reasons but in the end, out of a staff at Kirkby Fields numbering just over fifty, some thirty-seven came to Northampton.

Whilst all this was going on the buildings on the site were starting to go up. The well-known building firm Miller Bros and Buckley Ltd of Rugby had been appointed the main contractors and it had been decided that the new College would open at the commencement of the autumn term, 1972. This was a short building period and there were difficulties over site conditions and over the wintry weather in 1971–72. Although in the end the target date was achieved, as the Duke of Wellington said of the Battle of Waterloo 'it was a close-run thing'.

The difficulties over the nature of the ground were captured in a photograph taken by the *Chronicle & Echo* on the occasion of a site visit by the Committee. The photograph showed members of the Committee having to put their shoulders behind their bus and the caption over the photograph was 'The-Stick-in-the-Muds'. There were further difficulties created when one of the sub-contractors went bankrupt and at a vital moment the flow of certain essential custom-made components ceased.

The first students were received at the College before the buildings were ready and emergency arrangements to start courses had to be made. Some students begun their courses with unexpected 'teaching practice' in Northampton schools but morale was high and for the authority, the Governors, the staff and the students it was all a great adventure.

The opening had been arranged for the 10 November 1972 and the opener was to be the Secretary of State for Education and Science the Rt Hon. Mrs Margaret Thatcher, MP, who had links with the East Midlands and (through her family) distant connections with Northampton. The Northampton College of Education was in fact the only teacher-training college which Mrs Thatcher opened whilst holding office at the Department of Education and Science.

Two days before the opening there was a small fire at the College and it is alleged that the painters – putting right the damage to the decorations – walked out of the hall used for the opening as the guests walked in at the other end. One of the Governors also declared that as she drove into the car park to leave her car to attend the opening ceremony a representative of the firm responsible for tarmacing the car park held up his hand to stop her whilst the tarmacing machine laid the final cold surface on the place where she was directed to park. The College lawns for the day were provided by a firm nick-named by Alwyn Lodwick 'Rent-a-Sod' (who also provided lawns for the various schools and other openings in connection with the new town developments current at that time). The turves were laid, watered and rolled for the occasion and then taken up and moved to the next location at which a lawn was 'required'. They finally finished up as part of the lawn on the approach to the Principal's house at Nene!

In any event the great day came and the official opening took place. In welcoming the Minister of Education, David Walmsley coined the phrase with which he had to live thereafter: 'M'am, in welcoming you here today it will not surprise you to know that some people believe that Northampton is the hub of the universe'. Mrs Thatcher expressed her great pleasure at being invited and at all she saw. Sir James Miller (on behalf of his firm as builders) announced his intention to provide a sum of money which was used to start the 'Miller-Buckley Lectures' in commemoration of his firm's involvement in this project. Sir James Miller personally had had the distinction of serving both as Lord Provost of Edinburgh and Lord Mayor of London. The lectures he announced have been continued since their founding but are now known as the Buckley Lectures after Mr A. H. Buckley. The have attracted some of the most prominent figures in our national life as lecturers (see Appendix 9). As for Mrs Thatcher she accepted an engraving of the College drawn by Dennis Parrott, a staff member, as a memento of the occasion and went on to become the country's longest-serving prime minister of the twentieth century.

Four residential blocks having been built on the Moulton Park site, the issue of naming them was considered by the Governors. Various suggestions were made but in the end a consensus was reached in naming the halls after Kirkby Fields (Kirkby Hall), the John Clare Annexe, Northampton (Clare Hall), and two of the personalities associated with the development of education locally, Doddridge Hall and Dryden Hall.

Dr Philip Doddridge (1702 to 1751) was the son of a merchant, his grandfather (John Doddridge) had been one of the ejected clergy in 1662. He was educated at a School in St Alban's, and then at the Kibworth Academy later moving with that Academy to Hinckley in 1722. He became a Nonconformist Minister in 1723 and served in Leicestershire before becoming the Minister of the Congregational Meeting at Castle Hill, Northampton (1729). In 1730 he set up his Academy in the town to provide higher education tuition for the sons of Nonconformists who were denied such opportunities by the Universities of Cambridge and Oxford. He was active in other ventures, in 1738 he founded a charity school; in 1743 he was prominent in promoting the Northampton Infirmary (the original building is now the George Row Club and the successor building is that part of the Northampton General Hospital which fronts to Billing Road); and, in 1745 he assisted the Earl of Halifax to raise a regiment against any possible attack on the town by the Scottish Jacobite Army under Prince Charles Edward Stuart (the young 'Pretender'). Three hundred and seventy of Doddridge's hymns were published in 1755. These had been written in the first instance to illustrate his Sunday sermons and as *aides memoires* for his congregation. Many of these hymns are still in use today, such as: 'Hark the glad sound! The Saviour comes', Jesus, my Lord, how rich thy grace', 'O God of Bethel by whose hands', 'O happy day, that fixed my choice', 'See Israel's gentle Shepherd stand', and 'Ye servants of the Lord'.

Dryden Hall is not named after the Restoration poet John Dryden (1631 to 1700) but his descendant Sir Henry Dryden, Bart, of Canons Ashby, who was born in 1818. Sir Henry was educated at Shrewsbury and Trinity College, Cambridge. From his early years he showed great aptitude for drawing and an interest in archaeology. He developed a wide range of interests and skills coupled with a passion for things beautiful. He was one of the five non-Councillors elected to the Museums Committee. It was through this position he pressed for local science and art classes. An authority on ecclesiastical architecture and honorary curator of antiquities, costume and leatherwork to the Northampton Museum, he was in great demand as a lecturer. Sir Henry died in 1899 and his collection of books, notes and drawings was bequeathed to the Northampton Public Library.

The College of Education was launched as a teacher-training establishment in this way and promptly had to fight for its life and existence in an unfriendly world. The building of the College came at a time when a limited amount of financial resources were available to LEAs and almost immediately after the opening a period of contraction followed. The competition to survive was keen and indeed in some areas, deemed to be over-provided, college closures and college amalgamations began. Colleges at Liverpool, at Rugby and at Milton Keynes disappeared and Scraptoft became part of Leicester Polytechnic. Those who had transferred from Liverpool to Northampton had chosen better than they realised at the time. In the East Midlands (Derbyshire, Leicestershire, Lincolnshire and Nottinghamshire with Northamptonshire) there were those who regarded the Northampton College as the 'cuckoo in the nest'. Recognition of courses had to be fought for and sometimes was delayed to the frustration of the staff at Moulton Park. However, the steady support of Leicester University (and particularly Professor Jack Kerr, Professor L. C. Sykes and Professor G. H. Bantock), constant encouragement from the Governors and the help offered by the local HMIs meant that gradually Northampton won through and established itself. If in that period Northampton won a reputation for being somewhat aggressive and ambitious, it was in fact circumstances which dictated these matters rather than choice.

At their last meeting prior to Local Authority control of the College passing from the County Borough to the County Council the Governors each planted a tree on the campus as a farewell gesture and as a token of their belief in the future of Nene as a centre of Higher Education in the town and county.

*   *   *

On a personal note it is not often given to an individual as Chairman of an Education Committee and as Chairman of Governors to see a scheme of the size of the Northampton College of Education through from planning to completion, but this was my good fortune and both my son and daughter received their professional training at Moulton Park.

MEMORIES OF KIRKBY FIELDS COLLEGE OF EDUCATION, LIVERPOOL

Ron Smith

This is not a history of Kirkby Fields' College of Education. It is an account of my personal memories and impressions of life in the College where I taught from 1962 to 1972. As such, it is highly selective and partial. I consider myself extremely fortunate to have spent the last twenty years of my working life at Kirkby Fields and Nene College; both, I believe, true 'centres of excellence', both directed by a person of great ability and personality, both imbued with enterprise and friendliness and each with its own character and purpose. They say that distance makes the eye grow fonder. That may be so. But if my memories seem too good to be true at least they are honest.

Stalag 17

This was what a BBC Education Officer called the site of Kirkby Fields. He was addressing the assembled students and graphically described his first impressions – a formidable locked gate, fences all round, a collection of low wooden huts linked by great black overhead pipes, ten foot high, dominating the skyline. The students loved it!

At first sight the campus *did* resemble a prisoner-of-war camp. It had been built during the Second World War to house munitions workers and the original lay-out and many buildings remained. But after the war it became, in succession, an Emergency Teacher Training College, a college for training Malayan teachers and finally, in 1962, the Kirkby Fields' Training College. (The addition of 'Fields' in the title was a masterstroke and not unjustified.)

With these changes came a whole range of improvements and new buildings with the emphasis on light and space as well as ease of construction – a splendid library, new lecture rooms, a gymnasium and art room, a large glass-walled staff room, popularly known as the Fish Bowl. Perhaps, above all, new furniture and fittings transformed living conditions. The credit largely goes to Miss Danielli and Miss Lloyd-Williams, the Principal and her great friend and Deputy, with the generous support of Liverpool LEA. They fitted out all areas – students rooms, administrative block, staff and teaching accommodation with furniture, curtains, carpets and bedding that were cheerful, tasteful, comfortable and durable – the armchairs from the staff room are still in use in Nene College. Even the dreaded overhead pipes served their purpose well; they kept the rooms warm and dry although there was one occasion when a furniture van knocked down part of the structure, even that earned the students an extra week's holiday. With extensive well-kept grounds and playing fields the real picture emerged of a closely-knit community in an environment which, despite its obvious drawbacks, offered comfort and stimulation. And all this in Kirkby! Kirkby was a New Town built by Liverpool, with high-rise flats already showing signs of dilapidation and a bad reputation – the 'Z Cars' town, so it was said. There were obviously many people in Kirkby with social problems and the town was slow to develop amenities for sport, entertainment and relaxation. A large group of attractive young women living on the town's doorstep could have created problems but amazingly did not. The students found the schools and the children in Kirkby lively and exciting and they liked being close to and even a part of Liverpool in the heyday of the Beatles. Many stayed in the area after they had qualified – as indeed many do in Northampton. So there was much to be said for Stalag 17!

The Community

Perhaps the most striking feature of Kirkby Fields was its active community life. Numbers were relatively small. The students were all young women though the staff was roughly half male. Most of the time was spent on the campus; exit passes, particularly for weekends, were limited and it was costly in time and money to get into Liverpool. The result was that the students had very close friendly relationships among themselves – especially within their separate 'blocks' – and with the staff. The personal tutor system was extremely effective; we met our students regularly both in College and, for those of us who lived outside, at our own homes. Yet we were still addressed formally as 'Mrs', 'Miss' or 'Mr'. It took a little time to adjust to being called 'Ron' when we moved to Northampton and the 'Seventies'!

There were rules. We were in a transitional period between the times when women's training colleges were very strict and convent-like and the present more libertarian regimes. In general, the men staff were more easy-going than the women. We were sure that Miss Danielli had at times to adopt a formidable attitude to compensate for the men's complaisance and the students held her in considerable awe. Yet when she wished she could charm and enthuse them; her speeches at the formal College dinners were a delight to everybody. There was one public crisis; after a minor 'incident' one of the tabloids appeared with the headline 'Where it costs a pound to spend a penny'! It caused some excitement but blew over, though it possibly led the DES to subject us to a full-blown General Inspection – but more of that anon.

The shared social life was rich. Perhaps the outstanding thing was a stream of drama and music productions. The old drama programmes make impressive reading, ranging from *The Trojan Women* to the home-made *It's the Human Rights Show, Folk!*. Everbody attended. Two particularly stick in the mind; one was a Christmas play in the magnificent setting of St Chad's Church in Kirkby and the other a performance of *Noye's Fludde* with its superb singing and the local children, as animals, processing down the main hall over a spectacular waving sea. We had staff/student cricket matches (good for my batting average!) and athletics competitions. There were departmental trips and parties followed by coffee in the student blocks with staff wives and husbands joining in. And we seemed to be singing all the time, or at least on the buses coming back from trips and at parties, departmental, staff/student or staff! The favourites were Liverpool ('The Leaving of Liverpool') or social protests ('We shall overcome') songs. Richard (Fox) even persuaded me to join him in a couple of duets ('The Soldier and the Sailor' and 'The Chastity Belt') while Norman (Lake) gave his lecture on the Battle of Waterloo – 'Sam, Sam, pick up thi' musket'.

The highlight of these joint activities, combining close community living with serious study was Colomendy. This was an environmental studies centre run by Liverpool near Mold in North Wales. Every year we took the whole of the second year for a week's stay. During the day we worked hard in small groups covering a wide range of investigations in this rich area; then in the evenings, we enjoyed ourselves. We had good walks, swimming and the occasional game of darts in the local pub. The students mercilessly played tricks on the staff, locking them out of the shared sleeping area (huts again), placing odd pieces of underwear on flagpoles, raising false (usually) alarms about intruders. I was in charge one night and they all refused to go to bed until I had told them a bed-time story. But the most enterprising thing they did was an impromptu concert full of 'in-house' jokes and songs: the miming of the walk and mannerisms of a colleague of ours was brilliant, at once cruel and affectionate. It showed what a wealth of talent, imagination and sheer energy there was among them and how the appropriate atmosphere could bring it out. We were better people and better teachers for it.

Convivial times were not limited to staff/student ventures. As staff we came from widely varying backgrounds but we mixed extremely well. Staff parties were memorable. Everybody came, including wives and husbands; dress was formal; the food was magnificent and the 'entertainment' spontaneous and lively. Miss Lloyd-Williams, who at first sight seemed so efficient and serious, was particularly good at 'letting her hair down'. The first Christmas in 1962 was unforgettable. We were a small group then so the party was held in the library; in candelight with a resplendent Christmas tree it looked magnificent. There were presents from Miss Danielli for everyone. It was an evening of elegance, companionship and goodwill which typified all that was best in the College.

'Opening Windows'

The purpose of the College was to educate young women to become good teachers. I have spent so long trying to describe the social life because I am convinced that the sense of partnership between staff and students enormously enhanced the quality of the work done.

There seems to be widespread tendency nowadays to denigrate the teaching profession and the training of teachers in particular. My experience was that the good overwhelmingly outweighed the not so good. I was fortunate in that I joined the history department under Richard Fox and from that came the most enjoyable and rewarding teaching experience of my career. But we were not alone. A great deal of the teaching was imaginative and lively and it is my belief that we helped to mould a large number of superb teachers.

The formal qualifications of our students were not high. The early 1960s was a time when the demand for teachers was at its height (that was why the College was established) so that young people, and an increasingly large number of mature (officially over 25 years of age), were being pressed to come to training colleges, as they were then called. It was rare to have anyone with 'A' levels and special courses had to be set up for those who had difficulty with English and mathematics. Yet the quality of work produced was often outstanding and the development of virtually all students was remarkable.

Apart from a small number of BEd students in the latter years, everyone took a three-year course for the Certificate of Education. This had considerable advantages. The University of Liverpool (as the Leicester University later) allowed us a great deal of freedom in planning the Certificate courses so we were able to experiment and do imaginative things. As a result I think it is true to say that the majority of our students received a whole new perspective on learning. To take history, as I must, the Middle Ages came alive for them; they met an immense range of contemporary material – richly coloured manuscript pictures, troubadour songs, miracle plays at Chester and York, deserted villages, even the letters of St Bernard and the abortive love story of Abélard and Héloïse – pageantry not politics, diversity not dates! Their response was a delight and they learned a great deal.

And they worked hard. They all took two 'main' subjects, and wide-ranging programme of curriculum studies and three blocks of teaching practice in local schools. It was a heavy load culminating in rigorous examinations. Inevitably there were moments of stress but on the whole they responded extremely well. It was particularly pleasing to see how well the mature students did; lacking in confidence at first, over-anxious and over-conscientious, most of them came to find a new dimension and satisfaction in their lives and many became first-class scholars. The responses made by lowly-qualified young students and by mature women who had 'missed out' altogether in their younger days showed clearly what a wealth of talent there was – and probably still is – waiting to be tapped; and gave special pleasure to the work of teaching at Kirkby Fields.

It is easy, looking back, to exaggerate our success. But there is some objective contemporary evidence – our inspection. Since the days of payment-by-results a General Inspection has been a source of apprehension to most teachers and ours was not so different. For a week a horde (or so it seemed) of HMIs swarmed all over the College, not by any means with evil intent, in some cases with great charm and affability, but certainly with rigour and thoroughness. They were, I believe, most impressed. Perhaps they particularly liked to see teaching in small groups with plenty of discussion rather than lecturing to large passive assemblies.

One of the Inspectors said how nice it was to see students actually doing things! Most of all, I believe that Miss Danielli emerged with flying colours. Because of this inspection, I suspect, the DES was led to look to Kirkby Fields as a suitable body to join the last College of Education to be built in this country.

Town B

By the late 1960s the demand for new teachers was being met. The Liverpool area was very well provided with Colleges of Education and it was becoming increasingly difficult to find teaching practice places for our students – we had to go as far afield as Burnley to fit them in. So it became clear that changes had to be made. Rumours began to circulate and gradually it emerged that we were to be moved to this mysterious Town 'B'. The precise location was kept secret for months and there were all kinds of wild guesses before we finally knew – Northampton!

The process of change went on for two years. We had many visitors. I remember the visit of the top DES civil servant, an imposing, not to say formidable figure: A small but persistent student asked him to let her take him on a tour of the lavatories; he declined, she insisted and in the end he had to allow himself to be taken away to this inspection. Our 'girls' were made of stern stuff! But above all, visitors from Northampton, David Walmsley and Michael Henley, were prominent, with fellow councillors and fellow administrators; they were extremely friendly and clearly determined to make a success of the new College. Then, later there was Mr Skelton with his boundless energy and enthusiasm.

Dr Ogilvie was appointed as Principal and started in post a year before the College officially opened. So we came to know him and Wyn well from seeing them at Kirkby and at Lanercost, their temporary home in Northampton where we were often made welcome. I well remember my two first impressions of the new Principal; first, his amazing ability to remember names even of people he had barely met and, second, his tendency to pick up casual and often unthinking remarks and to ferret out what they really meant and what they implied. We soon learned that we should have to be on our toes!

Miss Danielli was appointed Deputy Principal but before the College opened she decided to retire. We were sorry about this because our relationship had been close and our regard for her great, as it still is. But I felt that she took the right decision.

Meanwhile Kirkby Fields was winding down. No new students were taken in after the decision to move was made so that only one group of students had to make the move. Feelings among the staff were mixed. We were all attached to Liverpool and some of us had wives or husbands happily employed there. It was the time of the first runaway inflation of house prices with Northampton well ahead of Liverpool. Some colleagues were quite unable to make the move. So it was a time of considerable uncertainty and anxiety; while we were keenly aware of the opportunity offered to us with a new College and all to look forward to, the difficulties loomed large in our minds.

But it all worked out remarkably well. It is right and fitting at this point to pay tribute to the Education Authorities of Liverpool and Northampton. Those colleagues who could not move were found suitable new posts in Liverpool. All those who came to Northampton were given appropriate appointments. The Northampton Development Corporation helped with student accommodation and with those of us who could not immediately move into the house of our choice. We were given generous help with removal expenses – certainly the first time most of us had experienced this. Even the massive task of organising the removal of virtually all our equipment was largely handled by Mr Skelton and his men. In every way it was a massive operation which was highly successful. So, in September 1972, we began a new demanding and exciting phase in our lives.

KIRKBY FIELDS COLLEGE OF EDUCATION PROSPECTUS

The College was established by the Liverpool Corporation in 1963 as a college for women. Students may choose whether they wish to be resident or non-resident for each year of their Course.

The College is situated eight miles North of the City of Liverpool on the outskirts of the new town of Kirkby, eight miles from the market town of Ormskirk, and fourteen miles from the popular seaside resort of Southport.

Most of the College buildings are wooden and within they are warm and attractive. Each student has a study-bedroom furnished in modern style. There are eight residential blocks each accommodating from 20 to 47 students. Each block has its own common-room, kitchen, drying-room, ironing-room and music-practice room In addition, there is a large Junior Common Room adjoining the Dining-Room. The Hall has a well-equipped stage, new Geography, History and Music Blocks were added in 1964; a Gymnasium/Sports Hall, a Sociology Block, an Art Block, a Mathematics Laboratory and additional hard-court surfaces in 1968.

Two full-time Tutor-Librarians are in charge of the Library which houses 45,000 books and offers attractive conditions for study. Considerable extensions to the Library were carried out in 1968.

Members of the College are able to enjoy the privileges of a University City with its cultural and social assets, and, in the case of Liverpool, all that a thriving industrial city with its attractive waterfront and extensive port and dock areas can offer. Library and museum facilities are excellent, as also are opportunities for lovers of music, art and the theatre. Kirkby itself offers a sports stadium second to none in the country. The area is rich in historical and geographical interests and the stretch of coastline from the mouth of the River Mersey to Southport offers untold opportunities to the naturalist. the Nature Reserve at Freshfield is used extensively by the College. Kirkby and the City offer particular scope for the comparative study of social conditions.

It is expected that the College will transfer to new purpose-built premises at Northampton in the Autumn of 1972. Students who are enrolled at Kirkby Fields College in 1971 will, therefore, complete their first year at Kirkby and their second and third years at Northampton.

The Northampton College will be a mixed community, and in the first stages of its development it is envisaged that the total enrolment will be 800. As the most recent college of education to be built in the country, the Northampton College will offer exceptionally good facilities to students in all areas of their training and in their cultural and social life.

The Northampton College will be a constituent college of the University of Leicester School of Education. Students enrolled in 1971, on the successful completion of their Course, will be awarded the Teacher's Certificate of that School.

List of Staff

Principal Miss B.Danielli
Vice-Principal Miss E.Lloyd Williams

The Rev E.Ackroyd	BA	Mr G.C.Lewis	MMus
Mrs A.F.Barlow		Mr A.R.Lodwick	
Mrs F.Binney	BSc	Mr R.J.Longhurst	BSc
Miss J.E.Blows	BA	Mrs M.S.Martin	MA
Mr S.Bowden	BA	Miss J.Moore	ALM,LGSM
Mr R.G.Burge		Mr S.R.Moss	MA
Mr B.J.Carter	MA	Mr W.S.Murray	Dip RADA
Mrs C.A.Challis		The Rev A.F.Osborne	BD,AKC
Mr P.S.Daniel	BA	Mr D.W.Parrot	ATD,NDD
Mr R.C.Davies	BMus, FRCO	Mr J.Reed	BSc
	LRAM,LTCL	Mrs M.C.Ridout	
	(CMT)	Miss D.L.Roberts	BA
Mr N.R.Dewhurst	BSc	Mr J.D.Roberts	MEd
Mr B.J.Dunnery	BA	Miss J.K.Roberts	BA
Mrs S.Evans	BSc	Miss M.A.Roberts	
Miss O.Eyton-Jones	BA	Mr G.E.Savona	BA
Mr A.W.R.Fox	MA	Mr C.T.Sherwen	ATD,NDD
Mr D.R.George	MSc	Mr R.Smith	BA
Mr D.G.Groover	MA,MFA	Mr K.Sutch	BSc
	Visiting Lecturer	Mr P.W.Sutcliffe	
	from San Siego	The Rev E.J.Turner	MA
	State College,	Mr J.S.Vale	BA
	California	Mr A.G.Williams	BA
Miss D.M.Hale		Mr T.Williams	BA
Miss A.W.Hall	BA,ALA	Mr C.H.Wild	MSc
Mr B.K.Hill	NDD	Mr F.A.Wragg	

Miss S.S.Hodgson	MA
Mr R.K.Jones	BA
Mr A.C.G.King	
Mr F.Kitson	BA
Mr N.B.Lake	MA

Senior Administrative Officer and Clerk of the Governors
Mr W.Segrave

Administrative Officer
Miss L.Williams

Principal's Secretary
Miss L.Jones

Senior Domsetic Supervisor
Mrs R.M.Smith

Domestic Supervisors
Miss M.C.Butterwood
(Domestic)
Miss R.A.Williams
(Catering)
Miss S.M.K.Williams
(Catering)

Extracts from the last prospectus issued by The Kirkby Fields College of Education, Liverpool, 1970–1.

HOW TO MOVE A COLLEGE OF EDUCATION FROM CITY 'A' TO TOWN 'B' IN ONE EASY LESSON

Leslie Skelton

When I left the police service in October 1971 and took up my duties as the Senior Administrative Officer of the Northampton College of Education, I was lodged in a tiny office in the former Annexe of the Leicester College of Education which was situated at the corner of Clare Street, Northampton. The Annexe was *not* part of the new College and along with Mrs Jean Hall (Residential Registrar) I was one of two persons employed as 'non teachers' by the new College. Dr Ogilvie was situated in a house called Lanercost in Cliftonville (about two miles away). I had a job, I had a desk, but I had no College as yet and nothing to put into it.

I attended a very early Governors' meeting and met the Principal of the Kirkby Fields' College of Education who was due to come to Northampton as the Deputy Principal. She was requested to liaise with me regarding the removal of the equipment, etc., from Liverpool. I was given a simple instruction by Mr Walmsley; 'Remove the College from Kirkby to Northampton'. I had left a Service where one is expected to stand on one's own feet and therefore this instruction was much to my liking. It is to the credit of the Chairman of Governors and the Chief Education Officer that they never once 'interfered' but constantly offered help if I needed it.

When I visited Liverpool I found myself in an area well-known to me from my early policing days. Kirkby was a deprived part of the City and it was much to my surprise that I found a very clean, extremely well-equipped small College. The standard of much of the furniture was exceptionally high; for example the furniture in the Senior Common Room was superb, and I moved it to Northampton in 1971–72, where it is still in use although I am led to believe there are now signs of the need to replace.

I made many visits to Kirkby Fields College and found that a removal plan was in the early stage under the control of the Deputy Principal, Miss Lloyd-Williams. She and I liaised and we had 'colour-coded' the plans, and the furniture to be removed from one College to another was suitably labelled.

The Library was small but still something of a major task. Unfortunately, the Librarian was not coming to Northampton and had left for another job so it was left to me to complete this move. I was able to call upon the services of Mr Victor Hatley, the Librarian at the College of Technology and Mrs Janet Wright, the Library Assistant at the Northampton Annexe, who visited Liverpool and arranged the move. We hired specialist library removal contractors who provided special containers, vehicles, etc.

In Northampton I was also making regular visits to the new College which was under construction and I had to set about planning and purchasing new furniture, fittings, bedding, curtains, carpets, etc., and was given a satisfactory budget to undertake this task. There were, of course, many snags with the building programme and the major delays were to the students' Halls of Residence and the staff residences. Eventually, however, we managed to get two of the four Halls of Residence fit for students but after I had drawn up an Operational Order for the Removal I was suddenly informed (on the Friday before the move on the Monday) that the buildings were not ready. Almost immediately I was told that the Government, hearing that Kirkby Fields' College was to be vacated, had commandeered the premises to accommodate the Ugandian Asians being evicted at that time from Uganda by President Amin. This meant yet another hurried visit to Liverpool. A fleet of vehicles was leaving Liverpool with nowhere to lodge at 'this end'. Walkers of Roade had been given the contract to remove everything from Liverpool and one can only state that they were excellent in every respect and most co-operative.

Upon arrival at Liverpool, I was informed by the Deputy Chief Education Officer for Liverpool that the Library had to be cleared immediately as this was to be used as the Reception Centre. I had no labour (most of the staff had been dispensed with at Liverpool) and the Education Department gave me a group of unemployed men to do the job. One wonders whether this was a good move; it certainly gave me problems. All the books from the Library and all the linen from the

Linen Store had to be lodged on the floor of the gymnasium (much to the dissatisfaction of the Physical Education Lecturer, Mr. Wragg). It was difficult to keep one's eye on what was happening and I am led to believe that more blankets went 'over the wall' than to the gymnasium. Eventually the 'Foreman' came to see me and asked if it was true that I was an ex-Chief Superintendent of Police. When he was given the affirmative answer he said, 'God, don't they trust anybody?' Things seemed to settle down after that.

The move started shortly afterwards and the College at Kirkby eventually was cleared but there were no facilities at Moulton Park and I lodged equipment of all types in the John Clare School, the Drill Hall, the Grammar School (Girls), Walkers' Garage at Duston and then Walkers placed the rest in a large hangar at Nether Heyford. It was stacked to the roof over a large area and the Superintendent Caretaker (Mr Tebbutt) and I used to visit it regularly to identify what was to go where. I repeat my compliments to Walkers, and particularly to Mr Dominick Browne, who placed the furniture, etc., where it was wanted. In all it is roughly assessed that 150 vans of furniture came from Liverpool to Northampton and over the next seven or eight months were removed to College. The contract was extended of course, but at today's prices it was done at a 'peppercorn rate'. One of the last loads to leave Kirkby was a van full of cleaning materials of every conceivable kind. These were still being used up to a short time before my retirement.

The opening day itself was something of an experience. I repeat that only two halls were ready for occupation and the students had to sleep two to a room. When Mrs Thatcher opened the College there were many false walls and curtains and banks of flowers hiding gaping holes. The car park was being laid as guests' cars were parked – but the most astonishing event of all was the 'garden' at the front. The Parks Department laid grass to a width of about 2 metres on either side of the entrance path and put shrubs on the outside of that and in the flower beds. They looked quite decent; particularly when one realises that the rest of the College was mud. One of the shocks one had the following day when attending College was to find that the 'garden' had gone.

This is a brief resumé of the exciting and demanding times. One would not have missed it for the world; the spirit of my staff was outstanding; they carried furniture, made beds, scrubbed floors, etc., – most of which was not their prescribed duty. Appointing cleaning staff was not easy in 1971–2 and one should not forget that we had also taken possession of eight houses on the Development Corporation Estate which, in itself, proved to be something of a nightmare to plan. It was a wonderful experience and I thank all my staff at that time for their efforts on behalf of the college in providing the Principal, the academic staff and the students with the best possible surroundings for study.

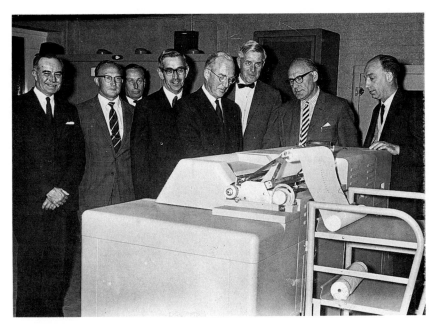

22 The presentation of the first computer to the College by British Timken. *Left to right*: E. R. Knapp, Hugh Marrack, Eric Jewitt, Stephen Bennett, Councillor T. Hayes Dockrell, H. A. Skerrett and Colin Paver

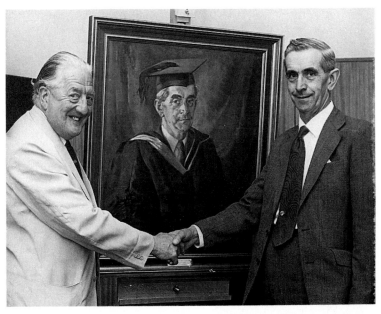

23 The retirement of Eric Jewitt in 1973: Alderman Harold Cockerill with Mr Jewitt and the portrait painted by G. B. H. Holland

24 Alex Parthenis with one of the Ward Models

25 Alderman Miss Carol Trusler

26 Gerald Fowler, MP, Joint Minister of State for Education and Science (who opened the extension to the College of Technology on 24 March 1970)

Errata

Photograph 27 shows Mrs. Ethel Skerrett.
It should show Mr. Harold Skerrett who
is pictured opposite.

27 H. A. Skerrett, OBE, BA, FHistS, Chief Education Officer for Northampton County Borough, 1950–68

Four Education Officers

28 George Edward Churchill, MA, Education Officer for Northamptonshire, 1950–74

29 Michael Henley, MA, Chief Education Officer for Northampton, 1968–74; and County Education Officer for Northamptonshire from 1974 to 1986

30 James Roy Atkinson, MA, County Education Officer for Northamptonshire from 1986 to date

Four Chairmen of Governors

31 David Walmsley, LLB, Chairman of the Governors of the College of Technology from 1969 to 1971; of the Governors of the College of Education from 1971 to 1974; and of Nene College from 1977 to 1981. The first Chairman of the College of Education and the second Chairman of Nene.

32 Dora Oxenham, CBE, MA, Chairman of the Governors of the College of Education from 1974 to 1976; and of Nene College from 1976 to 1977. The first Chairman of Nene.

33 Jack Morrish, Chairman of the Governors of Nene College from 1981 to 1985. The third Chairman of Nene

34 Gina Ogden, Chairman of the Governors of Nene College from 1985. The fourth Chairman of Nene.

35 Home Farm, Moulton Park, in the days that this was owned by the governing body of St Andrew's Hospital, Northampton

36 Tony Stimpson, ARIBA (Architect of the original buildings at Park Campus)

37 Leslie Skelton, MA, Clerk to the Governors of the College of Education and subsequently of Nene College, Chief Administrative Officer, 1971–86

38 Kirkby Fields College of Education, Liverpool

39 Miss Bridget Danielli, Principal
of Kirkby Fields College of
Education, Liverpool

40 Dr Kenneth Horne, DLitt

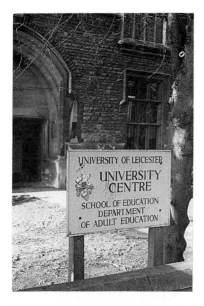

42 The Northampton Annexe

41 The University Centre, Barrack
Road, Northampton

43 The Corby Annexe

44 Sir Fraser Noble, MBE, MA, LLD (Vice-Chancellor of the University of Leicester) addressing those present on the occasion of the Official Opening of the Northampton College of Education on 10 November 1972. *Left to right:* Alderman Miss Carol Trusler, Sir Fraser Noble, Alderman K. R. Pearson (Mayor), David Walmsley (Chairman), Mrs Thatcher, Sir Hereward Wake, Bt, Mrs K. Pearson (Mayoress)

THE CONSORTIUM OF PRIVATE ARCHITECTS (COPA)

COPA is celebrating its fifth birthday in style. Give or take a week it coincides with the opening of Northampton's College of Education.

The Consortium of Private Architects was set up in the autumn of 1967 to handle projects that might be too big for a single small firm to deal with. The College of Education off Boughton Green Road is its latest and biggest offering and at over £882,000, it is also the largest project the Borough Education Authority has ever undertaken.

The first phase provides residential accommodation and facilities for 600 students These will come from the University of Leicester College of Education Annexe in Northampton and from Kirkby Fields College of Education Liverpool, which is closing down.

It is the type of establishment that used to be known as a Teachers' Training College (that term went out some years ago) and is one of the last of its kind to be built.

It was originally proposed four years ago and in the first phase accommodates 600 students. A start on the second phase to bring the total up to 800 students will be made next year.

Quadrangle

The main buildings are arranged round a large quadrangle and this fits in with the conception of a university-type situation based on the layout of some of the Oxford and Cambridge Colleges.

The focal point is the main entrance which can be seen from down the long drive.

A large slab of concrete, bearing the Northampton coat of arms overhangs the doors. In the same block are the library, main hall, lecture theatre, dining hall, common rooms and administrative offices.

What serves as the main hall is known as the Drama Studio – a large room with tiered seating for 330 (one year's full intake) with a large unraised stage area.

Air conditioning has been fitted, and sound has been taken care of by careful design and the fitting of acoustic panels and tiles on the ceiling.

Two sets of sliding doors are to be fitted so that when opened a large floor area, comprising the Drama Studio and the common room and bar, can be made available for social functions.

The buildings are grouped according to their distinct functions – teaching, residential, social. Either side of the entrance drive are the four three-storey student halls of residence. Students are provided with study bedrooms, and kitchen facilities are also located in the blocks.

Among the teaching buildings are a hexagonal Dance Movement Studio and an Arts and Craft block, which is built on factory lines, on an open plan basis using as few doors as possible. An area of 'un-scheduled space' which was not allowed for in the original estimates has been produced by economising on such things as corridors. The space that has been made available could be used as an extra teaching area or for exhibitions of students' work.

Mr Tony Stimpson was the COPA partner in charge of the design, working in association with Mr Leonard Howarth, the Borough Architect. The main contractors have been Miller Buckley Investments Ltd of Rugby.

Discussions

COPA is made up of Stimpson and Walton, Barker, Hammond and Cox, Rex Bryan and Pennock and Peter Haddon and Partners.

It is normal for one of the firms to take charge of a project but the resources of the other firms are available if necessary and regular discussions and exchanges of ideas take place between the different partners.

They are especially valuable. In this case the second phase of the college will be undertaken by Peter Haddon and Partners and it is important there should be continuity in the design.

COPA has already built two comprehensive schools for the County, a middle school for Northampton Borough as well as an old people's home at Daventry and a new block at St Crispin Hospital.

Extract from Trade Section of the
Chronicle & Echo, 11 November 1972

NORTHAMPTON COLLEGE OF EDUCATION

CASTELLO · FORTIOR · CONCORDIA

FRIDAY, 10th NOVEMBER, 1972

at 3-15 p.m.

NORTHAMPTON COUNTY BOROUGH EDUCATION COMMITTEE

OFFICIAL OPENING OF

NORTHAMPTON COLLEGE OF EDUCATION

The ceremony will be performed by

THE RT. HON. MRS. MARGARET THATCHER, M.P.

Secretary of State for Education and Science

FRIDAY, 10th NOVEMBER, 1972

NORTHAMPTON COLLEGE OF EDUCATION

History of Development

Approval in principle to a proposal to build a new College of Education in North-ampton was notified to the Education Committee by the Department of Education and Science in June, 1968. The proposal was seen as an important element in the programme for the expansion of the county borough, designation as a New Town and the establishment of a Development Corporation coming in the same year. Teacher training had, however, begun earlier. In 1966 the City of Leicester College of Education opened an Annexe; and in 1967 a University Centre, including a School of Education section, was established by the University of Leicester. Initially the new college was to be for 400 students, including Annexe students, but a prospect was indicated of later extension to accommodate 800 or possibly 1,200 students. A draft brief with detailed schedule of accommodation was submitted to the Department of Education and Science in November and agreed in December, 1968. The project was then formally included in the 1968-69 Preliminary List.

In November, 1968, the Education Committee authorised the appointment of the Consortium of Private Architects, Northampton, to undertake the main responsibility for the design of the new college. The Consortium has worked in association with the Borough Architect. Sketch plans received the Department's approval in January, 1970. Meanwhile, consideration had been given to a proposal arising from the projected closure of Kirkby Fields College of Education, Liverpool, for students and staff from this college to join the new Northampton college. When this proposal was adopted the plans for the first phase of the college had to be reviewed. Enlargement of the first phase to enable 600 students to be accommodated was agreed with the Department and revised sketch plans received approval in June, 1970. Work on site commenced in March, 1971, the main work of construction beginning in May of that year. Work is expected to commence next year on a second phase of the college to complete accommodation for 800 students.

Conception and Siting

The brief indicated that the college buildings should offer an environment providing maximum opportunity for self-education and self-discipline in a university-type situation. Accordingly in arriving at a solution to meet this requirement reference was made to the design and layout of certain Oxford and Cambridge colleges.

The buildings were to have unity that combined residential, teaching and social accom-modation. A focal point was called for close to the main entrance near to which should be situated the administration centre, dining and social areas and the library.

In locating individual buildings on the site of sixty acres, which includes wooded park-land, account had to be taken of fine well-established trees.

Building Layout

The brief suggested scope for the separation of buildings according to their distinct functions, namely teaching, communal use and student and staff residences. The requirement for a focal point has been met by emphasizing the entrance to the main building with a projecting lecture theatre facing the entrance drive. The library com-prises a first and second floor suite adjacent to this space and forms a dominant feature of the main quadrangle.

Four student halls of residence of three storeys each flank the entrance drive and form the west side of the main quadrangle. Single study-bedrooms are arranged in sets of forty-eight, sixteen on each floor. Fully-equipped amenity and utility areas on first and second floors are provided.

Apart from music and human movement suites which form the east wing of the main building, other major teaching facilities in the first phase are grouped into Education, Science, and Arts and Crafts Departments. The Department of Education closes the north side of the main quadrangle. The Department of Arts and Crafts which creates a more intimate space to the rear overlooking the music suite provides studio workshop facilities grouped around a central general activities area or inner court. The spaces that open from this area are for pottery and weaving with a studio for painting at first-floor level. The Department of Science and its ancillary greenhouses and dutch barn is placed on the periphery of the college complex.

The dining room is located overlooking the principal group of specimen trees across a terrace. The ground-floor junior common room also has this view, while the staff common room overlooks the main quadrangle.

Construction

The building is of traditional construction, the arts and crafts and main buildings including a reinforced concrete and steel frame. All buildings are faced in a metric, machine-made, chocolate-coloured brick, with features in precast exposed limestone aggregate slabs or grey slate hanging. Roofs are generally flat, apart from the human movement studio which has a hexagonal structural timber pyramid roof faced with slates.

Ceilings of teaching and public rooms are lined with acoustic tiles, except those of the main music room and dining room, which are of timber. Apart from some areas of fair-faced brick or blockwork, most walls are plastered and decorated to provide a foil for soft furnishings and later for college art work.

Statistics

Gross Contract Sum	£882,789.00
Total Floor Area	117,805 sq. ft.
	10,944 sq. m.
Teaching Floor Area	30,260 sq. ft.
	2,811 sq. m.
Net Cost	£6.24p per sq. ft.
	£67.17p per sq. m.

ORDER OF PROCEEDINGS

The Chairman of the Governing Body of the College
Councillor D. A. Walmsley, LL.B.
will open proceedings

———

The Principal of the College
Dr. Eric Ogilvie, B.SC., M.ED.
will introduce the College

———

The Chief Education Officer, County Borough of Northampton
M. J. Henley, M.A.
will ask the Secretary of State to declare the new College open

———

THE RT. HON. MRS. MARGARET THATCHER, M.P.
Secretary of State for Education and Science

———

The Deputy Chairman of the Governing Body
Sir Hereward Wake, Bart., M.C., D.L.
will thank the Secretary of State

———

The Deputy Chairman of the Northampton Education Committee
Alderman Miss C. M. Trusler
will ask the Vice-Chancellor to welcome the College
on behalf of the University of Leicester

SIR FRASER NOBLE, M.B.E., M.A., LL.D.
Vice-Chancellor of the University of Leicester

The Chairman of the Northamptonshire Education Committee
County Alderman A. L. Langham
will ask Bishop Graham-Campbell to dedicate the College

THE RIGHT REVEREND A. R. GRAHAM-CAMPBELL, C.B.E., M.A.

Sir James Miller, G.B.E., D.L., J.P.
will speak on behalf of the Building Contractors
Miller Brothers & Buckley Construction Limited

The Chairman will then conclude the proceedings in the Hall

GOD SAVE THE QUEEN

Following the conclusion of the proceedings in the Hall the platform party will go to the Main Entrance of the College where His Worship the Mayor of Northampton, Alderman K. R. Pearson, will invite the Secretary of State to unveil two plaques commemorating the Opening of the College.

Following the unveiling of the plaques, Alderman J. T. Lewis, T.D., D.L., a Governor of the College and Chairman of the Education Committee's Sites and Building Sub-Committee, will break the new College Standard.

Guests are requested to remain seated until the College Standard is broken which will be signified by a Fanfare.

GOVERNORS OF THE COLLEGE

Chairman
Councillor D. A. Walmsley, LL.B.

Deputy Chairman
Sir Hereward Wake, Bart., M.C., D.L.

His Worship the Mayor of Northampton
   Alderman K. R. Pearson
Alderman J. T. Lewis, T.D., D.L.
Councillor Miss M. Finch
County Alderman A. L. Langham
Professor L. C. Sykes, M.A., D.PHIL.
Professor J. F. Kerr, B.SC., PH.D.
Miss A. R. Lock, B.A., J.P.
T. Adams, M.ED., D.P.C.
J. L. Rawlings
Dr. E. Ogilvie, B.SC., M.ED.

Alderman T. H. Cockerill
Alderman R. P. Dilleigh
Alderman Miss C. M. Trusler
Councillor H. Fruish
County Alderman W. H. Hollowell
Professor G. H. Bantock, M.A.
Lady Hart
S. W. Hutchins
R. Smith, B.A.
Miss S. L. Smith
Miss E. M. Hitchfield, B.A.

Clerk to the Governors
M. J. Henley, M.A.

EDUCATION COMMITTEE 1972-73

Chairman
Councillor D. A. WALMSLEY, LL.B.

Deputy Chairman
Alderman Miss C. M. TRUSLER

Alderman T. H. COCKERILL,
Alderman J. T. LEWIS, T.D., D.L.
Alderman JOHN POOLE, O.B.E.
Councillor T. J. ANGIER
Councillor T. P. BAILEY
Councillor D. BAXTER
Councillor A. E. BILLSON, D.F.C.
Councillor E. COKER, J.P.
Councillor Mrs. J. DICKS
Councillor Miss M. FINCH
Councillor A. J. HARGRAVE
Councillor J. L. RAWLINGS
Councillor J. R. SEABROOK
Councillor Mrs. I. SHORT
Mrs. E. M. COLLIER
Mrs. J. M. A. CORRIN, J.P.
F. V. GROOME
Miss P. HENNINGS, M.B.E.
L. S. E. PIGGOTT
Mrs. E. H. WATSON

Town Clerk
A. C. PARKHOUSE, M.A.

Chief Education Officer
M. J. HENLEY, M.A.

Borough Architect
L. HOWARTH, A.R.I.B.A., M.R.T.P.I.

STAFF OF THE COLLEGE

Principal: Dr. Eric Ogilvie

Deputy Principal: Miss E. M. Hitchfield

Senior Tutor: P. W. T. George

Senior Woman Tutor: Miss E. Lloyd Williams

Teaching

E. Ackroyd
T. Adams
A. E. Axon
J. Bassett
Mrs. B. Bates
M. D. Bell
T. D. Bell
R. A. Billingsby
Mrs. F. Binney
D. J. Briggs
R. G. Burge
Miss J. A. Chapman
J. P. Davies
R. C. Davies
B. J. Dunnery
Miss B. J. East
R. P. Entwistle
A. W. R. Fox
D. R. George
Dr. Janet Harrison
B. K. Hill
G. V. Ilsley
A. C. King
F. Kitson
N. B. Lake
G. C. Lewis
A. R. Lodwick
G. C. Martin
J. S. Mason
J. S. MacDonald
Miss J. Moore
S. R. Moss
R. B. Munro
W. S. Murray
Miss J. Norman
Rev. A. F. Osborne
D. W. Parrott
M. V. J. Quigley
Mrs. M. C. Ridout
J. D. Roberts
G. E. R. Savona
W. G. Shaw
R. Smith
K. Sutch
Miss H. R. Tall
J. C. Vale

Miss J. K. Van Arsdel
M. R. Walley
A. G. Williams
F. A. Wragg

Administrative

P. Winterburn
Mrs. J. J. D. Hall
Mrs. M. P. Marriott
Miss W. Smith
Mrs. J. V. Wright

Secretarial

Miss A. Gilkes
Mrs. E. A. Mills
Mrs. M. G. Garrod
Mrs. A. Kent
Miss J. Messinger

Housekeeping and Catering

D. Barnes
Miss R. M. Hubball
Mrs. J. M. Newman
Miss D. Bilson
Miss P. Sawer

Medical

Dr. D. J. Campling
Mrs. E. A. Baird

Technical

R. Buckseall
R. J. Cook
B. M. Dun
Mrs. S. M. Perkins

Senior Caretaker

N. Tebbutt

Senior Administrative Officer: L. C. Skelton

'EXCITING VENTURE'—MRS THATCHER

Education Secretary Mrs Margaret Thatcher yesterday officially opened Northampton's teacher training college in Boughton Green Road.

She told the audience of more than 400 invited guests that she had very much enjoyed her visit to Northampton.

And she said that three things in particular interested her about the new college: that it would have advanced courses allowing some students to take B Ed. degrees; that it was concerned with the education of exceptional children, and could have courses for the education both of the gifted as well as for handicapped children; and that the college was co-operating fully to with local schools in working out its courses.

'I understand that local primary and secondary head teachers spent a full week in planning groups with the staff here before term commenced' she said.

'This is a very exciting venture, and this kind of co-operation can help colleges to find out what the professionals in the field really want and to train teachers to meet the real want, and to train teachers to meet the real and down-to-earth practical needs in the schools.'

Mrs Thatcher said that the Diploma in the education of exceptional children planned by the college was probably unique in that it was concerned with both the gifted and the physically and mentally handicapped child.

Turning from the courses at the new college to the buildings, Mrs Thatcher said: 'This college clearly owes a debt to the Chief Education Officer, Mr Henley, for the educational ideas he contributed to the design. The aim is to bring together residential, social and teaching accommodation to reflect the essential unity of college education.'

Good buildings were a great asset to education – but were not enough in themselves to guarantee good education. The teachers themselves had the greatest effect on the quality of education, she said.

And she concluded: 'Government decisions on the future of teacher training will be announced soon. I can not anticipate that announcement, but I can assure colleges that they will have new challenges to face.

'This college, with its particular blend of continuity and novelty and all the thought that has gone into it, should be well placed to meet these challenges.'

Mrs Thatcher unveiled a plaque to commemorate the opening of the college, and Alderman Jim Lewis, one of the college governors, broke the new college standard.

Extract from the
Chronicle & Echo,
11 November 1972

AN APPRECIATION OF DR ERIC OGILVIE

Richard Alcock

Eric Ogilvie was appointed to be Principal of Northampton College of

Education from September 1971. This was one year before the College
was due to open in entirely new buildings erected on 'sixty acres of partly
wooded parkland on the northern outskirts of Northampton'. The
College was planned for 600 students many of whom would come from
either Kirkby Fields College of Education, Liverpool or the Northampton
Annexe of the City of Leicester College of Education, both of which were
to close down.

In the light of subsequent developments it is interesting to discover
that one of the questions asked of him at interview was 'How would you
remove Colleges of Education from the monotechnic position?' He must
have answered it well! The interviewing committee were to look into
candidates for vision and they had the confidence and sense to choose Eric
Ogilvie.

Eric Ogilvie had already by that time had a distinguished and varied
career. Born in Yorkshire he was educated at Doncaster Grammar School
and served with the Fleet Air Arm during the war. He trained as a teacher
with distinction in Sheffield and rose to become Head teacher of a junior
school in Dewsbury in 1958. In 1962 he was appointed as Senior Lecturer
at Weymouth College of Education and four years later became Head of
the Education Department there. Having in 1970 secured his doctorate
from Southampton University with a thesis on 'Creativity Intelligence
and Concept Development' he was seconded in the academic year that
followed as Director of the Schools Council Project on Gifted Children.

There is no doubt that Eric Ogilvie was and remains deeply interested
in children's achievement, reflected very recently in the welcome he gave
to the Celebration of Primary Education, the exhibition for which was
mounted at Park Campus in the Summer of 1988. His publications
include *Gifted Children in Primary Schools, Problems of Gifted Children*
and *Individualisation and the Development of Talent.* He has continued
to lecture on the subject of gifted children and in October 1980 he was
honoured by an invitation as a Visiting Fellow of Mount Lawley College
of Advanced Education under the auspices of the Western Australian
Education Department. The College had established a centre for the
development of educational provision for Gifted Children and considered
that its work would be enhanced by the stimulus provided by our
Director. Since then the National Enrichment Research and Information
Centre has been established at Nene College.

In 1975 Dr Ogilvie was interviewed again and offered the appointment
as the Director of Nene College, to be formed out of the merger of the
College of Education and the Northampton College of Art and Technology.
The new college, no longer a monotechnic, was to embrace a wide range
of studies. Already the Director had widened his involvement on the
educational scene as a Member of the Board of Studies of the National
Association of Occupational Therapists and as an External Examiner to

the Royal College of Nursing. We can speculate that from this point at least the Director nurtured his belief that one day this College should be turned into a polytechnic by name as well as by nature.

One of Eric Ogilvie's particular strengths has been in public relations. Another has been that he has been able to seize opportunities and take initiatives at great speed. Bound up with this has been the success of the personal contacts he has developed. Not only have they been wide-ranging, bringing to bear the influence and benefaction of leaders of industry, trade unions, politics and the professions on the development of Nene College, Eric and Wyn his wife have always valued the strength and warmth of personal relationships and have been sociable and welcoming.

Their friendliness was evidenced from the very early days before the College of Education (and the Principal's House) were completed when they lived and worked from Lanercost in Cliftonville and established from that time a close working relationship with the Chief Education Officer and staff and with members of the Committee. There was then, and there remains, a strong belief on the part of Eric in the local and regional community and the sense that the College should be seen as a significant contributor and partner.

This has in no sense limited the wider vision and ambition for the College. The establishment of the Blackwood Hodge, now the Sunley Management Centre, the Leathersellers' Centre and the Timken Business and Innovation Centre together with the contact and exchange arrangements with France and Germany, owe a great deal to the qualities of Eric Ogilvie referred to above. The development of the three-year BA Combined Studies Degree in European Business which qualifies for direct admission to the final year of the Diploma Betriebswirt or European Diplome d'Etudes Supérieures Commerciales, Administratives et Financières may be an indication of the future direction to be taken by the College. Thus the College is set to go forward in strength and with confidence. Eric and Wyn will have much to contemplate from their home in Weymouth. They will leave behind many friends and admirers.

GLORIOUS AD-HOCERY

Dr Eric Ogilvie

It is undoubtedly appropriate that the title of this section be included somewhere in a book about the history of Nene College in Higher Education in Northamptonshire. An immediately obvious reason is that the very style of the book, bringing together as it does a number of different writers, all with their own uncoordinated and to some extent accidental viewpoints, is bound to lack the degree of coherence that might be expected from a more academic attempt at historical description and explanation. A second and much more vital reason is that there just is no other way to get a history written within the time and other constraints which we in Nene College have to live with. It is, I think, fair to say that if over the past sixteen or seventeen years every major decision that has been taken were to have been subjected to processes of co-ordination, rationalisation – aye – even criteria of efficiency, economy and effectiveness in relation to some clearly stated objectives, then there would probably have been only one single outcome. There would have been little to write a book about.

So runs the apologia for what follows. This account comprises a set of recollections which depends on nothing but an inadequate and highly selective memory. The incidents related are certainly not all the most important in the life of Nene College. For these the reader will need to look elsewhere in the book.

My personal involvement began of course with my appointment as Principal of Northampton College of Education in the spring of 1971. The post for which I applied described the College as a totally new venture. I would be able to appoint all my own staff, design my own management structure, determine the curriculum and, by and large, create a teacher training institution which would produce what I regarded as the ideal school teacher in the ideal teacher education environment. Terms like 'teacher training' as distinct from 'teacher education'; 'school practice' as distinct from 'teaching experience' would all be eschewed in a College which would see 'training' as a process applied to monkeys rather than men, and 'practice' as associated with simple mechanical conditioning-type activities requiring nothing but repetition. So much of teacher education had in my experience been teacher training that for me to be in a position to pursue a different approach, unshackled by the past, was to be seen as really the greatest opportunity and challenge that any professional teacher could wish for. Certainly I had never expected to find myself in such a fortunate circumstance, and for a week or two following my appointment I could hardly believe my good fortune.

The euphoria did not last long. It soon became abundantly clear that my job description had been written under one set of conditions, and that almost immediately afterwards, Government policy on teacher numbers had changed dramatically. In the space of a few weeks we moved from a situation wherein David Walmsley and Michael Henley had been urging colleagues to expand on and speed up plans for a new college, initially drawn on the back of an envelope; to a point where the opening of a new college for teachers was the last thing the Government wanted. Expansion had turned into contraction almost overnight, and I well remember Margaret Thatcher saying as much to me during her participation in the Opening Ceremony!

All that however was in the future. It ought not to have come as a shock since I had already discovered Michael Henley's great facility for ensuring that people would see the world if at all possible through rosy spectacles.

There are two main ways to get to Park Campus from the then somewhat seedy and, I assumed, temporary Education Office in Cliftonville Road. One led up through Kingsthorpe with its factories, shops and pre-war council estates; the other was the (then) new Ring Road which provided a very different image. Northampton appeared, not as an old-fashioned conservative market/shoe town, but as a modern, dynamic, growing, 'hi-tech' place looking to a future already sparkling bright. Amidst all this, the site of the new college seemed to rest in a countryside, a park-like environment quite outside the town itself. I was much amused to learn from Jack Coventon, the then Deputy County Borough Education Officer and later my good friend, that the longer more scenic route to Park Campus was deliberately chosen in order to impress candidates for the post of principal.

I cannot remember just how Michael Henley told me that my dreams of a *tabula rasa* start to the new college had vanished. I do remember how rapidly it became necessary to rethink the situation in the light of what amounted to a merger of three institutions. We had to accept students from Liverpool, from the Mature Student Annexe in Northampton and, of course, recruit a first-year group from a national catchment. A follow-on consequence was the merging of three groups of staff associated with the different students who were clearly coming together with very different ideas as to how the process of teacher (training) education should proceed. They had only a few months to reach some consensus of view about principles and construct an academic administration structure which would produce the goods on time.

Elsewhere in this volume, Richard Fox describes something of these hectic times from an academic point of view, as does Leslie Skelton from an administrative perspective. My part as Principal was merely to ensure that each separate party remained true to a very tight timescale and actually came up with the required results. There were no managerial rules that I or my colleagues could follow in any slavish way. Who my colleagues actually were became a constantly changing factor in that some who said they were coming from Liverpool Kirkby Fields' College did not, others in Northampton resigned, and so we were faced with a kaleidoscopic scene requiring some kind of control which had, on the one hand, to be rigid; and yet, on the other, be flexible enough to incorporate rapidly changing circumstances.

In the event, I issued a few general directives which amounted to little more than a simple statement of the task, and an agreement with individual senior colleagues that whatever action they thought to be necessary to accomplish their task should be taken without further consultation, and that regardless of outcome such action would have my personal support and be seen in fact as having been decided by me personally. I shall never forget one example of how this system worked. Leslie Skelton, my new Senior Administrative Officer had been asked to arrange for all the library books, equipment and so on, then in Kirkby Fields' College, to be transported into store in Northampton. Leslie had asked how he could identify what items should be brought and I told him to bring everything that was movable. It was not long before I received a telephone call from a near-speechless Principal of Kirkby Fields who, having extolled all the negative virtues of my very energetic, ex-Chief Superintendent of Police, Administrative Officer, ended her tirade with the statement, 'If I don't watch that man every minute he'll finish up taking the College lawns to Northampton'. I made all kinds of humble apologies and noises about the tight time-scale, the difficulty of maintaining proper communications, and even the excuse that people outside Education, and perhaps particularly members of the Armed Forces and Police, were apt to take their orders literally. Secretly, however, I was delighted that we were clearly going to start our new College with a goodly store of equipment of all kinds which would otherwise have taken years to accumulate. I did not tell Leslie Skelton about this episode until after the removals were complete, and it is amusing to recall that we actually considered bringing a whole gymnasium down from Liverpool but in the end reluctantly gave it up as an impractical proposal. We did nevertheless transfer a very substantial greenhouse from Liverpool to Northampton. The staff rebuilt it and I am glad to say it is still in use.

Of course not everything fell into place quite so easily. Academics are notoriously difficult to please as individuals or as groups, and curriculum/syllabus construction was unquestionably a headache to us all. The Chairman of one group which I had established, and who later was to become a person for whom I conceived the greatest professional respect, had on one occasion to be told quite bluntly that time was running out, and that if the kitchen was too hot there was an alternative to taking the heat. I know now that my complaints were never taken amiss and were in fact welcomed as being useful to all my colleagues who were responsible for hitting datelines and yet had to find some consensus amongst colleagues not all of whom could see the need for speed or compromise. And yet, compromise was inherent in the situation. To continue some courses which some students had already begun, and which differed from those of other students who were also partway throught a course would have been an immense task in itself. We had to accomplish that as nothing more than a sideline whilst we designed what we could regard as the most appropriate BEd degree in the country. Anybody who knows something of the history of CATE and what has been involved in the redesign of Teacher Education Courses in the recent past will appreciate just what my colleagues of those early days accomplished. I include in all this of course our colleagues in the University of Leicester. Professor Kerr, Professor Sykes and also Professor Bantock, a supposedly conservative rigid 'Black Paper' traditionalist in matters of Education, all actually responded to our needs as fast as we made them clear. At 'diversification' time later it became abundantly clear that having the choice of University or CNNA validation amounted to no choice whatsoever. The University took a straight-eyed careful and detailed look at our proposals which were written out quite briefly, whereas a visit to CNNA revealed one fact of life above all other, namely that obtaining validation would become a piecemeal gritty process taking an unconscionable length of time. We had no time! Only very speedy processes would enable the College to take advantage of the once-and-for-all opportunity to have new courses approved by DES outside the normal two/three year time-scale, and I still wonder how it was that the University understood our situation so well and responded so promptly. No words can express the debt which Nene College owes to Leicester University, of that I am quite convinced.

But I am anticipating the future. Whilst my academic colleagues were busy creating a new BEd degree and keeping to a strict time-scale, I was becoming increasingly aware that the College Building Programme was falling behind schedule. I had created a situation wherein students were being recruited for a start in September 1972 without their having any alternatives. Indeed, many had rejected offers of places in other colleges. The idea of being the first students in a new college attracted, I believe, a rather particular kind of student and as things turned out it was a good job that it did. We put back the starting date of term at least three times, and the paint in the Halls of Residence was still wet when the students ultimately arrived.

When Margaret Thatcher came to open the College things were still not much better. The future Prime Minister came dressed in a beautifully tailored suit and would, we knew, have to negotiate a number of doorways many of which had only been painted late on the previous evening. Leslie Skelton and I thus walked Mrs Thatcher through these 'wet paint' areas, one on either side, and trying to appear as if being shoulder to shoulder with the Secretary of State was as common and casual an event as having dinner. To this day I don't know if Mrs Thatcher smelt a rat (or the paint) but, if so, she certainly joined in the spirit of the enterprise in a way which perhaps explains to some extent why she later became Prime Minister. Despite the impossibility of anything but last minute planning – a whole wall of plaster had fallen off the previous day – the Ceremony went off without a hitch. A Governor commented 'Well, I've heard of the red carpet being rolled out for VIPs on these occasions but nobody has ever before rolled out a tarmac car parking space in front of me as I arrived!'

We can now take a leap in time. We merged the Corby Mature Student Annexe in our stride and all seemed set for steady expansion, and the peace of academic life. A monotechnic with a single mission was, it seemed, well on the road. How deceptive appearances can be! We had but one set of Northampton College of Education students. Even as these, our first students who had been so supportive and tolerant in the 'play-it-by-ear' conditions of 1971–2, were leaving us, the proud institution they had helped so much to establish was under a merger threat.* I cannot remember at just what point Michael Henley came to me and said, 'Eric, I want you to write a paper supporting the proposal that the College does not need and will not benefit from any merger with the other Colleges in the town' It now seems incredible that I should have written a paper in defence of a monotechnic which provided what I then genuinely regarded as a set of powerful arguments against the concept of a comprehensive college incorporating Further Education, Advanced Education and Higher Education.

Fortunately, (and I am here being very wise after the event) my paper was ignored or failed to carry any real weight. The Colleges of Art, Technology and Education were merged willy-nilly, and the various attitudes which prevailed amongst the different groups involved in the merger are best summarised in a cartoon of which I am inordinately proud and which is reproduced on the following page. This picture of College was sent to me months after the merger had occurred, and greatly encouraged me to think that the efforts we were all directing towards the creation of one unified, single-minded College, as distinct from some kind of tri-partite federated institution, were making real progress. This cartoon demonstrates that a point had been reached where we could look back and smile, even laugh, at ourselves, and at the feelings which were at some early stage no doubt expressed with perhaps some justice in some instances. I never discovered who drew this cartoon but I am glad now to have the opportunity to say that Nene College then had the benefit of staff with quite brilliant sparks of imagination coupled with a strong sense of humour. I know that these characteristics are essential qualities in the good teacher and am only glad that there is plenty of evidence that they still persist in the staff of 1989 when times are even tougher perhaps than they were in 1975.

But we should not minimise the problems of 1975. Colleges were being closed all across the country and many mergers were nothing more than thinly disguised closures. Of the three colleges in our training area we were the only one to survive in any real sense. Here again we were extremely fortunate in having Dora Oxenham as Chairman of the

---

* It is intriguing to consider whether the term 'merger' still today should carry with it, as it invariably did in those days, the notion of 'threat'.

County Council's Education Committee and Chairman of the College Governors. If she had not dedicated herself to the creation of a new comprehensive College of Higher Education, and persuaded a County Council, without the vast resources of many other local authorities, to spend a substantial sum of money to bring the merger about, then I have no doubt that Higher Education in any significant way would have vanished from Northamptonshire. Further Education, and especially Advanced Further Education, would also have been much more constricted than it is today. It is somehow disconcerting to think that Dora Oxenham managed what amounted to a Higher Education crisis locally so calmly and so well that the general populace of the Shire never knew that there was a crisis at all. Even many of those immediately involved failed to realise how closely we sailed to the wind before reaching safer waters.

The catchphrase of 1975 was 'diversify or die'. The merger could not be successful merely by changing a few 'go-it-alone' attitudes and continuing the course provision of the past. A new set of objectives and mechanisms for achieving them had to be established and, as had even by then become normal, all in a very short time-scale. A brand new set of Combined Honours modules was constructed as a basis for a BA and BSc degree package including the now little mentioned two-year Dips HE. The scheme was seen by others in the East Midlands Region as far too ambitious, one Polytechnic Director actually going so far as to say it was impractical! The fact is that not only has the original scheme largely withstood the test of time, but far more important, has provided a base upon which the present pattern of Higher Education has been constructed. The actual number of modules has, oddly enough, not altered materially. The newer modules are heavily weighted however in terms of student numbers. This surely demonstrates how profitable reaction to circumstances can be, always provided that it is speedy, positive, and guided by a careful examination of the relevant circumstances of the day. It is this latter element that converts reaction to proaction and mere 'ad hocery' to something more glorious.

Diversification meant, in 1975, little more than the creation of new courses and the expansion of older ones. It was already clear however that we would never be in a position to rest on whatever laurels might come our way. The need for change, preferably by straightforward aggregation of new activities to old, was met not by drawing up mission statements, but by infusing the whole College with a strong desire for change as a goal in itself. This approach is perhaps unlikely to find much support, even in our own management courses, but it has at least one demonstrable outcome; change does in fact occur, and in some directions which are seen by outsiders to be good only after the event.

It is true to say that several of our current success stories have been written in the teeth of opposition from so-called experts. I have already mentioned the Combined Honours Degrees but if space permitted similar tales could be told about our Nurse Training provision, our Health Visitors courses, our National Leathersellers' centre and, especially perhaps, Chiropody. The latter had already been usurped by another major institution in the East Midlands. By great good fortune a course for chiropodists had however never been mounted owing, I was told, to lack of resources. How easily we could have been put off! As is now obvious, Nene College's 'angels' in the Faculty of Science nevertheless trod where others were fearful, and we now have a thriving School of Chiropody which will be operating a unique course in brand new purpose-built premises as from March 1989.

Even more difficult to establish was what we now call our European Business Studies Degree. The most intransigent, intractable, self-opinionated senior HMI it has ever been my misfortune to meet, indeed the only one, reacted to our original proposal by saying that approval for any new European Business Studies Degree would be granted over his dead body, and even then it would be provided only in a Polytechnic. It was only by great good fortune that at one and the same time we had a Regional HMI with far greater vision. He thoroughly understood the need of a new institution, and moreover had flexibility of mind coupled with more than his fair share of creative problem solving ability. Thus he proposed a solution to our difficulties which became the fundamental base on which all our European contacts and programmes have been, and continue to be, established. I never watch 'Yes Minister' without thinking of how much we owe to that HMI. He stated publicly that in no way was he prepared to proceed against the advice of his specialist colleague, and he never did. But we none-the-less provided an extended Combined Honours Degree which was 'new wine in an old bottle'. Perhaps some equally creative PCFC official will shortly see the wisdom of allowing the College to complete the task of providing a qualification which so fully meets the needs of 1992. Of course there is a risk in giving such permission. Of course Nene College might not pursue the opportunity with all the vigour required. At least our past record should be enough to persuade a PCFC official to take a chance – if only for once!

It is appropriate to stress at this point that risk-taking ad hocery was not, and hopefully never will, become a managerised characteristic unique to Nene College. At the time the idea of a School of Chiropody was first discussed way back in 1979 both the local Health Authority and the County Council were served by people equally willing to back schemes apparently quite remote from reality and improbable of achievement. Luckily for us Councillors Jimmy Kane and John Soans, despite their widely differing political views and despite all the County Council's budget constraints were willing to give the College their blessing, albeit I am sure with hidden crossed fingers. Dr Bill McQuillan can doubtless tell a similar story of how hesitant we all were. If he can point to any single factor which persuaded us to press on then I should be surprised and grateful. Management ought to be an extract science and it makes me uncomfortable to think that it is not.

'How did Nene College become a centre for Management Training?' is a question often asked of us. The answer is both simple and complex. It demonstrates that accidental juxtapositions of previously unconnected events can give rise to more than an instinctive laughter reaction. As a consequence of the designation of Nene College as one of the five Institutions of Higher Education in the East Midlands it became clear that we ought to become, along with Leicester, Trent and Derby, a constituent member of the East Midlands Regional Management Centre. We made an application which was rejected on what we believed to have been the flimsiest of grounds. We were fobbed-off with seats on the Council but excluded from the Executive Committee and coming back from the meeting full of 'righteous' anger I determined, somehow or other, to establish a Management Centre of our own.

Shortly after this I had the good fortune, through the kindness of a colleague, to be introduced to the Chairman and the Managing Director of Blackwood Hodge plc. The occasion was actually a celebration of a golden wedding, so what began as no more than informal, indeed quite casual conversations, ended up with a large private gift from the Sunley Trust. We thus established a Centre which today is the envy of other Higher Education institutions, including many outside the East Midlands itself. Again it has to be stressed that warnings about viability and the need for caution were received from a number of sources which ordinarily would command respect, but again very fortunately, John Lowther, Jeffrey Greenwell, Michael Henley and David Walmsley gave strong support to the venture, without anything but faith in the future of Nene College to guide them!

And so I come towards the end of my chapter on the history of Higher Education in Northamptonshire. There is not the slightest doubt that none of the successful aspects of our activities can be said to be the result of long-term planning, careful predictions about the future, and specific research into market forces. I am thus convinced by our experiences that 'ad hocery' properly understood is a management strategy of immense power and should be subjected to a close academic analysis of its key components. It does not always work! We have failures and partial successes all along the line that somebody else must write about! I can only say that our Centre for Giftedness concept is still far from becoming an actuality in any real sense. The Innovation Centre took nine long years to reach its present state, and advances in other aspects of College life still await real progress. It might even be argued that the continuous change to which Nene College has been subjected and, more vitally, to which it has subjected itself, could have all have been affected faster or more beneficially in different directions from those we took. Naturally I do not believe that. Our change has been without decay in all that I see around. The 'Open Society' principle of management is an essential prop for 'ad hocery' to become glorious: perception, persistence, co-operation and crystal-ball gazing, all have played a part. It is not my intention here to denigrate attempts to plan the future. On the contrary, planning is also an essential part of ad hocery. There does however seem to be a strong belief in many quarters that if something is planned then it is bound to be, or become, good, efficient, economic, and effective. I wish life were that simple, but our experience in Nene College this far has not shown it to be so. We have to live by such tenets as: 'If it's easy don't bother with it; somebody else is already doing it', 'Aim for what others see as difficult or impossible', and 'If you can do it today, why did you not do it yesterday?' and, finally, 'Never plan and expect circumstances to fit: plan to fit the circumstances'. It is said that Napoleon, having listened to his senior general extol the virtues of an officer being recommended for promotion, commented, "Yes, I know he is a good soldier, but is he lucky?" Nene College has had more than its fair share of luck. This is perhaps best demonstrated by the very generous gifts it has received and continues to receive from such benefactors as Miss Margaret Lewis, Kenneth Horne, the Bernard Sunley Charitable Foundation and the Nene Foundation. These involvements by outsiders cannot be planned. They cannot be expected. They can only be hoped for. And yet they are quite indispensable and fundamental elements in any success story.

I began with an apologia. I would like to end with an apology. Very few names occur in this chapter simply because it is not possible to mention all those colleagues and friends whose contributions to the development of Nene College have been quite indispensable. I hope that somewhere, somehow a proper acknowledgement of the fact that Nene College is the result of co-operation and collaboration on a very wide scale can be produced. In the meantime, I would like to think that the City Fathers of Northampton take pride in what they started, as the County Council of the Shire takes pride in what it continued to develop so effectively. Their successors will undoubtedly follow in their footsteps.

* * *

There are two people who will not expect to be mentioned by name in this book when so many names have necessarily been omitted but these are two who many members of staff have said should be named.

Mrs Phyllis Thompson joined the College soon after it was set up and served until her retirement in 1988 as our receptionist. She was well-liked by her colleagues but, perhaps more importantly, she projected something of the aura of co-operation and friendship which was the hallmark of Nene to callers, and established that first 'good impression' which was so essential to the success of the College.

Ron Burge retired in 1980. He came to Northampton from Liverpool as the tutor-in-charge of horticultural studies but he was always more than that. In co-operation with Kew Gardens he grew exotic plants in danger of extinction in their South American habitat in his greenhouses at Moulton Park. He watched over the campus and produced many magnificent floral displays for special college occasions: all this in addition to instructing students and teaching children in the schools in the county.

7 The Formation of Nene College

Michael Henley

Great things come from sharing energy and talent. Nene College was formed through just such sharing. Soon after the announcement of the initiative of the central government of the day (in Circular 7/73) a wide range of representative opinion and advice was sought by the Education Committee for consideration by them and by the Governors of the several colleges concerned. The Governors of other county colleges were consulted and also the District Councils. A conference of heads of secondary schools in the county, including the independent schools at that time providing places for the LEA, to find out their views was held in June 1973. The heads had much practical advice to offer concerning the aspirations of their school leavers. Representatives of industrial and commercial enterprise, public and private, came together in July 1973 and gave an assessment of existing higher and further education provision made from their standpoint together with their opinions about future county needs. Trades Councils and Chambers of Commerce also responded fully to the invitation to provide their evaluation of present and future education and training requirements and what a new institution should aim to achieve. Every effort was made to miss no one out. From the start Nene College was seen as belonging to Northamptonshire and as part of its overall education service.

Various options were considered and initially there were preferences for outcomes other than the one finally chosen. There were two sites to consider: the present Park and Avenue Campuses. What was the scope for looking to one site as the base for future development was a question that had to be addressed. Another question, even more crucial, was what should be considered in terms of scale, particularly in relation to student numbers and spread of courses, to be as sure as possible about potential viability in the longer term compared with the existing strong establishments of the kind in the East Midlands. The views of the Regional Advisory Council for Further Education in the East Midlands

(RACOFEEM) on this aspect were important. This Council supported the Northamptonshire proposals and made representations to the Department of Education and Science on behalf of the region in their favour, after extensive ground work had been done.

The case for further development of provision for higher education in Northamptonshire was strong because of the planned substantial increase in population in the county. There was also concern to maintain a teacher training presence, which in the context of the 1973 White Paper could be retained only if there were other higher education students working alongside the intending teachers. The monotechnic frame for teachers training was to be dismantled. There was an existing impetus towards growth in advanced further education in both the College of Technology and the College of Art. It escaped no one's notice on the staff of these two Colleges and the College of Education that the proposals of the central government in 1973 offered just the opportunity already looked for in Northampton. Moreover collaboration between the County Borough and the County over course development in these colleges over many years meant that there was a familiarity with the educational issues possessed by the key figures who were to deal with planning the formation of Nene College.

The financial issues were less clear than the educational ones. It was evident that a new development of the kind envisaged would increase the expenditure of the LEA. It was not evident how far central government would compensate for this through its various grant provisions. In principle, the expansion of higher education in the public sector would increase the expenditure of all LEAs. Why not therefore benefit directly in Northamptonshire from this expansion as well as sharing in the obligatory increase in expenditure and the rate increase? There was no reason. As is generally the case in education, financial considerations afforded very limited guidance on such matters of major policy.

The College of Education had been successful in attracting students and its reputation was growing as a place where students gained a sound knowledge of theory and the right kind of practical experience. Both the County Borough which was responsible for its management and the County Council fully supported the College of Education seeing it as a major resource for teacher in-service professional development for the two LEAs. This resource was underpinned by the work in this field directed by the School of Education of the University of Leicester particularly at the University Centre in Northampton. One view about the future was that the College of Education had the potential to grow into a free-standing institution of higher education through both diversification of its courses and multiplication of student numbers following its own momentum. The site it had was large enough to allow for sufficient extension of teaching and residential accommodation. The

The Development of Nene College

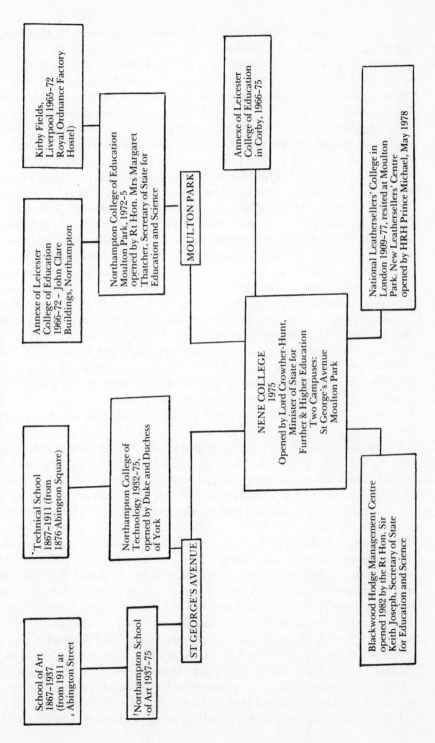

Kirby Fields, Liverpool 1965–72 Royal Ordnance Factory Hostel)

Annexe of Leicester College of Education 1966–72 – John Clare Buildings, Northampton

Northampton College of Education Moulton Park, 1972–5 opened by Rt Hon. Mrs Margaret Thatcher, Secretary of State for Education and Science

MOULTON PARK

Annexe of Leicester College of Education in Corby, 1966–75

National Leathersellers' College in London 1909–77, resited at Moulton Park. New Leathersellers' Centre opened by HRH Prince Michael, May 1978

'Technical School 1867–1911 (from 1876 Abington Square)

Northampton College of Technology 1932–75, opened by Duke and Duchess of York

NENE COLLEGE 1975 Opened by Lord Crowther-Hunt, Minister of State for Further & Higher Education Two Campuses: St George's Avenue Moulton Park

School of Art 1867–1937 (from 1911 at , Abington Street

'Northampton School of Art 1937–75

ST GEORGE'S AVENUE

Blackwood Hodge Management Centre opened 1982 by the Rt Hon. Sir Keith Joseph, Secretary of State for Education and Science new buildings had been designed to allow for enlargement. At first sight the prospect was not unattractive.

There was also a view expressed on behalf of the longer established Colleges of Art and Technology that the buildings and site in St George's Avenue provided the basis for a new institution of higher and advanced further education and that all three colleges did not necesarily have to join together in order to meet the central government requirement. Both older colleges in the not too distant past had offered courses leading to degrees and final professional qualifications. These were mainly part-time courses but they had enjoyed the support of large numbers of local people now practising in a range of professions in town and county. There was need to persuade the Governors of the Colleges of Art and Technology that the loss of separate identities would not lead inevitably to a reduction in the status of their courses when run in a larger institution. There was particular concern expressed about the future of courses in art and design. The deliberations on such issues were not simple to manage. The staff involved were very anxious indeed when the proposals for merger were first put to them. Arrangements to transfer a number of non-advanced courses from these colleges to the new College of Further Education in Northampton had been successfully made. Such transfer could be taken on a stage and rationalisation was a strategem that both County Borough and County Council favoured. There was encouragement coming from the New Town Development Corporation and from business interests concerning increase in local provision of advanced professional and technician qualifications a number of which would be located at the Avenue Campus in due course.

Given the planned increase in population for Northamptonshire as envisaged in the early 1970s it was suggested by a number of persons that consideration should be given to the establishment of two new institutions. Indeed circular 7/73 suggested that the minimum population in a catchment area for a new institution was reckoned as 250,000 compared with over 500,000 in Northamptonshire then. One would be formed from the College of Education through diversification of its courses to provide other degree courses besides those leading to the BEd. The other would concentrate on the provision of advanced vocational and professional qualifications except on teaching. Analysis of reasonable predictions of student numbers into the 1980s and beyond demonstrated, however, that when making comparisons on a national scale the projected institutions would have weak and vulnerable positions during their formative years. There was a perceived danger that relatively small numbers in most of the courses to be offered meant continuity from year to year could not be guaranteed strongly enough to prospective students, who would therefore be inclined to choose larger institutions and thus gain a sense of security.

Initially it was mooted that the College of Agriculture should join with the other three colleges in forming a new institution. The Governors of this College were willing to consider the option which they discussed fully. In the event the distinctive functions of the College of Agriculture were thought to be best maintained outside the proposed merger. Certainly this College later realized the great potential it had for growth on its own account.

It was the view amongst the officials of the Department of Education and Science (DES) that a new institution formed from three colleges would be relatively small seen on a national scale. These officials were not inclined to encourage the colleges in Northampton to go in separate ways. It was above all clear that a place was seen in Northampton for a new institution.

Northamptonshire was not well served in a geographical sense by the university or polytechnic provision in the region. The declared policy of Central Government was to improve the geographical distribution of higher education places and to do so by the creation of new institutions in the non-university sector. The way forward in this direction had to be by means of collaboration with the Department of Education and Science. In September 1973 the new Education Committee reached agreement on a proposal to merge the colleges of Art, Education and Technology. Once agreement had been reached at local level on a single new institution formed from all three colleges energy could be devoted to the creation of a development plan. In May 1974 the Secretary of State affirmed agreement in principle to the merger of the three colleges and to implementation from September 1975.

The final shape of the development plan would be influenced by the Director of the new institution and its steering committee. Successful implementation of the development plan would be in the hands of the governing body and the LEA. It was necessary to choose a new Director as soon as possible. The Principal of the College of Education had been in post for three years. The Principal of the College of Technology had only recently been appointed. Both were formidably equipped with academic qualifications and were running well-esteemed colleges. The Principal of the College of Art was soon to retire and was not in contention for the Director's post. It was not considered necessary to advertise the post outside the county; there was no expectation that candidates of superior qualifications and experience could be found elsewhere. Once the choice was made negotiations were begun with all staff in the three colleges concerning arrangements to fill the posts in the new staffing structure for Northamptonshire's first College of Higher and Further Education: Nene College.

A merger working party was formed. Its membership included representatives of existing staff, student unions, LEA and the several professional bodies involved. Sub-committees of this working party addressed central issues, e.g. course planning, establishment matters, library resources, publicity and communications.

The creation of the new governing body required consultation with business, academic, professional and trade-union organisations. Even though many Governors of the pre-merged colleges were to lose their positions, there was enthusiasm and devotion shown immediately towards the cause of the new college. From the first, Nene College was seen as possessing a fine heritage of local commitment and voluntary service from persons successful in the many walks of life in Northamptonshire. This meant that the first governors could build their own work on strong foundations just as the staff could. Nene College was created as a logical outcome of existing achievement belonging to Northamptonshire. The other colleges were supportive and could associate their own expectations of growth with those of Nene in conditions of mutual strength and a shared vision of post-18 education in the county. These colleges were represented on the new governing body.

As it became the convention that the Chairman of the Education Committee should be Chairman of the Nene College Governors, there was a strong linkage in the political dimension between the College and the LEA over all matters of policy and resources for the College. For a number of years the convention introduced at the formation that the Deputy Chairman should be a senior member of the opposition party (the Chairman being from the majority party) was maintained. Unlike schools up to now, a college needs a governing body in order that its constituency is understood and is enabled to have representatives brought together for a common purpose. Nene College courses covered a wide range, wider than any other institution in the county and reflective of all facets of the interests of the population of the county. The courses were designed to meet the needs of a market and the College Governors had a crucial role to help with interpreting that market to the Director and his colleagues. There was also the paymaster to think about and the role of County Councillors to interpret the paymaster position and offer mediation where necessary was effective for the College.

It was recognised when the governing body was designed that the structure was important. It was also recognised from the first that the persons appointed to support that structure had to be well chosen for their energy, credibility outside the College and imagination. The College Governors were given substantial powers which unless well used could inhibit growth and achievement. Bureaucracy (in its pejorative sense) had to be eschewed. The object was to release energy. The Director had to be given freedom to mobilise the talents of his colleagues and backing to encourage him to innovate, promote change and development, and to express his judgements freely and frankly. The Director was in day-to-day charge of an organisation larger than all but a few, private or public, in the county. The quest for maturity in the deliberations of the Governors began at once and once gained the condition was not released.

At the formation stage, as will have been observed, great care and attention was given to all issues affecting the climate or context in which the new institution was created. The opinions were valued of all parties obliged or invited to participate in this work of change. Steps were taken to demonstrate that this was so whenever the immediate follow-up in action after meetings or consultations did not make the position clear. This meant individual discussions with key people, additional correspondence, availability of key personnel, especially the Director-designate and the County Education Officer. At the level of final policy decision the key person was the Chairman of the Education Committee, Mrs Dora Oxenham.

A major consequence of the concern to achieve a friendly context in which to form the new college was that relationships amongst staff were empathetic. The loss of energy through addressing conflict that was caused to staff was kept at a low level because the decisions on the establishment were made openly. Moreover exceptional arrangements were made to assist the relatively few persons for whom the new institution appeared not to offer continuity of opportunity and career progression; there was a special budget to support early retirement. As a result energy was given almost entirely to the task of policy design, course building, management and team building, and of gaining acceptance for the new resource being created for the county and country. There was much attention given to revision of conditions of service, to the formulation of new rules and procedures and to the budgetary process including negotiations with officials of the Department of Education and Science. The approach on all sides was positive and the determination to succeed was strong.

External circumstances helped. The expectation for growth in the combined activities of the three predecessor colleges was strong. In other words the career expectations of staff were heightened rather than lessened if there was a change in prospect immediately or in the course of a few years ahead. There was no expectation of contraction in the volume of work that Nene College would handle compared with the aggregate of the work of the three existing colleges. Planning was meticulous and the data base was strong; the growth trends were thoroughly analysed and the findings were made the basis of the first five-year plan. Secondary head teachers were consulted and their opinions canvassed concerning school-leaver expectations or desires about post-18 educational opportunity. The Colleges of Further Education at Corby, Kettering, Northampton and Wellingborough shared in the planning because of well-established arrangements for the co-ordination of non-advanced work in the two LEAs existing until April 1974 and then combined. It was also found helpful at the time that the Chairman of the new Education Committee was a very experienced and senior County Councillor and the County Education Officer, the former Chief Education Officer of the County Borough. Between them they were able to recognise quickly distress signals when they were made, particularly by persons or organisations belonging to their former respective authorities. Not many merged institutions elsewhere in the county were successfully launched like Nene College, and no doubt the personalities of the key people counted significantly in making the Northamptonshire arrangements work out so well.

On the teacher training side, pre- and post-experience, a standing committee was established to advise on course content and style and to serve as a monitoring device on how well client needs were being met. The College, the LEAs Education Departments and the County's teachers were represented together with the School of Education University of Leicester on this standing committee. The College tutors were willingly influenced by the outcomes of the Committee's deliberations.

One idea that was not taken up was to have a Curriculum Development Centre (CDC) located at Park Campus. The five-year plan envisaged a base of 550 to 650 initial and in-service teacher education and training students. This meant there would be an ample range of tutors to support a CDC but it required space and there was no immediate prospect for new or adapted buildings coming on line for this purpose. Instead a strong group of Teachers' Centres were established by the LEA and school-focused in-service teacher education grew in the county assisted by links with Organisation for Economic Co-operation and Development (OECD). Nene College contributed in a major way to these developments as time went on.

Throughout the formation stage the University of Leicester gave encouragement and took practical steps to secure that the necessary systems of academic validation for the new courses and expanded existing courses were in place as required. The partnership with the University had already developed into a strong one as teacher training had flourished in the County in the previous decade or so under its direction. There was consideration given to creating a fresh start with the proposed combined degree courses by recourse to the Council for National Academic Awards. The high satisfaction the LEA had with the partnership with the University (with areas of activity indeed other than teacher training only) meant however that the lobby for the alternative had no case of substance to submit. The enthusiasm for what was proposed by the LEA on the part of the Vice-Chancellor and the professors who were involved in academic planning with College and County Education Department staff ensured that complex and time-consuming procedures affecting also RACOFEEM and DES were dealt with most efficiently.

The approach to the task of forming Nene College was systematic. There was a mission statement. Task groups were formed, e.g. to draft the Articles and Instrument of Government; to plan the consultation process; to prepare the data base on which to found future development; to meet with officials of the department of Education and Science. The task groups were located in the existing colleges or in the Education department, and interacted with elected members of the County Council and Education Committee. Included in the membership were representatives of various County Council departments besides Education, according to need.

The importance of the choice of the name for the new institutions should not be underestimated as a factor in the formative stage. 'Nene' was chosen for its county-wide connections and for the idea it gave of links beyond Northamptonshire. Thus the name stood for a unifying concept. The name was recommended to the Education Committee and the Governors by the Chairman and the County Education Officer who jointly were inspired one day in the summer of 1974, when reflecting on educational development in the County, while looking across the Nene Valley during a break in a programme of visits to schools and colleges. The name should be pronounced 'Nene' as first intended, not 'nen', but at the formation stage (as subsequently) this matter quickly became a conversation piece.

DEVELOPMENT OF HIGHER EDUCATION IN THE NON-UNIVERSITY SECTOR, CIRCULAR 7/73: AN OUTLINE PLAN FOR THE ESTABLISHMENT OF A COLLEGE OF HIGHER EDUCATION IN NORTHAMPTON TO SERVE THE NEW COUNTY OF NORTHAMPTONSHIRE, NOVEMBER 1973

County of ·Northamptonshire, County Borough of Northampton Education Committees

Foreword

The proposals set out in this document have been formulated in agreement with the present Education Committees of both Northamptonshire County Council and Northampton County Borough Council, the Governors of the Colleges, and the Chairman of the new Northamptonshire County Education Committee. A working party with a membership including the Principals and staff representatives of the Colleges is to develop the proposals in further detail. A further report including appropriate additional detail will be submitted after 1st April 1974 following consideration by the new County Education Committee.

M. J. Henley,
County Education Officer Designate

Development of Higher Education in the Non-University Sector, Circular 7/73

Northampton College of Education;
Northampton College of Technology;
Northampton College of Art

Proposal to merge the above three Colleges

1. *General statement of Opportunity and Need*

The opportunity for development in accordance with the guide lines of Circular 7/73 is seen to arise from the following main considerations.

(i) The presence of three major establishments located on two sites relatively near to each other and possessing their own course growth potential in an area of substantial planned population increase.

(ii) The scope for development of premises on both sites, and particularly on the site of over sixty acres of the Northampton College of Education.

(iii) The capacity through the proposed merger for quick development of higher and advanced further education courses of a wide range with a strong vocational bias within a single institution with an initial target full-time equivalent student population of 3,200 plus a curriculum development centre.

(iv) The need to correct the disparity in provision of higher educational places in Northamptonshire compared with the rest of the East Midlands Region and the fact that there is regional recognition of need for this correction, especially as planned population increase in the combined area of Northampton County Borough and the present administrative county of Northamptonshire is from the 1971 figure of 468,000 through an estimated 1973 figure of 498,000 to 640,000 by 1981 and 785,000 by 1991.

(v) The firm and clear support for the proposed development received from the existing governing bodies, and Heads of Secondary Schools, and Principals of other establishments of further education in the present County Borough and County.

(vi) The absence of other higher education provision available now, or planned within a radius of 30 miles, and the existence of good road communications within the proposed catchment area for non-resident students who will comprise the great majority of the enrolment.

2. *Outline Statement of Present Provision and the Proposed Development*

(i) Northampton College of Education is in process of current enlargement to provide for a total of 800 students including those on degree or advanced diploma courses. The Northampton Colleges of Technology and Art (which share the same site and other common facilities and services in adjoining buildings) have between them 600 full-time students within a total full-time equivalent student body of approximately 1,100. Thus the starting base is a full-time equivalent student body of nearly 2,000.

(ii) There are currently 1,600 full-time students from the present County Borough and administrative County following degree and comparable courses elsewhere and over 1,000 students following courses of initial teacher training mainly elsewhere. It is estimated that school population increase (which is projected from 87,700 in January 1973 to 132,000 in 1981 and 159,300 by 1991) and a strong local trend towards larger numbers following 'A' level courses will nearly double the present number of 2,600 students as above described to 5,000 by 1981. It is proposed to develop the local provision of nearly 2,000 full-time places in the present three colleges by rather more than 50 per cent to 3,200 full-time places through the merger by 1981, the bulk of the increase to be for students following degree, comparable courses, and courses for the proposed Diploma of Higher Education.

(iii) The courses envisaged for development include degree, diploma, certificate, post-graduate and post-experience courses together with a proportion of non-advanced courses and fall into the undermentioned categories:—

Arts and Social Sciences
Pure Science
Expressive Arts
Initial Teacher Training
In-service Teacher Training and Education Studies
Applied Science/Mathematics
Leather Technology
Building and Construction
Business and Management Studies
Engineering
General Studies
Pre-Diploma Art
Printing
Graphics
Fashion
Non-Vocational Art.

Details of student numbers for the above categories are given in Appendix III.

In validation of courses as they develop the University of Leicester has indicated willingness to expand its present programme, and it is further envisaged the C.N.A.A. and the Open University will collaborate together with other appropriate national professional and examining agencies currently operating with the Colleges of Technology and Art.

(iv) To achieve development on the above lines making an estimate of cost on the basis of current prices a capital investment in buildings and site development of £2,650,000 is envisaged spread over three programme years 1975/76, 1977/78 and 1978/79. The required land is in the ownership of the education authority.

3. *Some other Aspects of Proposed Procedure of Development*
(i) Following the full consultations at local, area and regional level and the

emergence of a consensus of opinion that lines of development as indicated above are appropriate, steps have now been taken to establish a working party which includes the Principals of the three Colleges and other staff representatives to consider the proposed time table in more detail. The working party will work in close consultation with the existing academic boards. HM Inspectors will continue to be fully consulted at all stages.

(ii) Preparation of an Instrument and Articles of Government will be put in hand shortly and it is envisaged that the establishment of a Governing Body and the appointment of certain key staff including a Principal or Director and a Chief Administrative Officer can be completed during the academic year 1974-75. At the same time, or during 1975-76, the existing governing bodies would be wound up.

(iii) Appendices attached give details as undermentioned:

Appendix I Calculation of estimated New Accommodation and Site Requirement

Appendix II Calculation of estimated Building Costs on a Phased Basis

Appendix III Analysis of Projected Student Numbers.

M. J. Henley
November 1973

Appendix I: Calculation of Estimated New Accommodation and Site Requirement

A. *New Accommodation*

The calculation of estimated new accommodation required is based upon provision being made for:

1 An additional 1,150 FTE students

2 The transfer from the College of Technology/College of Art of 450 FTE students elsewhere

3 Additional library, academic and non-academic staff workrooms, partly by new building and partly by adaptation, necessary to bring the present accommodation at the College of Technology and College of Art up to recommended standards, together with other extensive internal adaptations.

4 A Professional/Curriculum Development Centre for the initial and in-service training of teachers. (This will provide accommodation for 200 FTE students on in-service training courses not included in the total of 3,200 given in Appendix III).

5 Residence for an additional 400 students to allow 20%-25% of full-time and sandwich students (it is estimated that the total of these in 1981 will be 2,600) to be resident.

B. *Sites*

1 *College of Education Site* To accommodate the additional 1,150 students referred to above on the College of Education site at a 1 : 1 plot ratio and to provide on the same site additional residential accommodation for 400

students and the Professional/Curriculum Development Centre allowing for the extra car parking needed and for land for Environmental Science the following area will be necessary:

For 1,150 students	1.32 ha
Residence for 400 students	1.20 ha
115 car-parking spaces	.24 ha (1 space per 10 additional students)
Land for environmental science	.81 ha
Total	3.57 ha

The total site area is 24.9 ha. Therefore ample space is available.

2 *College of Education Site* (or site for a new college available in the South of Northampton) To accommodate the 450 transferred students referred to above, allowing for car parking, the following area will be necessary:

For 450 students	.41 ha
45 car -parking spaces	.09 ha
	.50 ha

3 *College of Technology College of Art Site* To accommodate the additional building referred to above, a small area will be required. This is available.

Appendix II: Calculation of Estimated Building Costs on a Phased Basis

Taking as a basis the requirements outlined in Appendix I the total building costs are estimated as follows:

1.	Provision for the additional 1,150 FTE students, i.e. 12,210m² at the present College of Education, Cost Limit of £97.31 per m²	Net Cost	£1,188,155
2.	Provision for transfer of 450 FTE students elsewhere allowing 9.25 m² per student, i.e. 4,162 m² at the present Colleges of Further Education non-specialist accommodation, cost limit of £99.16 per m²	Net Cost	412,753
3.	Provision of additional accommodation at College of Technology/College of Art totalling 479 m² at £99.16 per m² and adaptations to 25% of the useable area – i.e. 4,230 m² at £35 per m²	Net Cost	195,548
4.	Provision of a professional/curriculum development centre of 1,000 m² at £97.31 per m²	Net Cost	97,310

5. Provision of residence for an additional
    400 students at £1,415 per Residential
    Cost Unit   Net Cost   566,000

		£
Summary of Total Costs:-	1.	1,188,155
	2.	412,753
	3.	195,548
	4.	97,310
	5.	566,000
Total Net Cost		2,459,766

It is proposed that building be phased as follows:

1975–6 Starts Programme £
Provision for an additional 400 places,
College of Education Site   413,271
Residential places for 140 students   198,100
Professional/Curriculum Development Centre   97,310
New Library Building, first stage of adaptations
  College of Technology/College of Art   121,523
                        Total Net Cost   830,204

1977–8 Starts Programme £
Provision for an additional 400 places,
College of Education Site   413,271
Residential places for 140 students   198,100
Provision for 450 FTE students
  transferred elsewhere   412,753
                        Total Net Cost   1,024,124

1978–9 Starts Programme £
Provision for an additional 350 places,
College of Education Site   361,613
Residential places for 120 students   169,800
Remaining adaptations College of Technology/
  College of Art   74,025
                        Total Net Cost   605,438

Summary of Phased costs:

	£
1975–6	830,204
1977–8	1,024,124
1978–9	605,438
Total	2,459,766

Appendix III: Analysis of Projected Student Numbers

1. *Present College of Education: Estimated FTE student numbers 1981 (all advanced courses)*

Initial Teacher Training	600
Other courses – Arts and Social Science	520
Pure Science	180
Expressive Arts	100
Total	1,400

2. *Present College of Technology: Estimated FTE student numbers 1981**

	Advanced courses	Non-advanced courses
Applied Science/Mathematics	110	200
Leather Technology	90	15
Building and Construction	300	145
Business and Management Studies	200	160
Engineering	300	290
General Studies	100	40
Totals	1,100	850

Grand Total Advanced and Non-advanced courses   1,950

3. *Present College of Art: Estimated FTE student members 1981**

	Advanced courses	Non-advanced courses
Pre-Diploma Art		70
Printing		70
Graphics	30	50
Fashion		30
Non-vocational Art		50
Totals	30	270

Grand Total Advanced and Non-advanced courses   300

* No evening only or short course students included.

Summary of estimated FTE student numbers 1981

1.	Present College of Education	1,400
2.	Present College of Technology	1,950
3.	Present College of Art	300
		3,650
	Less transferred courses	450
	Total	3,200

Note: i. The above distribution does not necessarily reflect the ultimate distribution of students on the existing two sites when building additions have been completed.

ii. For in-service training students see Appendix I A 4.

NENE, NEN (OR NINE?)

*The Nene: What is the Proper Name of our Northamptonshire River –
Nene or Nen?*

It should be remembered that our forefathers before last century paid little
attention to spelling. There was no correct way of spelling, and therefore no
incorrect way. The same word would be spelt in two different ways in the same
line in all probability, if it should happen to come twice. The printing press, and
especially newspapers, gradually standardised spelling, and then dictionaries
appeared, and now there is a right way and a wrong way of spelling most words,
but not all.

Early spellings of the name of our river are therefore no guides to correct
present day usage. In Speed's map of Northamptonshire (1610) there are a
hundred spellings of places different to what is the custom to-day. Ancient
spelling does, however, help us to the pronunciation at the time, for every writer
tried to write phonetically.

A writer fifty years ago said that children in schools were taught that four rivers
empty themselves in the Wash, and one of them is the Nen. They were taught also
that the chief tributary of the Nen is the Nene, and that Northampton stands at
the confluence of these two streams, the Nen and the Nene. Naseby is regarded as
the birthplace of the river, that is of the Nen. In county maps of last century, and
the century before, it is called Northern Water and Naseby (or Naisby) Head. The
other stream is called the Western Water. Bridges calls it the Nyne.

The pronunciation of this name 'Nyne' was certainly 'Neen.' Owing to the two
streams having names so near akin, and further being of almost the same size and
importance, confusion arose as to the proper name of the united river. Those who
knew the Nen tributary called the augmented river the Nen; those who were better
acquainted with the Nyne tributary called the river the Nyne. And as there was so
little difference between the sounds 'Neen' and 'Nen,' the names were never sorted
out, the confusion was never ended.

Therefore when in 1755 there were renewed attempts to make the river
navigable, it was nearly invariable in the proceedings of the Commissioners to
find 'the River Nine or Nen' or 'the River Nen, alias Nine.' Occasionally,
however, as early as 1755, we find 'the River Neen' in its news columns. In 1759
the 'By-laws and Orders' quote the Act of Parliament of Queen Anne for making
navigable 'the River Neene, or Nine.' There is thus plenty of variety in the
spelling.

The lock which Sir John Langham gave to the navigation at the paper mill,
Northampton, was completed in 1760. The commemoration stone built in the
lock spelt the name 'Nene'. In Yaxley church, near Peterborough, is a memorial
stone to Thomas Squire, who helped in making the river navigable. It is spelt
'Nene' on the stone. The old formula 'Nine or Nen' continued with the
Commissioners until about 1820, though occasionally the name Nine was
dropped. At this time the Northampton Mercury used the form 'Nen', and
continued to do so for twenty years at least in both its news and advertisement
columns. Then the name Nene came up again, and in 1852 The Nene Valley

Drainage and Navigation Improvement Act was passed. Since this time Nene has become more usual, and to-day is almost invariably used.

From the foregoing it would appear to be now incorrect to write 'Nen' for the river below Northampton, and that 'Nene' is the only correct form. The name Nene would also be correct if applied to the Naseby stream or Northern Water. To avoid confusion the other stream should be called Western Water.

TLM, Northampton

The river was formerly called the Nine, as is evident from a map of the Wadenhoe estate of about a century ago. It is there styled the Nine or Nene. It would be interesting to know why the name was changed. The river is said to have its source in nine springs.

G.S. Ward Hunt

In a publication entitled 'The Curiosities, Natural and Artificial, of the Island of Great Britain' circa 1770, the Nene is written Nen, and in a later work 'England and Wales' by Thomas Dugdale (which, although not dated, was published soon after the death of King George IV) it is called the Nen, or Nine, but no mention is made of the origin of the name.

Nene appears to be the modern spelling for this river.

L.H. Chambers
Extracts from the *Northampton County Magazine*,
Vol. 3, 1930

Letter from John H. Thornton

Recently the River Nene seems to have been one of the major items of local news – with its floods, its diverted course, its barrage and recreation area and the bestowal of its name on the new College of Higher Education. It would therefore appear to be an appropriate moment to inform newcomers to this part of Northamptonshire that the correct local pronunciation is 'Nen' and not 'Neen.'

As a schoolboy is Kettering and Wellingborough nearly 60 years ago I never heard anything else but 'Nen' and it was not until after the Second World War that I realised that 'Neen' was starting to creep into radio announcements, particularly when the item of news was about Peterborough.

Accordingly three years ago I decided to find out where the change from 'Neen' to 'Nen' took place and armed with a tape recorder I covered the river from its mouth near Sutton Bridge in the Wash to Irthlingborough and talked to anybody I happened to meet on the bank, young, middle-aged and old.

From Sutton Bridge to Peterborough no-one had any doubt – 'Neen' it was and 'Neen' it always had been, or so they said! Between Peterborough and Oundle there was some doubt; the older inhabitants of Waternewton still called it 'Nen' generally but both names were used; a retired schoolteacher always called it 'Neen' and so did the schoolchildren. Towards Oundle, 'Neen' was generally used.

Between Oundle and Thrapston there was again some doubt; at Pilton (near Lilford), Wadenhoe and Aldwinkle, the old said 'Nen', the young said 'Neen'; and at Thrapston itself a young man on the east side of the town had no doubt that it was 'Neen' whereas on the west side, another young man said 'Nen'. From then on 'Nen' was the only name used.

I had the impression from my research that with the influx of new population from other parts of the country and also with the disappearance of local village schools and local village schoolteachers, the map spelling of 'Nene' was being taken at its face value and that within a few years the 'Neen' pronunciation could reach Northampton.

Possibly the reason for the change in the first place was that the Ordnance Survey maps changed the spelling from 'Nen' to 'Nene' between 1873 and 1883 and in doing this a long-standing tradition of spelling variants was being continued. As part of my research I checked on the spelling over a thousand years, first in documents and then in maps – and to my surprise I found no less than 13 including; Nen, Nene, Nin, Nine, Nyn, Nyne, Neen, Neene, Neane, and Nien. And as late as 1895 the northern branch from Northampton to Naseby was called 'Nene' and the western branch to Staverton 'Nin'.

Possibly the most interesting observation was made to me by an elderly lady living in Northampton after she heard me lecture on the subject; she said that as a schoolgirl in Wisbech before the First World War she always called the river 'Nen' and so did everyone else; this suggests that 'Nen' is the traditional pronunciation for the whole length of the river. However, when I was asked recently by the BBC about the matter (apparently they always get rude letters whether they use 'Nen' or 'Nene') I replied that the correct pronunciation was the local one for the area concerned; they must have taken me at my word since a few days ago when the new barrage was mentioned in the News the announcer said 'Nen'.

Incidentally, in your report (March 26) on the river's new course the opening words were, 'From today the River Nene will never be the same'; I think the reply might be: 'It never was!' The course of the river beyond Peterborough has been changed several times and in fact it is only comparatively recently that it has reached the sea under its own name; in mediaeval times it divided near Peterborough, one arm joining the Welland at Crowland and the other the Ouse, first at Benwick and later at Outwell (near Kings Lynn).

Published in the
Chronicle & Echo,
14 April 1975

MRS DORA OXENHAM, CBE, MA

An address by the Public Orator of Leicester University (Professor L. J. Herrmann) on the occasion of the award of the Honorary Degree of Master of Arts to Mrs Dora Oxenham on 9 July 1984

Northampton and Northamptonshire owe a great deal to our second honorand this afternoon, Mrs Dora Oxenham. She served on the County

Council for over thirty years and was its first woman chairman from 1969 to 1972. She has been deeply concerned with numerous aspects of life, work and leisure throughout the county, but her closest links with the public sector were always in the world of education. She was especially involved in the fate and future of the county's village schools, a constant target for change and closure throughout her time on the Education Committee, of which she was Chairman from 1974 to 1977. It was during her tenure of that office that Nene College came into being through the amalgamation of three of the county's institutions of further and higher education, and she became the Founder Chairman of the new college's Board of Governors in 1975. The creation of Nene College, which, as some of its own members may be surprised to learn, today sports no less than thirty-six different telephone numbers in the current Northampton Area telephone directory, was largely due to her perspicacity and support, and she is with us today as one of the founders of the institution which has brought this ceremony to the town.

Mrs Oxenham was born in Derbyshire but grew up in Northamptonshire, and was educated at Kettering High School. The daughter of a farmer, she married a farmer and is very much a country woman, now more anxious than ever to help preserve the rural character of the county; she has only recently retired from the Chairmanship of the Northamptonshire Rural Communities Council, and was for many years Chairman of the Environment Committee of the East Midlands Planning Council. During the same period she was Vice-Chairman of the Corby Development Corporation of which she had been a founder member, and she was one of those who ensured that the growth of Corby would not occur at the cost of massive spoliation of the surrounding countryside.

She was, however, the only member of the Corporation to marry the first Chief Architect of Corby New Town, who had moved to the position of foundation Professor of Building at UMIST in 1957. Mr Oxenham died in 1965 and Mrs Oxenham has been Mrs Harper since 1971. To confuse the issue still further Dora Oxenham is also known to many as just 'Mrs Northamptonshire', for she has been taken to its heart by the county as much as she herself has taken the county to her heart. Nearly four decades have passed since she was first elected a County Councillor. She was urged to stand for election in 1946 by a delegation from four villages. She accepted that invitation because she felt deeply that local government stands at the grass roots of democracy, and that those roots needed support and strengthening after the dread example of the rise and fall of Nazism in Germany. Mrs Oxenham has certainly done more than most to strengthen local government in this county, and it is fitting that we should honour her at this inaugural degree ceremony, a notable event in the history of the county town and its College.

LESLIE SKELTON, MA

An address by the Public Orator of Leicester University (Dr M. A. Khan) on the occasion of the award of the Honorary Degree of Master of Arts to Mr Skelton on 13 July 1987

In 1972 the Northampton College of Education emerged from some muddy fields in Boughton Green Road, Moulton Park, Northampton with four people about a hundred van loads of equipment, eighty students from a closing Liverpool college and a budget of about £24,000. Out of this Nene College, associated with the University of Leicester, developed by mergers and new developments to a thriving institution with over six hundred staff roughly equally divided between teaching and non-teaching, about sixteen thousand students on the books and a budget approaching £10,000,000. This is a remarkable achievement, even if we ignore the fact that we live in days of shrinking budgets in higher education. It requires administrative skills of the highest quality. Nene College has been fortunate to have Leslie Cooper Skelton as its Chief Administrative Officer to keep the show on the road and at the same time to oversee the new developments. It is particularly remarkable in view of his non-academic background.

Leslie Skelton comes from Glossop in Derbyshire and went to Lord's School in Bolton – a private school specialising in commercial subjects. At the age of 15 he left to become a police cadet in Bacup and this turned out to be the start of a long and distinguished career in the police force. After a couple of years he returned home to help look after his ailing father and worked with the Weights and Measures office. After a year he joined the St Helen's Borough Police as a constable and undertook office and patrol duties. In 1941 he joined the Royal Air Force for flying duties and became engaged in Flying Training Command until he was grounded after a slight flying accident and transferred to the army as a member of the Seaforth Highlanders.

When he was released after the war he returned to the police service. There he went through many departments in many parts of the country and finished up with the rank of Chief Superintendent in the Dorset police. On the way he held a number of training posts. He was an instructor in Warrington, went to the National Police College at Bramshill, was Deputy Commandant of the Police Training College in Folkestone, started a new college at Nutfield, and then moved to the police training centre at Chantmarle, Dorset, as Commandant, where one of the lecturers in education was Dr Ogilvie, who was subsequently appointed head of the newly formed College of Education at Northampton.

This development obviously excited him, and in 1971 he applied for and was appointed Senior Administrative Officer of the newly formed

Northampton College of Education so assisting in establishing the new teacher training college. His contribution here has been enormous. There were new buildings which had to be equipped, staff to be appointed and eventually in November 1972 the building was opened by the then Secretary of State for Science and Education.

In September 1975, along with the College of Technology and the College of Art in the town, the College of Education was merged into a new College of Higher Education to be known as Nene College, offering degrees to be validated by the University of Leicester. He has been central to the growth of the college ever since – merging an annexe in the town and one in Corby, which was formerly attached to Scraptoft. He assisted in the inauguration of the Leatherseller's Centre and the Blackwood Hodge Management Centre. The secret of Leslie Skelton's success is his obvious enjoyment of the job – responding to the challenges, and the development of the students all of whom he loved and amongst whom he made many friends whom he visits all over the world.

Leslie Skelton has had two outstanding careers. Sadly, he will not be enjoying the retirement he planned with his dear wife Doris, who passed away only a few months ago and who shared his labours and triumphs. But as one might expect, Leslie has found something else to do. Like the good criminal returning to the scene of his crimes, he has resumed his association with the police. He is combining his experiences with the police, in an educational establishment, in Gilbert and Sullivan, and in cabaret to organise a series of road shows all over the country on Crime Prevention for the Local Authorities, Chief Constables, and the Home Office.

He has also taken on board service as the Hon. Secretary of the Northamptonshire Record Society which is itself contemplating currently a 'move' from Delapre to Wootton Hall.

In honouring him today, we thank him for the efficient and inspired execution of administration of this college and providing the firm platform from which it can move forward strongly into the next decade.

'LET NENE COLLEGE DEVELOP IN FREEDOM'

A plea that Nene College, Northampton, be allowed to develop in a free and open manner with support from local government rather than favouritism from central government was made by its director, Dr Eric Ogilvie, at the college's inauguration yesterday.

Nene College – formed by an amalgamation of the three Northampton colleges of Art, Technology and Education – has existed since 1973 but is now able to confer BA degrees. The inauguration ceremony of unveiling a plaque was performed by the Minister for Further and Higher Education, Lord Crowther-Hunt.

In a forthright speech to nearly 300 local dignitaries and educationists, Dr Ogilvie said they did not wish the college to be regarded as a new baby to be given favoured treatment, nor should it be surrounded by barriers.

'Exclusiveness is the enemy of education . . . . there are powerful sources in society tending towards the erection of barriers so as to close down opportunity for advancement and keep us all in what others conceive to be our proper stations,' he said.

'We want students to come to Nene College because we have been able to offer a range of worthwhile opportunities and no other reason'.

First speaker at the ceremony was Mrs D. P. Oxenham, Chairman of the Governors, who said local industry and commerce in an expanding county would benefit from the college. And Lord Crowther-Hunt followed by saying that there had been much local initiative in Nene being the first college of its kind following the 1973 Act.

Lord Crowther-Hunt was presented with an axe with a blunted edge by president of the student's union, Peter Hallam, who suggested it might be a symbol against cuts in education. The Minister, however, regretted its bluntness, saying it could have been used for cutting red tape.

Other speeches were given by chairman of the County Council, Councillor R. E. Warwick and the Mayor of Northampton, Councillor J. Gardner.

Extract from the *Chronicle & Echo*, 14 October 1975

'WE DON'T WANT SPECIAL TREATMENT' - DR OGILVIE

The new Northampton Nene College, born out of the amalgamation of the Colleges of Art, Education and Technology, was inaugurated by Minister for Further and Higher Education, Lord Crowther-Hunt.

The Mayor of Northampton, Councillor John Gardner, the chairman of Northamptonshire County Council, Councillor R. E. Warwick, and the president of the students' union, Mr Peter Hallam, were among the guests, together with the chairman of the governors, Mrs D. P. Oxenham and the college's director, Dr E. Ogilvie.

Dr Ogilvie said Nene College faces new tasks which sooner or later would require additional resources. But it was not weak, not inexperienced and did not seek special treatment which could not be clearly and straightforwardly related to whatever tasks the community wished it to carry through.

The college had a highly-diversified and well-qualified staff, which was matched by an equally energetic and responsible student body.

They did not want that growth to depend upon artificial defence mechanisms or weighted in their favour. They did not want that growth to depend on the deliberate setting up of barriers to proper student choice, as for example a central government edict that students should find their further and higher education only near at home, or that particular kinds of courses could run only in certain kinds of places.

They wanted students to come to the college because they had been able to offer a range of worthwhile opportunities to them, and for no other reason.

Dr Ogilvie said he believed that the future of the country depended upon an immediate expansion of further and higher education in any direction which could be seen to be relevant. In their efforts to provide what was truly relevant, they must guard against exclusive and closed systems.

Dr Ogilvie said the college would strive to be an open institution worthy of an open society and it is hoped to provide courses at many levels rather than few.

It has become an associated college of the University of Leicester, and through their joint efforts, had constructed a new range of courses, including a Diploma of Higher Education.

Extract from the *Mercury & Herald*, 23 October 1975

8 Nene College, Northampton, 1975-89

Richard Fox

Although it may appear premature to be writing a history of so young an institution as Nene College the period 1975–89 has a completeness in two respects. The creation of Nene College emanated from the White Paper of 1972 and its designation as a Higher Education Corporation independent of the County Council derived from the White Paper of 1987 and the subsequent Education Reform Bill. Dr Eric Ogilvie was its only Director during this period and its development and character was formed by the imprint of his personality and educational values.

The first phase of the reform of higher education during the 1960s had doubled the number of universities and established thirty polytechnics in furtherance of the Robbins principle that all who were qualified should have access to higher education. The smaller colleges of technology and art continued primarily as providers of part-time higher education to a local market. Simultaneously there was an enormous increase in teacher training places leading to the creation of Kirkby Fields' College of Education in Liverpool, an Annexe of the City of Leicester College of Education in Northampton and their incorporation into the last College of Education to be built, the Northampton College of Education.

The second phase, heralded by the White Paper of 1972, sub-titled 'A Framework for Expansion', sought to extend the availability and uptake of higher education by the creation of new institutions of higher education within a reduced demand for teacher training. At the nub of the proposals was the need also to integrate teacher training into the mainstream of higher education provision as recommended by the James Report of 1972, and to create multi-disciplinary institutions which could diversify and expand.

Northampton was a designated new town. Under local authority re-organisation there would be one county authority for education from 1974. The Colleges of Technology and Art had aspirations for expansion into higher education. The College of Education was required to diversify. The Department of Education and Science signified that it would welcome merger proposals. The times seemed propitious for the development of higher education provision in a wide range of disciplines in a new college. The future beckoned. As an act of faith and confidence in the future each college as early as 1973 began to formulate ambitious development plans.

Every institution takes pride in its character and autonomy. The College of Art stated that it 'had a character, spirit and identity all its own which it must retain at all costs.' Mergers unavoidably create problems of personal status. It is remarkable therefore how quickly and willingly each institution planned for a merged future.

This was in part a realistic recognition of the wishes of the Department of Education and Science and the preferences of the Local Education Authority. The White Paper had also warned Colleges of Education that if they were to 'find a fuller and firmer place in the higher education family their staffs must face major changes and be involved in much closer assimilation into the non-university sector of further and higher education. This could mean that a college which expands and diversifies would not be easily distinguishable from a polytechnic.' The White Paper envisaged an increase in students from 204,000 in 1971 to 335,000 in 1981 in spite of a reduction in teacher training places from 114,000 to 65,000. It stated that a relatively greater increase in the regions was desirable and that, although it had been policy to concentrate advanced further education in polytechnics to achieve economies of scale, it considered an institution of 1,000 to 2,000 students sufficient to offer a suitable range of courses. Such a prospectus appeared to offer enormous potential to a new multi-disciplinary college of higher education in an area of rapid economic expansion. The euphoria of the White Paper induced in staff an expansionist outlook. The vision of future opportunities prevailed over sentimental regard for the past.

There was great scope for development. The Colleges of Technology and Art had no full-time advanced students. The College of Education had not completed one cohort of students.

The College of Technology's Development Plan for 1973–83 envisaged increasing the percentage of Advanced work from 28 per cent to 72 per cent by a combination of the expansion of advanced courses and the transfer to the College of Further Education of 450 full-time equivalent students. New courses to be introduced in the early phases of the plan included Higher National Diplomas in business studies, building, mechanical and production engineering, estate management, civil engineering, electrical and electronic engineering; Higher National Certificates in construction engineering, applied physics, applied biology and medical laboratory techniques; the Diploma in Management Studies; the Certificate of Qualification in social work and the Diploma of Higher

Education. The final phase of the plan proposed degrees in building, civil engineering, engineering and combined science; Higher National Diplomas in town planning and materials science and Diplomas in highway engineering and public health engineering. This plan in retrospect appears excessively ambitious, but at the time matched the spirit of the White Paper and staff expectations in a developing environment.

The College of Art had more modest plans and did not aspire to degree or Higher National Diploma courses. But it wished to diversify at professional and college diploma level into landscape architecture, theatre design, textiles, ceramics, illustration, photography, graphics and fashion; more lateral than vertical development.

The College of Education had the advantage of already offering a wide portfolio of subjects in the Certificate in Education and Bachelor of Education Degree courses. It was able to propose a modular Diploma of Higher Education, Bachelor of Arts and Bachelor of Science combined studies honours degrees with over twenty subjects encompassing the humanities (English, history, French, American studies and religion), the expressive arts (art, music, physical education, dance and drama), the social sciences (psychology, sociology and social studies), life and environmental sciences (biology of man, environmental biology, earth science, geography and environmental studies) and the mathematical sciences (pure mathematics, applied statistics and computing). It sought to extend the subjects available, in collaboration with the Colleges of Technology and Art, to land utilisation and the management of natural resources, plant and animal physiology, astronomy, pollution and conservation, soil science, urban studies and European studies. It contemplated the eventual provision of single honours degrees in social science, English and history. It looked towards a Post-Graduate Certificate in Education and an enormous expansion, in keeping with the White Paper's proposals, of in-service teacher training with a purpose-built Curriculum Development Centre, Child Study Centre incorporating a nursery unit and a Centre for Exceptional Children.

Michael Henley was able to incorporate these grand designs in a plan submitted to the Department of Education and Science in November 1973 for the establishment of a new College of Higher Education with a target of 3,200 full-time equivalent students of which 80 per cent would be advanced by 1981. In anticipation of a favourable reply from the Department of Education and Science a Joint Course Planning Committee of the three colleges met monthly during 1974 to marry, refine and develop the separate development plans. Degrees in economics, law, physics, chemistry, geology, biology, mathematics, psychology and geography were added to the list of desirable new courses.

Optimism was tempered by the terms of Circular 6/74 which offered the general approval of the Secretary of State to courses wholly or mainly constituted of elements already taught provided no additional staff was required. The affirmative reply of Hugh Harding of the Department of Education and Science in September 1974 to the Local Education Authority's proposals included the cautionary warning, 'The Authority's views on the need for new resources if the amalgamated institution is to realise its full potential have been noted. The Authority will understand that any proposals for major building projects will have to be examined in the light of the economic situation prevailing at the time.'

More promising was the good will shown by the University of Leicester on the recommendation of Professor Geoffrey Bantock and with the support of the Vice-Chancellor, Sir Fraser Noble. Following a Declaration of Intent in 1973 the appropriate structure for the validation of the Diploma in Higher Education and Bachelor of Arts and Bachelor of Science honours degrees was established in 1974. The process of validation through Boards of Studies, the Committee of Collegiate Studies and Senate was completed in time for a first intake to these courses in September 1975.

The validation of honours degrees, other than for teacher training, in associated institutions was a new venture for the University, undertaken at a time of financial uncertainty. With minor exceptions staff at Nene College and the University were congenial partners in validation. The developing relationship over the years particularly at subject level was a source of strength to the College and was enhanced by the fortuitous withdrawal from university validation of St Paul's, Rugby, which closed, and the City of Leicester College of Education at Scraptoft, which amalgamated with Leicester Polytechnic. A special relationship has developed between Nene College and the University of Leicester, which fully justifies those who facilitated the speedy response to the original request for the validation of diversified degrees. Two Quinquennial Reviews and a full inspection by Her Majesty's Inspectors have authenticated the quality of the combined studies degrees at Nene College.

Looking back over the years and comparing the plans for course development with what has been achieved there must be a sense of disappointment, of unfulfilled potential. Of the original proposals for degree and Higher National Diploma courses from the College of Technology only two have been achieved, the HNDs in engineering and business studies. The Faculty of Art and Design has only two full-time advanced courses. The areas identified for diversification in the College of Education's plans have not materialised. Yet the College achieved its target of 3,200 full-time equivalent students, of which 1,800 were advanced, only one year later than that envisaged in Michael Henley's submission to the Department of Education and Science in 1973. By 1988 it had 4,200 full-time equivalent students of which 2,700 were advanced.

It is a record therefore of both frustration and success. The key factor has been the one referred to in Hugh Harding's letter of September 1974, 'the economic situation prevailing at the time'. From the time of Nene College's establishment economic circumstances have been inimical to the needs and aspirations of a developing institution. The rosy glow of the White Paper of 1972 gave way to a bleaker landscape of high commodity prices, a record (still) balance of payments deficit and hyper-inflation before Nene College had even admitted any students and a visit to London from the International Monetary Fund followed shortly afterwards, presaging even further retrenchment.

The hopes and expectations derived from the White Paper that a new multi-disciplinary institution of higher education would be enabled to diversify to the point of polytechnic status were replaced by a recognition that growth would be incremental rather than spectacular and that the College would have to create its opportunities. How the College managed to achieve expansion in an unfavourable environment during a period of scarce resources and an elaborate and constricting approval system is the main theme of this chapter.

*   *   *

It had the inestimable advantage of the unequivocal and enthusiastic support of the County Council, demonstrated by the happy decision of successive chairmen of the County Education Committee also to chair the Governors. The harmony of relations between the College and the Authority is illustrated by the request of the College in 1984 to increase the representation of the local authority on the governing body, acceded to by the Department of Education and Science though with some disbelief.

The College was given a new name, the choice of Dora Oxenham, the chairman of the County Education Committee, its first chairman of governors and a committed supporter of the College. 'Nene' symbolised its county allegiance and, to those with geographical expertise, its approximate location. It also provided a never-failing lubricant to conversation with guests anxious to know the correct pronunciation. We have the authority of the BBC, on the occasion of 'Any Questions' being held in the College, that there are seventeen 'correct' ways of pronouncing 'Nene'. Official policy is that the current chairman of the governors is infallible in this respect.

The extensive discussions and sensitive appointments before the merger avoided bitterness and created among senior staff cordial and co-operative relationships. Dr Eric Ogilvie, formerly Principal of the College of Education, was appointed Director and Dr Ron Garnett, previously Principal of the College of Technology, Deputy Director.

Arthur Beavan and Arthur Angus respectively formerly Principal of the College of Art and Deputy Principal of the College of Technology, became Assistant Directors.

The academic structure comprised six Schools. Those of Humanities and Education and Social Science recruited nationally to the Certificate in Education and taught the disciplines traditionally associated with initial teacher training. The School of Science and Mathematics, Management and Business Studies had a major interest in teacher education but encompassed part-time vocational training in the molecular sciences and in business, management and office studies respectively at both advanced and non-advanced levels. Art and Design recruited locally for full-time vocational courses in graphics, printing, design crafts and fashion and prepared students for admission to polytechnic diploma courses. The School of Technology offered continuous part-time training from craft to technician and professional levels in construction, mechanical, electrical and civil engineering.

The College's origins determined its character. Each element was considered an integral and valuable part of the whole and expected to flourish within the new institution. Unlike the polytechnics which tended to shed their non-advanced work, Nene College expected all flowers to bloom. Expansionist and responsive in outlook it refused to be selective in its development. TVEI, CPVE and YTS (the Technical and Vocational Education Initiative, the Certificate of Pre-Vocational Education and the Youth Training Scheme) had equal legitimacy with the Diploma in Chiropody or the Diploma in Management Studies. The College has successfully combined two roles; that of providing education and training for employers, employees, young people and adults in Northamptonshire and that of a major contributor to the national provision of full-time degrees and Higher National Diplomas. It has not been deterred from its comprehensive approach by the penalties imposed since 1984 on mixed economy institutions.

* * *

The first major problem facing Nene College after 1975 was the decision of the Department of Education and Science to reduce by 60 per cent the number of initial teacher training places by closures, amalgamations and reduced maximum permitted intakes. The maximum permitted intake of Nene College was progressively reduced from 300 to 255 to 180 and finally to 120. The Certificate in Education was to be replaced by the Bachelor of Education degree, admission to which required the conventional matriculation requirements and, additionally, passes at ordinary level of the GCE in both mathematics and English language.

The College had simultaneously to compete for its quota from the diminishing pool of qualified school leavers wishing to train for teaching and attract to its combined studies courses enough students to offset the decline in teacher training numbers. The College comfortably achieved its teacher training targets while the Certificate in Education was available but when this was withdrawn intakes slumped to 80 in 1980 and 95 in 1981. Total enrolments for initial teacher training went down from 826 in 1975, representing 86 per cent of the College's full-time advanced students, to 267 in 1982.

Diversification was the prerequisite of survival and viability for all subjects engaged in teacher training. Bachelor of Education students were taught in common with combined studies students, a contribution to viability but insufficient in itself. Combined studies degree students specialised in one subject and acquired a broad education by studying three or four other subjects in complementary or contrasting disciplines. A student's programme of studies could be changed at the end of each year. The combined studies degree had to offer a sufficient range of subjects to provide the choice and flexibility which would attract applicants yet enrol enough students on each subject to fulfil the Secretary of State's conditions of approval. There was therefore an inherent necessity to extend its subject range and increase its enrolment targets. The subjects initially approved by the Secretary of State and validated by the University of Leicester were those appropriate to prospective teachers. It was essential to extend the degree into other areas. applied statistics, American studies, development studies, law, fundamentals of business practice, molecular science, materials science and fossils and evolution were all added to the subjects available by 1982. These gave an additional dimension to the degree, facilitated the development of coherent programmes of studies but, even more important, anticipated the immense increase in demand for business-orientated degree studies. The crucial success of this diversification is evidenced by enrolments of 672 on the combined studies degree in 1982 compared with 72 in 1975.

Diversification was not confined to the combined studies degree. The Higher National Diploma in business studies, introduced with an intake of 26 in 1976, had 162 enrolments in 1982. The Certificate of Qualification in social work with enrolments of forty-eight was first offered in 1979. The closure of Milton Keynes College of Education benefited Nene College by the transfer in 1981 of the Certificates in District Nursing and Health Visiting with thirty-seven students. The Higher National Diplomas in leather technology, engineering and graphic design were introduced in 1977, 1981 and 1982 respectively. All these courses were approved only after persistent applications by the College with the support of the County Education Authority and local industry. Approval for the Higher National Diploma in business studies was attained in spite of intense competition from other institutions. The Certificate of Qualification in social work was only rarely validated outside universities and polytechnics.

The importance of this diversification is shown by the fact that enrolments of full-time advanced students in 1982 exceeded by 417 those in 1975 in spite of a reduction of 559 in initial teacher training numbers. Initial teacher training occupied 86 per cent of the College's full-time students in 1975 and 19 per cent in 1982 when the combined studies degree accounted for half of all full-time advanced enrolments.

A major factor in gaining the approval of the Secretary of State and validating bodies was the complementarity of the programme of diversification. The presence of psychology and sociology in the degree course was essential for the validation of the courses in community health and social work. Economics, fundamentals of business practice and law complemented the multi-disciplinary Higher National Diploma in business studies. The Higher National Diploma in graphic design was unviable without the printing courses and the National Diploma in graphic design. The Higher National Diploma in engineering depended on the National and Higher National Certificates. The College by design was developing horizontal and vertical links between its courses to their mutual strength.

The success of the College in adding within the first seven years of its existence nine full-time advanced courses and eight new subjects to the combined studies degree, each requiring an incubation period of up to four years between the original application and the first intake, so protracted were the approval processes and so rigorous the scrutiny of HMI and the validators, is the more remarkable when the severe financial restraints operating throughout this period are taken into account. A reduction of 260 hours per week of staffing was required for example in 1980. Only through increased efficiency could resources be released for new developments. It was no surprise to discover when unit costs were published that Nene College was 12 per cent below the national average for all public sector institutions of higher education.

Eric Ogilvie, the Director, exuded confidence in the future of Nene College. He was dedicated to growth and tended to see only opportunities where others identified problems. The expansionist ethos of the new college earned it the soubriquet 'Jaws'. But his reports to the Governors between 1980 and 1982 indicate his concern that development would be vitiated by financial stringency. 'There are great uncertainties' his report in June 1980 reads. In the following February he writes 'There are challenging times ahead'. He was disturbed by the low teacher training recruitment, the Secretary of State's refusal to approve the Higher National Diploma in engineering, the threat from the Regional Staff Inspector to the combined studies degree which was having difficulty in meeting the conditions of enrolment for the third year of the course, the demands for resources by the validators of the health visitors' certificate and by the reduction in the College budget. Yet amid the forebodings he took exceptional delight in the creation of the Blackwood Hodge Management Centre, munificently endowed by the Sunley Foundation. It provided a facility of high quality not only to its clients but for the College as a whole. Its story is told elsewhere in this book but the timing of its impact on the College cannot be overlooked here. It showed imagination and affirmed the intention of the College to fulfil its potential as a provider of quality courses in a quality environment. Closely orientated to the needs of commerce and industry and self-financing in its operations it was a harbinger of things to come. It became operational in October 1981 and was officially opened by Sir Keith Joseph in March 1982.

Along with the Management Centre the most frequently visited part of the College is the National Leathersellers' Centre. The Centre was built with a gift of £500,000 from the Worshipful Company of Leathersellers and opened by HRH Prince Michael of Kent in 1978. It is given a separate chapter in this book to mark its unique international standing.

Another initiative taken by the Director was the formation of the College Court in 1978. The capping of the Advanced Education Pool in 1980 and the deliberations of the Oakes Committee pointing to more centralised control and planning showed the need for friends who would support the College's aspirations. People distinguished in scholarship, the arts, industry, commerce and the professions gave freely their advice on the development of the College and use their influence to support its aims.

When asked what he had achieved during the French Revolution the Abbé Sieyes is reputed to have replied, 'J'ai vécu'. The College did more than survive during the period 1975 to 1982. It had established its position as a major provider of higher education and had acquired an identity, and a portfolio of courses which gave it a sense of security and confidence to meet the changes and challenges of the new National Advisory Body for Local Authority Higher Education established in 1982 to plan and fund higher education. Its most important asset, however, was its reputation for being an institution large enough to offer a varied academic experience and social life but small enough to merit its caring reputation and friendly atmosphere. Former students who had enjoyed their college life and work were the best guarantors of future enrolments. An increasing number of applicants had applied to Nene College on the recommendation of a friend or teacher. Its qualities were becoming known.

With Government cuts affecting all universities and colleges, Nene opened a do-it-yourself bookshop in June 1981. This was not handyman's paradise but a bookshop designed and constructed as part of a project for the School of Technology by a group of Construction Industry Training Board students under the direction of Mr Derek Holland.

The original bookshop was too small to cope with the expanding curriculum and so the scheme was devised with the Concrete Association providing cement and concrete free. This was pumped over the top of the buildings from the front forecourt using a special crane and pipes. All this work was done with the blessing of the Construction Industry Trade Union (normally all building undertaken by Construction Training Board students has to be demolished after assessment when it is part of the college courses). The cost was £5,900 and this represented a 'saving' of about £8,000.

Professor Leslie Sykes, who had been so helpful to Nene in its early days and who had been closely associated with the University of Leicester Bookshop, cut the ribbon to declare the bookshop open, saying: 'Bookshops are indispensable in any institution of Higher Education'.

* * *

The period 1982 to 1989 was one of steady but continuing growth. If during the period from 1975 to 1982 Nene College can be described as an emergent institution then after 1982 it can more aptly be termed a developing one. The College looked forward to the first planning exercise of the National Advisory Body with confidence. The Government's stated aims were cost effective, high quality provision. It was anticipated that the most efficient institutions would be favoured and the most expensive penalised. In the event the less efficient were protected and advantaged. Every institution was required to submit plans for student admissions on the basis of a 10 per cent reduction in funding. Since it was apparent that future funding would be based on target student numbers, those institutions with high costs were able to trim their budgets without a corresponding reduction in student numbers and even, by proposing higher staff–student ratios, propose an increase. Nene College did not have that option. It was obliged to identify savings of £440,000, mostly in academic and support staff. All part-time courses, teacher training and courses of direct vocational relevance were exempt from reductions in intakes. The whole reduction was to be borne by the two courses with the most buoyant intakes, the Higher National Diploma in business and finance and the combined studies degree. The former was pegged to an intake of 75 and the combined studies degree, intakes for which had erupted from an average of 125 during the late 1970s to 290 in 1982, would be limited to an intake of 200 necessitating the withdrawal of French and the study of religion and the removal of final year studies from physical education, art and geography. There was much anguish, even though it was possible through planned re-deployment of resources to propose an overall maintenance of student numbers within a reduced budget.

This initial setback was the prelude to the development of a collaborative relationship with the officers of the National Advisory Body leading to an acknowledgement of the cogency of the argument that Nene College's situation in an area of rapid economic expansion entitled it to special consideration and an understanding of the legitimacy of the College's development plans. Regular dialogue constituted a partnership in planning. The College was sensitive to the National Advisory Body's priorities and the National Advisory Body became responsive to the College's needs. There was regret at the demise of the National Advisory Body and of the fruitful working relationship which had been established.

Even though the second planning exercise predicted a reduction in funding of at least 5 per cent the period 1986 to 1989 represented the most continuous and rapid growth in the College's history; and this in spite of an approval system even more restrictive and stringent than before. The diversification of the previous decade gave the College a platform for growth provided there was the student demand.

It had long been the College's ambition to offer a discrete business studies degree. This was allied to the Director's determination to encourage an international outlook through association with European institutions. Negotiations were started in 1982 for a joint study programme within a European Business Degree with the Fachhochschule of Rheinland-Phalz at Trier. A Treaty of Co-operation was signed with the University of Leicester in September 1984 whereby the final year of a European Business Degree could be taken as a post-graduate diploma by students from the Fachhochschule who had completed their Diploma. Reciprocally Nene College graduates of the European Business Degree would qualify for admission to the final year of the German Diploma. In order to gain the approval of the Secretary of State it was necessary to offer the European Business Degree as a programme within the combined studies degree. The first intake was in 1986. The first graduands and diplomates will receive their degree certificates at the Degree Congregation in 1989. A parallel arrangement was also made with the Ecole Supérieure de Commerce at Poitiers whereby Nene graduates in European Business would join the final year of the DESCARFE, a prestigious qualification in the field of business. Mutual visits and shared teaching are integral to the course. It was most imaginative to devise such academic co-operation in anticipation of the closer integration of the countries of the European Community. The degree matched the idea of the time with applications far in excess of places.

Also innovative was the diploma in chiropody. This was first proposed in 1981, and developed as a joint venture with the District Health Authority and the active encouragement of Her Majesty's Inspectorate. The School of Chiropody was opened by the Rt. Hon. Peter Brooke, MP,

Minister of State for Higher Education, in 1985. After a successful appeal a new unit providing clinical training facilities for chiropodists was completed in the grounds of Northampton General Hospital in 1989. The initial scepticism of the Board of Chiropody turned to unqualified approval when it reviewed the course in 1988.

The part-time Bachelor of Science degree in health science studies, introduced in 1984 as a post-experience qualification for those in professions supplementary to medicine, was the first in the country. Its success and sustained demand owed much to the active involvement of the University of Leicester and particularly to Dr Kenneth Jones. One of the major achievements of the College is to have established from nothing a flourishing programme of community health care.

Undoubtedly one of the striking advances during the second half of the 1980s was the dramatic increase in part-time provision in management, business studies and related professional qualifications. The success of the Northampton Development Corporation in attracting commerce and industry to the region was matched by the College's response to their education and training needs. The number of students enrolled on part-time courses in accountancy, management, banking and business increased from 367 to 633 between 1984 and 1988. From being a dependency of Leicester Polytechnic the College achieved CNNA validation in its own right for the diploma in management studies. Enrolments on the certificate and diploma courses increased from 49 in 1984 to 228 in 1988.

* * *

Very many people have combined full-time employment with technical training on a day-release basis qualifying over the years for National Certificates and Higher National Certificates. From 1985 those with the ability, persistence and motivation could continue their part-time studies to achieve a Bachelor of Science honours degree. It was first awarded for chemical science and will shortly be extended to computing and business and finance. One of the prime duties of Nene College is to meet the continuing education needs of the people of Northamptonshire. In 1988-9 5,451 students were enrolled on part-time or evening-only courses extending over an academic year. Another 4,357 students enrolled on shorter courses.

There was a rapid extension of computer-aided learning and computer courses. A National Diploma, Higher National Certificate and Higher National Diploma in computing were successively introduced. Information analysis was included in the combined studies degree and computing. The number of students taking computing at advanced level increased five-fold within four years. Hands-on computing experience became a part of virtually every course. Massive investment in computer hardware amounting to £750,000 over three years barely kept pace with demand. Within five years the number of computer technicians and programmers increased from four to twenty-three. Students and staff had to get used to the new and ugly language and print-outs of information technology.

During the 1980s initial teacher training was the most scrutinised and the most radically reformed of the College's courses. The bad news that secondary training was to be withdrawn from 1983, another blow to recruitment, was balanced by approval to offer a Post-Graduate Certificate in Education which the College had been seeking since 1975. There was gradual recovery from the low enrolments of the early 1980s and by 1989 the intake was above target and the largest since 1976. Enrolments in 1989 were more than double those eight years previously, testimony to its resurgence. Her Majesty's Inspectors, after two partial and one major inspection extending over two years, confirmed its quality. So thorough and fundamental was the reform and renewal of the Bachelor of Education degree that at one time three degrees were operating at the same time. The exhausting and exhaustive processes of inspection, validation and accreditation culminated in the Council for the Accreditation of Teacher Education's seal of approval for its combination of academic rigour and professional relevance in 1988. The College acquired a reputation for the excellence of its early years education and training.

To achieve a well-designed and professionally-orientated Bachelor of Education degree a decision was made to teach it separately from the combined studies degree. The distinctiveness and coherence of the course now took precedence over the James Report's recommendations that prospective teachers should study alongside other students. The withdrawal of two hundred full-time equivalent Bachelor of Education students from the combined studies degree course could have undermined its viability. Its earlier and continuing diversification in response to changing demand paid dividends in terms of the increase in applications from 255 in 1978 to almost 2,000 ten years later to the extent that the course, with its proliferation of 'no vacancy' signs, resembled a sea-side resort at the height of the season. This freedom from dependence on late applicants was a tribute to the national standing of the course. With twenty-five subjects and six inter-disciplinary units organised into twelve coherent programmes of studies it has proved its ability to compete effectively with universities and polytechnics.

The quality of the course was given independent ratification by HMI after a major inspection in 1985. Particularly gratifying were the comments in the report that the well-defined aims of the degree placed emphasis on the preparation of graduates who can think independently and use skills flexibly rather than on the acquisition of subject content. Students were provided, within a progressive educational experience, with a variety of perspectives and different skills.

In his response to the Green Paper 'Higher Education into the Nineteen Nineties' of 1978, which stated that 'it is clear that the era of rapid expansion is coming to a close and may be succeeded by a decline', the Director, in pleading for a commitment to higher education by the County Council, argued that 'knowledge was the central capital and crucial resource of the economy in an increasingly complex and technical society' and that Nene College should be supported to promote 'the wide applications of high technology and encourage innovation'. In his Report to the Governors in June 1979 he advocated the establishment of a Business Advisory Centre, the goals of which should include stimulating awareness of the opportunities for starting up new enterprises, encouraging individuals and firms embarking on new business ventures in Northamptonshire and providing technical information, advice in management and finance and practical assistance in dealing with design, development and manufacturing problems. A job description for the Head of the Centre was provided, for good measure. Four years later he invited the Governors 'to support what is no more, at the present time, than an expression of hope' an Innovatory Centre. In 1988 the hope was realised. With the support of the County Council and the Northampton Enterprise Agency, a generous gift from the Timken Foundation and a range of sponsors, the Timken Business Innovation Centre was in full operation with every starter unit occupied. The College's technical expertise was readily available to those trying to make a modest but important contribution to the regeneration of the economy.

The College has been a continuing client of the Land and Buildings Department of the Local Authority. There was hardly a year when buildings were not being designed, altered, built or officially opened; the National Leathersellers' Centre in 1978, two residential blocks in 1980, the Blackwood Hodge Management Centre in 1981, a Computer Centre in 1983, a teaching block for social science, environmental science laboratories and library extension in 1985, the fitness and information technology extension to the Blackwood Hodge Management Centre in 1986, the Timken Business and Innovation Centre in 1988, and the School of Chiropody in 1989. These are physical symbols of expansion, enterprise and sheer doggedness on the part of the Director and the Authority in the face of national restrictions on capital expenditure.

The non-advanced sector of the College which accounted for 40 per cent of its work and 20 per cent of the county's further education provision has been relatively neglected in this history. This is partly because for most of the College's brief history it was fortunate not to live in 'interesting times' as the Chinese proverb puts it. A continuous stream of craftsmen, bricklayers, carpenters and joiners, plumbers, welders, motor mechanics, painters and decorators, were trained to the highest standards as the number of national prizes awarded to students testifies.

Many medallions and silver trowels adorn the mantelpieces of
Northamptonshire. Other students, in civil, mechanical and production,
electrical and electronic engineering, progressed to the higher education
sector. The striking and original posters advertising plays at the Royal
Theatre, Northampton, were designed by students in the Faculty of Art
and Design, which, in response to criticisms from the Business and
Technician Education Council, revitalised itself in the mid-1980s under
Paula Shirreff and set standards of professional competence in graphic
design and fashion that attracted commissions and sponsorship from
industry and enabled students to win prestigious national competitions.
The winds of change which had registered an uncomfortably high force
in higher education began to affect further education increasingly. The
Training Agency, formerly the Manpower Services Commission, demanded
new standards and methods of training. YTS students numbered over 500
in 1988. The College prepared young people for the Certificate in Pre-
Vocational Education and engaged in the Technical and Vocational
Education Initiative. It pioneered distance learning schemes in lift
technology, site management, telecommunications and leather technology.
Its AL courses enabled mature re-entrants to education to achieve the
qualifications they needed for higher education. Park Campus was more
closely associated with full-time students recruited from Britain, Europe
and the world. Avenue Campus continued its historic role within Nene
College of servicing the needs of the local community and industry for
education and training in craft and technology.

* * *

The spirit which infuses an academic community and determines its
character is revealed not just by its academic achievements and course
development. The social and cultural activites it generates can be a surer
guide to the quality of life it offers its students.

Students can express their musical talent in a variety of ensembles
ranging from madrigal choir and recorder group to brass band and full
orchestra. In-house recitals and concerts have been supplemented by
performances from such as Kent Opera, Corelli Strings, the Nene
Consort, the Kronos and Carlton String Quartets, the Romani Trio and
Michael Hext. In May 1983 the College was host to the televised
Barclaycard Composer of the Year competition. Marcia Wragg's talent
for enthusing dancers and non-dancers alike is demonstrated in the
annual dance production, a highlight of the pre-Christmas festivities.
The London Contemporary Dance Company, the Phoenix Dance Company
and Extempore Dance are among those who have performed at the
College.

With over a hundred students taking drama, their provocative,
searching and stylish presentations punctuate the year as do the visits of

small professional companies. Major College productions of plays, musicals and Gilbert and Sullivan have included a brilliantly perverse version of *Iolanthe*, where the fairies were translated into ladies of easy virtue. It was a small step to progress to *The Beggar's Opera* and *The Threepenny Opera*. As writer-in-residence the College has had the poet and translator of Persian classics, Dick Davies, and Ian Watson, an author of science fiction. Anna Maria Stanczyk, the concert pianist, and Christopher Brown, composer of children's operas, have been musicians-in-residence. The College has been host to 'Master Mind' and 'Any Questions'. The College also hosted the teams competing in the 'Its a Knockout' contest relayed from Northampton.

Each year during the autumn term David George has presented the 'Science and Society' series of lectures by distinguished scientists. The Miller-Buckley Lecture with speakers of the eminence of David Bellamy, Sir George Porter, Magnus Pyke, Tony Soper and Jack Scott is endowed by the firm that built the College of Education.

The Executive Lunchtime Seminars at the Blackwood Hodge Management Centre give local businessmen the opportunity to hear national leaders of commerce, industry and the professions. For eleven years the Nene Lectures, inaugurated by John Frain when Deputy Director, have provided a series of lectures each of which is devoted to an aspect of the College's work such as management, the humanities, technology, art and design and social science. The series on humanities included Melvyn Bragg, Alasdair Milne, David Puttnam, David Lodge, Antony Hopkins, Joan Bakewell, Michael Bognador and Richard Hoggart. There have been regular art exhibitions in the Corridor Gallery. Each year the Higher National Diploma in graphic design presents its final assessment at the Derngate and students of fashion display their originality and flair at Cinderella-Rockerfellas with sponsorship from Barclaycard.

In these ways the College has served the intellectual and cultural interests of the general public. What is known as the 'hidden curriculum' has flourished at Nene College. The Students' Union has promoted a wide range of social and sporting events and activities. Forty-five student societies operate under its aegis. There have been particular successes in basketball, football, rugby and the national Moot Competition for students of law.

This brief history of Nene College has of necessity been selective in recording the challenges and difficulties it has faced and the progress it has made towards gaining a national reputation as a major institution of higher education, developing its links with the local community and providing a successful and enriching experience for its students.

Fourteen years is a brief period on which to reach a judgement. Many of the aspirations expressed in the first development plans may not have been realised but the Centre for Giftedness, a special interest of the

Director, was established in 1979 and now has the imposing title of the National Enrichment Research and Information Centre. Both the national organisations which promote the study of giftedness located their headquarters at Nene College in 1979.

The College has had to be adaptable to changing national policies and demand. The College is in sixteen of the nineteen subject groups of the National Advisory Body (only agriculture, catering and librarianship are missing). It may lack critical mass in any one area but by teaching a range of disciplines comparable to that of a polytechnic has been able to respond to changes in student demand or in the priorities of the national planning body. The achievement of sustaining a College, in an environment unpropitious to expansion, which managed to increase its number of full-time equivalent advanced students from 1,200 in 1980 to over 2,600 in 1988 and its total full-time equivalent students from 2,389 to 4,200, cannot be gainsaid. Some reflection on the reasons for this is appropriate.

'A pleasant, well-maintained, cultured environment, conducive to study' is how HMI described Park Campus. Applicants are undoubtedly attracted to the handsome buildings on a human scale and to the surrounding parkland with its noble trees. But they also notice the students and staff are at ease in their relationships. On the occasion of the retirement of Alex Parthenis (the then Dean of Technology) Harry Myers, of Her Majesty's Inspectorate, said he always found Nene College a very friendly place. It is an unregulated and well-regulated College. Students sign on their enrolment forms to abide by the rules of the College. But there are no rules nor any necessity for them. Eric Ogilvie insists in his welcome to new students that everyone is a member of an academic community, that there is no 'us' and 'them' at Nene College and that this applies to relations between students and staff and between academic staff and administrative and manual staff.

Success might be attributable to the remarkable increase in productivity of the teaching staff. Staff student ratios increased from 9 : 1 in 1981 to 14 : 1 in 1988, an improvement of over 50 per cent. They comfortably exceed the National Advisory Body's target of 12 : 1 and the Audit commission's target for the early 1990s of 11.4 : 1. This is even more creditable when it is realised that the funding methodology has penalised Nene College each year by a sum amounting in 1989 to almost £500,000 because of its proportion of non-advanced work.

The whole-hearted support of the County Council has been crucial in seeking approval for new courses, ventures like the Business Innovation Centre and improved funding. The College owes much to the interest taken in the welfare of the College since 1975 by County Councillor Dora Oxenham, and by County Councillors Terry Angier, Mary Bland, Allan Bradley, Graham Fordyce, Harvey Fruish, Owen Granfield, Jimmy Kane, John Lowther, Jack Morrish, Bill Morton, Alan Northen, Gina Ogden,

John Soans, Janet Thomas, and (both as a Councillor and as a non-Councillor) David Walmsley. The Education Reform Act has changed the relationship of the College to the Local Authority but it is to be hoped that it has not wholly severed it.

Recognition should also be given to the 'effective, professional and encouraging relationship', as HMI expressed it, with the University of Leicester. Each year since 1984 the splendour of Degree Congregation has brought colour to the Derngate Centre in Northampton and honour to luminaries of the County followed by the conviviality of a strawberry tea on the College lawns.

The College has been fortunate in its benefactors such as Sir William Shapland, Kenneth Horne, the Worshipful Company of Leathersellers, the Nene Foundation, the Timken Trust, the T.D. Lewis Trust, the Kingsthorpe & Manor Trust and Express Lifts, which have given support extending from student bursaries and the endowment of fellowships to the funding of major building projects.

The location of the College has been to its advantage and was a main argument in the College's submission for designation as a polytechnic. During the life of the College the sub-region within a 25-mile radius of the College was for a time the fastest growing area in Western Europe in terms of increases in population, job opportunities and commercial and industrial expansion. Three of the four most rapidly growing counties in England were Northamptonshire, Buckinghamshire and Cambridgeshire.

Other factors which have benefited the College include the willingness of over 300 representatives of commerce, industry and the professions to serve on its consultative committees and the international links developed by staff with institutions in Trier, Poitiers, Charleroi, Sweden, Belgium, Spain, Portugal and Florida.

As primarily a teaching institution the College's research activities have been limited but the establishment of a Research Committee with appropriate funding has resulted in the appointment of three Research Assistants and support for sixteen collaborative research projects in areas where the College has special expertise, including investigations into children's sense of time, pain relief through the use of nerve stimulation techniques, biochemical aspects of saliva in relation to stress and trends in sexual attitudes in a European context. The promotion of scholarship has been a continuing concern. Since 1975, 170 members of a staff of 300 have been awarded higher degrees or professional qualifications with financial assistance from the College.

But whatever advantages the College has enjoyed from circumstances or its friends what credit is due must go primarily to the Director, Dr Eric Ogilvie, and his immediate colleagues. During a period when the benefits of higher education were no longer taken on trust, when almost as many institutions of higher education closed as survived, when course development was difficult and funding barely adequate, when the economical needs of the country took precedence over student demand, his leadership and the talents of his staff have enabled Nene Collage to flourish. They have laid the foundation for the further enhancement of higher education in Northamptonshire and the fulfilment of Nene College's historic mission.

There is a group of individuals intimately concerned with the development of the College who, because they have served as second-in-command do not come as sharply into focus as perhaps they otherwise might. Obviously it is not possible to mention everyone but specific reference should be made to the Deputy Principals.

Dr E. M. Hitchfield, BA, PhD (1972-4): was the Deputy Principal of the College of Education. Elizabeth Hitchfield has been a leading figure in the field of teacher training and the author of one of the standard student textbooks on the theories of Piaget. When the amalgamation that took place in 1975 was under discussion, Miss Hitchfield felt her future lay in teacher-training and she obtained a post with Warwick University. Since then she has moved to Oxford University. From time to time she visits us or we see her at concerts at the Derngate Centre. It is always a delight to meet up with her.

Dr Ron Garnett (1975-7): was the first Deputy Principal of Nene College (having previously been the Principal of the College of Technology). His considerable contribution is summarised on p. 84.

Dr John P. R. Frain, MA, MTech, PhD, MIEx (1978-85): started his working life in industry and then transferred to teaching. He became the HMI for Further and Higher Education in the East Midlands and in that capacity had oversight of the development of Nene in its earliest days. Eventually John Frain decided to move out of the Inspectorate and become our Deputy Director. We always felt that it was a tremendous compliment to Nene that he came to us. John Frain was a charming man. It was a constant delight to be in his company socially but behind the charm of a former sales director of a nationally known firm lay real knowledge and expertise. His friends and contacts both in the educational world and in industry were legion. His tact and diplomacy were legendary. It was a very real loss (but no great surprise to his colleagues in view of his talents) when he moved on in 1985 to run his own ship as the Principal of the amalgamated college now known as the South Merseyside

College, Liverpool. There he has been an outstanding success in a difficult situation. At Nene he was particularly involved in carrying out the Director's ideas (and the Governors' wishes) in the setting up of the Blackwood Hodge Management Centre and also in the initial contacts with Poitiers. Some idea of the extent of John Frain's work-load can be gauged by the fact that since he left in 1985 it has been necessary for Nene to have two Deputy Directors.

Dr Graham H. Clark, BSc, PhD, CChem, FRCS, MBIM (Deputy Director Resources, from 1985): came to Nene from the North-East Surrey College of Technology where he was Head of Department having previously served as a Principal Lecturer at Huddersfield Polytechnic. Graham Clark is a chemist but at Nene he has had primary responsibility for resources. Outside the life of the College he has a reputation as a golfer but this is only what one would expect of a Scotsman educated at Edinburgh University.

A. W. R. Fox, MA (Deputy Director Academic, 1985–9): Richard Fox was one of those who came to Northampton from Liverpool when the Kirkby Fields college closed and was transferred here. He has contributed the first section in this chapter on Nene College from 1975 to 1989, writing from personal experience of the events he describes. As a colleague in this particular project and as a personal friend who shares a love of classical music it is invidious to say very much more other than to pay fitting tribute to one of the hardest working 'chiefs-of-staff' one might find anywhere in the academic world.

DR KENNETH HORNE, D.Litt.

An address by the Public Orator of Leicester University (Dr A. J. Meadows, MA, DPhil, MSc) on the occasion of the award of the Honorary Degree of Doctor of Letters to Dr Kenneth Ellison Horne on 7 July 1986.

You may remember the children's rhyme which begins: 'If all the world were paper, and all the seas were ink'. People who work in academic life sometimes have the impression that all the world *is* paper. Certainly, we are unlikely to underrate the importance of paper in the running of the world. In these terms, our first honorary graduand must be considered one of the more influential people in this country, since a significant fraction of the paper we use is handled by his firm.

In one sense, he was born into the business, for the firm's activities as a paper merchant were begun by his father, whom he joined for a short period after leaving school. However, the counter-attraction of higher education proved too much, and he entered King's College, London, to read for a degree in history. He not only obtained a good degree: he met his wife, who was also taking the history course. Unfortunately, the need to support himself financially by working between lectures overstrained his health, and he contracted TB. When he left hospital, the consultant warned him strictly to leave London and lead a quiet life. Characteristically, he immediately accepted a strenuous teaching post at a London Grammar School. His wife was appointed to a post at the same school, which operated an early form of equality – all teachers, regardless of sex, were called 'Sir'.

After the war, Mr Horne's father, realising that he must soon retire, begged him to take over the firm. The paper business in those days was taught on the job, and Mr Horne must have been one of the first graduates to be employed in it. He asked so many questions to try and discover the way things worked that he initially made himself unpopular in the trade. His colleagues were accustomed to their activities being accepted, rather than investigated. Ultimately, this intellectual curiosity led him to write an introduction on *Paper for Books*, which became a standard text. He also applied some of his school-teaching background to the firm's products. He had taught a course on economics, and had become particularly interested in the idea of monopoly. He now asked himself whether there was any chance of creating a monopoly in the paper business, where conditions were actually competitive. The answer he came up with was to have the paper mills make new types of paper according to his specification to which he attached his own brand names. When these caught on, as they rapidly did, he held an effective monopoly for these papers.

During his early years with the firm it remained in London – close to the publishers clustered round the British Museum, who were important paper purchasers. Visits to his wife's family in Yorkshire led to contacts with the major printers there, and, eventually, to the establishment of a Yorkshire office. Next, the Midlands were covered from a branch in Leicester, and the firm now has a network of branches round the country. By the mid-1970s, the growth of trade outside London and the need for better accommodation had convinced Mr Horne that he should move away from the city. It is gratifying that, after considering Milton Keynes, he decided Northampton provided a better central focus. The move allowed him to build the first ever specially designed, computerised warehouse for paper handling. Much of the work on computerising the firm's activities was carried out in-house. Some of the software involved was written by his eldest daughter, and some of the operations come under his eldest son. This ceremony is being held within a mile of what is probably the largest paper merchanting warehouse in the world, and certainly the one with the most efficient delivery system. Some idea of the scale of operations can be derived from the firm's turnover figures. Starting at a very low level in 1947, when our honorary graduand took over, they rose to £850,000 in 1961, to £9 million in 1971 and £130 million last year.

The clear moral we should draw from this story is that an academic training is by no means a hindrance to business intitiative. It is certainly pleasant to observe that a degree in history can lead to profitable employment. However, the story would be incomplete if it were left there. Mr Horne has become a well-known figure in Northamptonshire in roles other than that of major employer. He has, for example, been a leading spirit in the renovation of the ancient church of the Holy Sepulchre nearby here. But most noteworthy, and of special importance to us, is his great involvement in the activities of Nene College. The design that his firm uses on its products is the hunting horn. Though conceived before the move to Northampton, it symbolises very well the close relationship between our honorary graduand and the old hunting country of the Midlands in which he has settled. In this year – which has been especially labelled 'Industry Year' – it is particularly pleasant to say, Mr Vice-Chancellor, I ask you to admit Kenneth Ellison Horne to the honorary degree of Doctor of Letters.

THE NATIONAL LEATHERSELLERS' CENTRE

Dr David George

The National Leathersellers' College, London, owed its origin to the attempts made in 1893 to start a class of technical instruction in leather manufacture at the Borough Polytechnic in South London. This effort was initiated by the Worshipful Company of Leathersellers and evening lectures in the subject were organised at the Herold's Institute, a building which, under a clause of a scheme controlled by the Charity Commissioners, was lent to the Borough Polytechnic by the Governors of the Herold's Foundation. The scheme was a great success and with further financial support from the Leathersellers' Company the building was altered to provide more suitable facilities and a director was appointed. In 1895 four evening classes were provided.

The success of the tanning school led to its further expansion and its importance to the leather trade was recognised in 1898 by the inauguration of a research scholarship. Ten years later the Leathersellers' Company built a College in Tower Bridge Road, Bermondsey, London. This College was opened in 1909 and during the years that followed became famous throughout the world for training leather technologists, many of whom have since occupied some of the most important posts in the industry. The College was known during this period as the Leathersellers' Company Technical College and later as the Leathersellers' Technical College. In 1951 the Minister of Education established the College as the National College for the Leather Industry and the College was re-named the National Leathersellers' College. In 1955 the Minister of Education formally opened new extensions to the college.

Changes in the size of the UK leather industry made it necessary to centralise and unify education and training and in 1976 the Secretary of State gave approval to the establishment of a National Centre for Leather Education within Nene College, Northampton. Through the generosity of the Worshipful Company of Leathersellers, who made a grant of £0.5 million and the Northampton County Council, who provided land and the services of their architects' department, a new building was created to house the National Centre. The grant given by the Leathersellers' Company was a further example of the support given to education by the Company over many years. This support was recognised when it was agreed to call the new Centre the National Leathersellers' Centre.

In September 1977 the National Leathersellers' College, London, merged with Nene College, Northampton, to form with the Department of Leather Manufacture, Nene College the Division of Leather Technology. In May 1978 the new National Leathersellers' Centre was formally opened by His Royal Highness, Prince Michael of Kent who is an Honorary Liveryman of the Leathersellers' Company.

Many students take up a career through a course of Higher Education without having explored the opportunities accorded by this fascinating, challenging and rewarding industry. This is surprising since leather is very much a part of everyday life and is always in demand for fashion, sport, industry and general comfort. Whatever the type of leather being made, or the kind of skin being used for the purposes, the processes a tannery employs are treatments of a natural material, essentially a mixture of proteins possessing unique chemical and physical properties. In other works, leather manufacture is a technology based on protein chemistry.

The use of hides and skins dates from palaeolithic times, though exactly how man learned to turn these putrescible materials into flexible, non-putrescible leather is a matter for conjecture. Although the industry is one of the oldest known to man modern leather science dates from the beginning of the present century. Since then the scope of the subject has increased steadily and as knowledge of protein chemistry and of other natural and synthetic products used in the industry has advanced, so the leather technologists have had to become familiar with a large number of pure and applied sciences, and with the constitution and properties of a wide variety of materials. Before the technologist can hope to produce leather, he must understand the nature of the materials he uses, the way in which they react, the methods of controlling this reactivity, the methods of analysing and testing his finished product. With this knowledge as a basis he had then to become familiar with all the practical tannery processes and machine operations which are necessary to achieve his ends, including those for the preparation of skins for tanning, the tanning processes themselves and the many subsequent operations involved in the dyeing and surface coating of the leather.

The study of the reactions occurring during leather manufacture involves the student in a fascinating and challenging subject which applies the strict discipline of the pure sciences to the practical manufacture of an article possessing aesthetic appeal as well as utilitarian value. However, while fundamental leather science has a fascination of its own, the purpose in studying it is, in the end, to produce a better leather, using processes which have been long established as well as new ones. Because many aspects of leather manufacture overlap other technologies and sciences, attention has to be paid to chemical engineering, polymer science, microbiology and mechanical engineering amongst other things. In addition to these disciplines a student, on leaving Nene College, should be capable of initiating new developments through research and development.

The successful student who possesses a qualification in leather technology usually has no difficulty in finding a suitable post within the industry. There are excellent opportunities for overseas travel and senior positions in the leather and allied industries in production, quality control, management and marketing are currently occupied by many former students from both Northampton and London. The students' Corium Club has members throughout the world and forms quite an 'old boy' network. They produce an annual magazine, hold social events and are well known for their sporting prowess.

Leather technology is a multi-disciplinary subject and as such benefits from other departments within the faculty of sciences as well as from business studies and management courses offered. Much has been said about the growing 'ecumenism' between industry and education. The new emerging technologies require a changed work-force consisting of 'knowledge' workers rather than manual workers and in consequence industrialists are looking much more expectantly at Higher Education to develop personnel with the necessary knowledge and perception for a new age.

The National Leathersellers' Centre is fortunate in having an active and supportive Advisory Committee made up of members from the leather and chemical industries. The United Kingdom leather industry is in a healthy situation and is renowned for producing some of the finest leather in the world with much being exported. The leather and associated chemical companies together with the Worshipful Company of Leathersellers give considerable support to the Centre financially and by way of gifts of hides, skins, chemicals and prizes.

The Centre also works in co-operation with the Leather Manufacturers' Research Association which has recently opened nearby and an additional bonus is the Museum of Leathercraft which has recently moved to Northampton. This, coupled with the close proximity of the Shoe and Allied Trade Research Association at Kettering, means that Northampton has become a world centre for education, research and development in leather production and usage.

The College library holds a unique collection of international books and journals on leather and related subjects and parallel to this the College bookshop now holds a most comprehensive stock of books for sale covering the same specialities.

The seven teaching staff and four technicians are well qualified and experienced. They undertake consultancy work and research. This has included many overseas visits especially to developing countries, which is both good marketing for the College but also excellent diplomacy for Britain. Staff regularly attend international leather conferences and trade exhibitions. At the present time there are two research assistants working in the Centre. One is writing a doctoral dissertation on goatskin improvement, while another is investigating computer-controlled tannery processing.

The major course offered by the Centre is the two-year full-time diploma of the Business and Technician Education Council. For this course applicants should have an 'A' level in chemistry as well as 'O' level mathematics, physics or biology. Other courses vary from the short in-service training courses which are gaining in popularity to a one-year post-graduate course for those with a degree in chemistry, chemical engineering or biology, to block-release courses.

The specific aims of these courses are as follows:

(a) to provide an appreciation of the scientific method, a sound understanding of the basic principles of chemistry and an awareness of the fundamental importance of the physical properties of materials, statistics and chemical engineering;

(b) to apply these principles to the scientific study of leather production process control and leather quality;

(c) to develop confidence in the application of these principles to the solution of problems in leather technology;

(d) to clearly communicate the results of experiments;

(e) to operate scientific instruments and apparatus to obtain reliable scientific data;

(f) to introduce students to the practical problems associated with leather manufacture by the preparation of a variety of commercial leathers in the college tannery;

(g) to give an appreciation of the problems and workings of management;

(h) to be a springboard for further studies in leather technology.

In other words, we are trying to turn out good practitioners, and not just theorists, who are trained to think, solve problems and work independently, who would be competent troubleshooters for the leather industry. Above all, we hope to produce young men and women who have been educated holistically.

At the present time there are 380 students from twenty-three nations in the Centre and this brings to the College an international heritage of culture and tradition. Since the Centre opened eleven years ago sixty-eight countries, ranging from Australia to Zimbabwe, have sent students to the Centre for training. These overseas students are sponsored by their governments, home tanneries, United Nations agencies or the British Council.

As to the future change is certainly in the air. The staff of the Centre are developing distance learning material at first certificate level. This will probably replace the first year of the block-release course and thus cut down costs. A Master's degree will possibly be offered shortly in association with the University of Leicester chemistry department. The Centre plans to undertake more research and consultancy work as well as offering more short income-earning specialist courses.

The dreams of automated leathermaking become more of a reality every year as systems and plant are developed to remove manual labour. But, particularly, the micro-computer has opened up so many new possibilities in streamlined production from automated dye recipe production and chemical mixing to fully computer-controlled beamhouse and tanning operations. Additionally, the pressure to minimise sulphide and chrome usage and discharge in the effluent is bringing in a galaxy of new unhairing and tanning technology, not to mention the move towards water-based finishing systems to meet environment-protection legislation. It is an exciting period but it will demand a new type of leather technologist with new skills and a sensitive awareness of his environment.

GEORGE WILLIAM ODEY, CBE

George Odey was born in 1900 and educated at Faversham Grammar School and University College, London. Throughout his adult life he maintained an interest in education and an interest in tanning.

From 1922 to 1925 he was Assistant Secretary of the University of London Appointments Board. Then in 1925 he joined the firm of Barrow Hepburn, serving as Chairman of the Group from 1937 to 1974. During the Second World War he represented the Ministry of Supply in

Washington in connection with negotiations for the joint purchase of hides. He was similarly involved in negotiations with the South American countries over leather supplies to the United Kingdom. It was for this work that he was made a Commander of the British Empire in 1945.

From 1947 to 1950 he was MP for Howdenshire and from 1950 to 1955 the MP for Beverley, where he lived. In recognition of his public services as a Member of Parliament and as an East Riding County Councillor from 1964 to 1974, George Odey was made an Honorary Freeman of Beverley. He was also appointed Deputy Lieutenant of Humberside in 1977, was the Commodore of the House of Commons' Yacht Club in 1954, President of the International Tanners' Council from 1954 to 1967 and of the British Leather Federation in 1965.

George Odey was a leading member of the Worshipful Company of Leathersellers and Chairman of the Governors of the National Leather-sellers' College, Bermondsey. From the point of view of Nene College it was his influence and his support which eased the transfer of the Bermondsey College to Northampton and laid the foundation for the success of this move.

George Odey died on 16 October 1985 and is remembered by many of those associated with Nene not only for his vision but also for many quiet personal kindnesses.

SIR KENNETH NEWTON, Bt, OBE, TD

Sir Kenneth Newton was born on 4 June 1918 and succeeded his father as the 3rd Baronet. He was educated at Wellington College, Berkshire, and in 1936 joined the family firm, James Garnar and Sons, founded by his great-grandfather in Bermondsey, London. Then followed three tough years learning all there was to know about the practical side of making leather. In 1939 the Second World War intervened and Sir Kenneth served until 1945. He was in the Territorial Army with the British Expeditionary Force and was evacuated through Dunkirk. He then served as a Company Commander with the Eighth Army in the Desert Campaign. During the invasion of Sicily he commanded the amphibians known as 'DUKWS' – the first operation in which these vehicles were used. For his services Sir Kenneth was awarded the MBE. During the following campaign in Italy Sir Kenneth was promoted to Lieutenant-Colonel and was then made responsible for training RASC companies in amphibious warfare pre-paratory to the invasion of France in 1944. He ended the war with a posting to India in preparation for the attack in the Far East expected on Japan.

After the war James Garnar started to acquire other companies, and in

1981 the Group (which had become Garnar Scotblair Ltd) merged with Booth (International) Ltd to become Garnar Booth Ltd – at that time becoming what was probably the largest and most diverse leather-producing group in Europe.

Sir Kenneth (who was made a Director of the firm in 1942) became Managing Director in 1966 and Chairman in 1972. He was awarded the OBE for export achievement in 1970. He relinquished the role of Chief Executive for Garnar Booth Ltd in 1976 but remains Chairman of the Company. As such he is one of the industry's best-known elder statesmen.

His links with Northampton followed the acquisition of the local firm of Messrs Wilson and Tilt Ltd by Messrs Garnar Booth and these links have been strengthened by Sir Kenneth's involvement with Nene College. He is a Governor, a member of Court and Chairman of the Leather Industry Advisory Committee of the College. As such he has been a major (if not the major) driving force in the development of the National Leathersellers' Centre in Northampton since its opening in 1978. When the Leathersellers' College in Bermondsey was closed due to road-widening schemes planned for that part of London, Sir Kenneth (with the late George Odey) was responsible for persuading the Worshipful Company of Leathersellers that the activities previously carried out in Bermondsey should be transferred to Nene.

Sir Kenneth was President of the International Council of Tanners from 1972 to 1978; President of the British Leather Federation in 1968–9; he is a Liveryman and Member of the Court of Assistants, Leathersellers' Company (Master 1977–8) and of the Worshipful Company of Feltmakers (Master, 1983). Sir Kenneth is Chairman of the Board of Governors of Colfe School, Lewisham.

THE SUNLEY MANAGEMENT CENTRE
FORMERLY THE BLACKWOOD HODGE MANAGEMENT CENTRE

Sir William Shapland and Dr Tony Berry

The period following the end of the Second World War saw a major growth in the population and business activities of the town of Northampton and its surrounding area. Situated in the centre of the country with the building of the first motorway, the M1, and the establishment of Milton Keynes as one of the new towns, it attracted many new businesses both large and small. Many realised that this growth in business was also creating a need for trained personnel, particularly at mid-management and top management levels, in order to ensure the success of the new ventures. Two men in particular decided to do something about it.

The late Bernard Sunley, from small beginnings, established by the

1940s a fairly large building and construction business (he built over a hundred airfields for the RAF during the war). Following the end of the war he realised that there would be a boom in construction work all over the world because of the need to make good the ravages of war and to provide the infrastructure to support the improvement in living standards that would be demanded in all parts of the free world. He therefore set up a new company, under the name Blackwood Hodge, to operate in most parts of the free world and to hold franchises from manufacturers for the sale and servicing of heavy construction and mining equipment. He established the United Kingdom centre for that business in Northampton. By the late 1950s the business had grown very rapidly and was operating in more then thirty countries around the world. This growth created a tremendous demand for trained personnel and particularly trained managers, and to meet that demand Bernard Sunley decided to create a management training centre in Northamptonshire. To that end he purchased a large estate and mansion, known as Collingtree Grange, from one of the shoe-manufacturing families in Northampton. The plan was to set up a training school for the production of Blackwood Hodge managers. Unfortunately, the difficulty and cost of recruiting teaching personnel and of finding a leader for the organisation resulted in the deferment of the establishment of this training college and, on the untimely death of Bernard Sunley in 1964, it was abandoned.

The other man who saw the need for management training and education in Northamptonshire was Dr Eric Ogilvie. Under his direction Nene College expanded in the 1970s and he realised that it would be necessary to supplement the Faculty of Mathematics, Management and Business in the College with practical training in business management in a Management Centre. The only way that he could set up a Management Centre was to organise the financing of the physical facilities from the public sector and ensure that the operation of the Centre was self-supporting so that no part of the operation should be a financial burden on the Northamptonshire County Council Education Department. In the course of his searching for this finance he met William Shapland, who had succeeded the late Bernard Sunley as Chairman of the Blackwood Hodge Group of Companies and who was also a trustee of the Bernard Sunley Charitable Foundation set up by Bernard Sunley in 1960. The result was that the Charitable Foundation agreed to provide approximately £1.5 million to construct and equip a Management Centre to be operated as part of Nene College to provide management education and training on a commercial basis under the name the Blackwood Hodge Management Centre. The Centre was opened on 7 October 1981 and this represented the realisation of the dreams and ambitions of the late Bernard Sunley, a very successful business entrepreneur, and of Dr Eric Ogilvie, a very successful and farsighted educationalist.

The Centre was built to a high specification and was specially designed to provide the most up-to-date facilities for both residential and non-residential students. A two-storey residential wing provided thirty-two self-contained single study bedrooms. The main building contained the necessary lecture, syndicate and tutorial areas with fully equipped dining-room, kitchen, bar and lounge. The non-residential sector included seminar, syndicate and staff rooms and a high technology lecture theatre seating up to a hundred delegates. The Centre was located on a specially landscaped site within the Moulton Park Campus. The Centre operated as an integral part of the Faculty of Mathematics, Management and Business and control was exercised by the Dean of the Faculty, Dr Tony Wood, assisted by the Centre Director, Stan Thorley.

The first year saw a steady growth in the volume of business offering tailor-made courses, open seminars and Centre facility hire. At the end of eighteen months, the Centre had met its financial target and was making an operational surplus. This growth was sustained throughout the subsequent years with contracts from local businesses, the Manpower Services Commission, professional organisations and gradually the Centre began to attract interest from national organisations. Throughout these years, the Centre operated with a small nucleus of permanent staff and a larger circle of associates selected for their expertise in a particular field.

By mid-1985 it became clear that the Centre had reached its capacity and work commenced on a £250,000 extension that would increase the number of seminar rooms and administrative offices and add an information technology suite and a health and fitness centre. The cost of this work was financed by the Sunley Foundation. The extension was officially opened on 25 January 1986 by Sir Keith Joseph, Secretary of State for Education and Science, who came a second time to the College having officially opened the Centre on 19 March 1982 (following its opening for 'business' six months earlier).

The Management Centre has always been a part of the Faculty of Mathematics, Management and Business, and the Head of the Centre has always reported directly to the Dean of the Faculty. However, the Management Centre has always had a special place within the Faculty. Its magnificent facilities and services are not at all typical of higher education; the requirement to operate as a separate profit centre created unique pressures and requirements, not least of these being the need to operate the Centre 48 weeks of the year, with a core of academic staff working to nominal 36-week per year contracts. The meeting of financial targets by both facility hire staff and programme directors always involved goodwill and that extra commitment.

In 1985 certain major changes in personnel affected the Centre;

Dr Tony Wood was appointed Director of Luton College of Higher Education, his secretary Miss Amanda Yates became personal assistant to a local managing director, and Miss Katie Parkes, Administrative Manager, left the Centre to start a family. A new team was thus established. Dr Tony Berry, previously Assistant Dean, was appointed Dean of the Faculty and thus charged with the overall direction of the Management Centre; Mrs Sheila Plowright became the Dean's secretary, and Mrs Julie Welsby was appointed Administrative Manager. Continuity of operations was sustained through Stan Thorley as Centre Director and Peter Norris as Head of Management Development.

By this time in the life of the Centre, a considerable portfolio of clients had been established both in terms of facility hire customers and those organisations that had utilised management development programmes. The list included Alfred Dunhill, Audi Volkswagen, Avon Cosmetics, British Sugar Corporation, Carlsberg, Levi Strauss, Merseyside Police, Pianoforte Supplies, Robert Horne Group, Royal Pioneer Corps and Saab UK.

In terms of management programmes, the Centre was providing open courses to meet identified managerial needs, seminars to meet current organisational and managerial issues, programmes designed and run by the Centre's staff for a specific client, and joint ventures, many of the latter programmes involving in-company training. Initially in its life, the core team of lecturers based in the Centre specialised in human relations but progressively after 1985 greater use was made of the marketing, financial and computing expertise of Faculty staff.

Dr Michael Smith was appointed Head of Management Development in September 1988 to succeed Peter Norris. Dr Smith rapidly expanded the portfolio of management development programmes and the range of business services, also relying heavily on Faculty staff. The fruits of co-operation became evident in the identification of the Management Centre as the first local support centre for the MBA distance-learning programme operated by Henley Management College. This has provided a first-class staff development opportunity for all Faculty management staff and provided added impetus to the development of the Faculty's own MBA programme scheduled for 1989–90.

In the belief that a leading Management Centre must provide not only good management education and training provided by fully qualified teaching personnel, but also first-class living and catering facilities, the Centre has since its inception provided and maintained very high standards in the residential accommodation provided. In addition, it maintains kitchen and dining facilities under the direction of Monsieur Guy Pautrat, a French chef of the highest calibre, to ensure the serving of first-class meals both for residential and non-residential students at the Centre.

In the Dean's office, there is a Visitors' Book which has recorded those people from public and private sector who have visited, and contributed to the life of, the Centre. Even the most cursory turning of its pages reveals major figures in the worlds of education, commerce, public and political life, including His Royal Highness the Duke of Gloucester, the Earl Spencer, Air Marshal Sir John Sutton, the Earl of Dalkeith, Len Peach, Lord Boardman, Brenda Dean, Norman St John Stevas, Denis Healey, Shirley Williams and Adrian Cadbury. Many of these visitors were particularly associated with the Executive Lunchtime Seminars organised and run by the Centre, which have, since their inception, proved to be very popular events.

Nene College Northampton

BLACKWOOD HODGE
MANAGEMENT CENTRE

Official Opening

By
The Right Honourable Sir Keith Joseph Bt, MP
Secretary of State for Education and Science

Friday 19th March 1982 10.45 am

THE BLACKWOOD HODGE MANAGEMENT CENTRE

HISTORY OF DEVELOPMENT OF THE CENTRE

On the 15 April 1980, The Bernard Sunley Charitable Foundation announced that it was making one of the largest single donations ever made to an educational establishment in the United Kingdom. £1.7 million was being donated to Nene College, Northampton to establish a new centre for management education and training. The centre would fittingly be called the Blackwood Hodge Management Centre, thus linking it with the multi-national industrial organisation founded by the late Bernard Sunley in 1941.

The announcement was the outcome of enthusiastic collaboration between the Trustees of the Sunley Foundation, the Northamptonshire County Council and the Governors and staff of Nene College. Building commenced immediately, the foundation stone being laid by Mr William Shapland, FCA, the Chairman of the Foundation's Trustees and of Blackwood Hodge Limited. Now that the building is completed it provides the College with a purpose-built residential centre comprising study bedrooms, lecture rooms, syndicate rooms, tutorial and interview areas; computer, teletext and reprographic facilities; dining facilities, lounge and bar areas.

The Centre aims to:

create a range of courses and seminars which will help managers and supervisors to become more effective in their organisations and to stay abreast of the many changes — legislative, economic, technological and social — which influence the business environment;

work in close co-operation with organisations to devise exclusive programmes directed towards their individual needs;

provide an appropriate and extremely comfortable setting in which organisations can undertake their own training programmes.

In addition to the College Court and the Board of Governors, the Centre is guided in its development by its specially constituted Advisory Council which is comprised of people of national and international standing drawn from all types of private and public sector organisations.

THE BLACKWOOD HODGE MANAGEMENT CENTRE

ORDER OF PROCEEDINGS

At the Drama Theatre Park Campus

Welcome to Sir Keith Joseph and other Guests by
COUNCILLOR JACK MORRISH
CHAIRMAN OF NORTHAMPTONSHIRE EDUCATION COMMITTEE AND NENE COLLEGE BOARD OF GOVERNORS

A Short Address by
MR WILLIAM SHAPLAND FCA
CHAIRMAN OF TRUSTEES OF THE BERNARD SUNLEY CHARITABLE FOUNDATION

Introduction of Sir Keith Joseph by
MR M J HENLEY MA
COUNTY EDUCATION OFFICER

An Address by
THE RIGHT HONOURABLE SIR KEITH JOSEPH Bt MP
SECRETARY OF STATE FOR EDUCATION AND SCIENCE

Vote of Thanks to Sir Keith Joseph proposed by
MR D A WALMSLEY LL B
VICE CHAIRMAN, NENE COLLEGE BOARD OF GOVERNORS

Vote of Thanks to other Guests Proposed by
DR E OGILVIE B.Sc(Econ) M Ed FRSA
DIRECTOR, NENE COLLEGE

At the Blackwood Hodge Management Centre

Dedication of the Centre by
THE VERY REVEREND RANDOLPH WISE
DEAN OF PETERBOROUGH

Unveiling of a Plaque commemorating the Opening of the Centre by
THE RIGHT HONOURABLE SIR KEITH JOSEPH Bt MP

TOUR OF THE CENTRE

Prior to, and following, the proceedings at the Drama Theatre, the Northamptonshire Music Schools will provide a musical interlude.

After the ceremonies at the Centre, guests will be able to tour the premises from 12.15 to 1.00 pm and during the early afternoon.

THE BLACKWOOD HODGE MANAGEMENT CENTRE

BLACKWOOD HODGE MANAGEMENT CENTRE ADVISORY COUNCIL

W A Shapland Esq (Chairman)
M Abrahams Esq
L Baxter Esq MBE
N S Boggon Esq (Deputy Chairman)
Sir John Boyd CBE
M L Dove Esq
H Ford Esq
Dr J P A Frain
R S Garnett Esq MBE
P W Goodwin Esq
A J Greenwell Esq
Professor D R Harper CBE
B V C Harpur Esq
Professor P M Jackson
A Jauncey Esq

R P Jones Esq
E R Knapp Esq CBE
W C C Mackay Esq
H G Marrack Esq
J E Morrish Esq
Dr E Oglivie
D S Pyke Esq
B G Pearse Esq
L Teeman Esq OBE
S Thorley Esq
O Tynan Esq
A Van Beylen Esq
R D Williams Esq
Dr A J Wood

COUNTY EDUCATION OFFICER
M J Henley MA

DIRECTOR — NENE COLLEGE
Eric Ogilvie BSc(Econ) MEd PhD FRSA

DEPUTY DIRECTOR — NENE COLLEGE
J P A Frain MA MTech PhD MIEx

ASSISTANT DIRECTOR — NENE COLLEGE A W R Fox MA

SENIOR ADMINISTRATIVE OFFICER and
CLERK TO THE GOVERNORS — NENE COLLEGE
L C Skelton

BLACKWOOD HODGE MANAGEMENT CENTRE STAFF

DEAN
A J Wood BSc PhD FIMA

ACADEMIC STAFF

S Thorley MA MEd FBPsS MBIM (Director of Studies)
S B Barnes Dip Phys Ed DMS
P J Brown B Met DMS MBIM
A C Cozens FMS MIIM MBIM
H Critchell FMS MIIM MBIM DMS
B L Jongman Cert Ed

P W Norris MSc FIPM
D W Pickton MA Dip CAM Dip M G Inst M
B Read MSc MIPM
Mrs V Rowland BSc(Econ) MSc MIPM
L C Saward BSc PhD
C C Suter BTech DipM MInstM MABE AIPM MBIM

Teaching Associates currently involved in programmes include:

H R Ballantyne
D M Bradshaw
A P Broadway
I C Callard
R P Entwistle
Mrs D Hayes

M R Hermann
I Spiby
Mrs N Webb
L Williams
B Vickers

Client Liaison Officer Mrs P Jones BA MSc   *Press Officer* R Hill Adv Dip Ed

ROBERT HORNE FELLOWS

W Sirs JP
G Turner

W Goldsmith
Professor B Taylor

NON TEACHING STAFF

Miss K R Parkes MHCIMA Cert Ed (Administrative Manager)
Mr E Brown
Mrs J Brown
Mrs S Collins
Mrs A Cox
Mrs A Dickens
Mr A Hancock
Mrs E Hever

Mrs J Lainchbury
Mrs S Laste
Mrs R Moghadam
Mr J Parbery
Mrs M Redmond
Mrs W Stevens
Miss A J Yates BA

ARCHITECTS Northamptonshire County Council
Director of Land and Buildings John Gammans AA Dipl Dip TP
Head of Building A J Ede ARIBA
Project Architect A J Healey BA(Arch) RIBA
Clerk of Works P Osborne

CONTRACTORS
Main Contractor Bernard Sunley and Sons Ltd
Contracts Manager A E Swain
Site Agents K Dickens, P Holding

Catering by CAS International Catering Limited with a team
headed by L Dabbs, G Pautrat, Mrs M Wright

Throughout its life the Centre has been aided and supported by its Advisory Council under the chairmanship of Sir William Shapland. The members of the Council are a mixture of senior members of key public authorities together with managing directors or their representatives from key major local companies. At times Council meetings have been stormy, involving the clash of public and private sector cultures. Out of the work of the Advisory Council has come tremendous support for the Centre and its work, not only in the form of advice and participation in management programmes but also in hard financial sponsorship.

The operation of the Centre under the name Blackwood Hodge has resulted in some problems because the name conflicts with the name of the Company, which is still operating in the area. It was therefore decided early in 1989 that as the Management Centre together with Nene College moves towards independence and corporate status, that the name of the Centre should be changed to 'The Sunley Management Centre', thus associating the Centre with the successful entrepreneur who had the dream of a Management Centre in Northampton forty years ago.

SIR WILLIAM SHAPLAND, LLD, FCA

An address by the Public Orator of Leicester University (Professor A. A. Dashwood) on the occasion of the award of the Honorary Degree of Doctor of Laws to Sir William Shapland on 8 July 1985

For more than twenty years Sir William Shapland presided over one of our country's most successful businesses. He has also been a dispenser of charitable funds on a prodigious scale for whose enlightened patronage Town and Gown in Northampton have reason to be grateful.

William Shapland joined the accountants, Allan Charlesworth & Co., in 1929 as the office boy. He had been the second choice for the job but the preferred candidate turned it down. According to Machiavelli, the two ingredients of greatness are *fortuna* (luck) and *virtu* (ability). If luck smiled on young William's entry into the firm, a dazzling display of ability ensured his rise within it. He qualified initially as an Incorporated Accountant (a branch of the profession accessible, then, to a young man without private means) and was placed first in the final examinations of 1935. Now a manager in the firm, he was recognised as a contender for a partnership; but for this he would have to requalify as a Chartered Accountant. Nothing daunted, he submitted to a second set of articles and examinations, and in 1946 repeated the trick of coming top in his finals. The same year he became a partner in Allan Charlesworth.

However, scaling the heights of his profession was not enough for Sir William. In 1955 he retired from Allan Charlesworth and embarked on a new career in business as deputy to his friend and former client, Bernard

Sunley. Between them they were responsible for bringing to the United Kingdom the technology to found an industry in heavy earth-moving equipment. Sir William was Managing Director of the Bernard Sunley Group from 1964 to 1968 and chairman of the flagship company, Blackwood Hodge, from 1964 to 1983. Under his tutelage Blackwood Hodge grew from its base in Northampton into the world's biggest company in the business of selling and servicing earth-moving equipment, with operations in twenty-nine countries. Other interests of the Group included building and real estate development. A more unusual venture, a source of real pleasure to Sir William, but less profit, was the creation of a ski resort, Isola 2000, in the French Alps.

The prosperity of their business offered Bernard Sunley and William Shapland an opportunity for munificence they were not slow to exploit. The Bernard Sunley Charitable Foundation has an endowment which enables it to dispose of some £2.5 million each year. Sir William has been a Trustee of the Foundation since 1960, and in his retirement it enjoys his undivided attention. His policy is to support large-scale building projects, mainly for the purposes of education and medical research.

For those present here the Blackwood Hodge Management Centre at Nene College will surely rank as the most excellent gift of Sir William's charity. The Centre was built by the Bernard Sunley Charitable Foundation at a cost of £1.8 million; and through the generosity of the Foundation, it is currently being extended. Sir William's aim was to ensure the provision in the Northampton area of modern and flexible education for management at all levels. Four years after it opened its doors not only has the Centre spaciously achieved that aim but – an object lesson to its customers – it has begun to operate at a profit. As Chairman of the Centre's Advisory Council Sir William has been a party to that spectacular success.

Sir William was knighted in 1982 and has received many other honours. For his services to medicine he was made Honorary FRCS in 1978. He was elected a Waynflete Fellow of Magdalen College, Oxford, in 1982 and University College, Buckingham, awarded him an Honorary DSc last year. Today it is our turn to honour him as a creator of wealth who has also shown that he understands how wealth may be used creatively.

THE TIMKEN BUSINESS AND INNOVATION CENTRE

Mike Furminger

The centre, the brain child of Dr Eric Ogilvie, Director of Nene College, was born out of the 'Pre Launch Event' on 11 March 1986. This led to plans for a practical centre being compiled by Andrew Castley, at that time the college's project leader. The Northamptonshire Enterprise Agency (through David Mann) acted as the development agent.

Start of work on site, September 1987;
Michael Furminger started as the Director of the Centre, 1 January 1988;
Building hand over, 1 July 1988;
Building full, October 1988;
Formal opening, 1 November 1988, by Mr Jack Timken, President of the Timken International Fund.

The Timken Business and Innovation Centre is an exciting new development for Nene College in keeping with the growing size and status of the College. The Centre has 6,300 sq. ft of space (580 sq.m.) and has been specifically designed to meet the needs of small or new starter businesses and to assist their rapid growth. These new knowledge-based businesses will be able to call upon the full range of services in the Centre as well as those services of Nene College that they may require. This £400,000 Centre was partially funded by donations from the Timken International Fund through its Nene Foundation.

The Centre, opened in July 1988, is located in an attractive green-field site, the Park Campus of Nene College, Northampton. On the same Nene College site the Northamptonshire Enterprise Agency have constructed five business starter units, each of approximately 2,000 sq.ft (610 sq.m), which form the first phase of the Northamptonshire Enterprise Park.

The Management Centre, Nene Innovation, has the following functions;

(1) to encourage the growth of new start up businesses, particularly in knowledge-based areas, for example – science, engineering and technology;
(2) provide a physical focal point for enterprises with common needs;
(3) to operate the Northamptonshire Centre for Technology Transfer within regional, national and European networks;
(4) to provide resources for training in the region and an access point for assistance in all aspects necessary for successful business development.

A range of common services is provided by Nene Innovation including:
● Reception telephone answering service;
● Secretarial, word processing and reprographic facilities;
● Fax, telex;
● A local area network capable of linking individual units to the Centre's word processing and computer system and to the College's central computer services;
● Main services of heat, light, electricity and telephone.

The Centre also provides an academic area of some 560 sq.ft (52 sq.m), adjacent to this are two seminar rooms of 140 sq.ft each (13 sq.m). Linking the three areas together is the coffee area, which is available for informal meetings. The businesses within the Centre have first priority on the use of these facilities but they are available for general hire.

The Centre Director is based in an open plan office along with other support staff. The shared reception service provides the first contact in both the business and the management of the Centre. The reception service intercepts telephone calls in the appropriate company's name if required.

The Centre also has a large exhibition area of approximately 600 sq.ft (56 sq.m), situated near the entrance to the building so that visitors to the centre can look at product displays before meeting their contacts. The Centre also has a shared toilet and cloakroom area, including a toilet for the disabled.

Use of specialist equipment located within the Centre or Nene College may be contracted separately and, if desirable, may be temporarily moved into the units. The College wish to encourage this practice since the use of this equipment in a commercial environment provides a valuable educational experience for vocationally orientated students.

The creation of employment and wealth are the main objectives of Nene Innovation. Nene Innovation is in a unique position to succeed as it operates within a purpose-built architect planned Centre with the full resourced support of Nene College, a major higher education institution.

The Centre's aim is to bring together all the technological resources of the area to provide a spawning ground for new businesses. It acts as a point of contact for businessmen, industrialists, academics and experts in all fields. The informal environment of the Centre encourages the exchange of views and the development of innovative ideas. Nene Innovation intends to link the skills of Nene College and all the participating members in the Timken Business and Innovation Centre, to create a new force in the economy of the region into the next decade and beyond.

WARD J. TIMKEN

Jack Timken joined the Timken Company as a Project Manager in 1968. In 1977 he was named Director (Corporate Development) and in 1985 Director (Human Resources Development). He is a native of Canton, USA, and a graduate of the University of Arizona (1966). He undertook the programme for Management Development at Harvard (1977) and was Sloan Fellow at the Stanford Graduate School of Business in 1984-85. He is President of the Timken Company Charitable Trust and serves on the governing bodies of a number of foundations which support civic, educational and charitable causes.

THE CHIROPODY CENTRE

Linda Merriman

The Northampton School of Chiropody is a joint venture between Nene College and Northampton Health Authority. The establishment of such a school was first proposed in 1980. However, it was 1985 before the school took its first students. From the outset the school was seen as differing from other schools of chiropody. Unlike the majority of the others, which were solely housed in educational premises, the educational content of the Northampton course is taught at Nene College and the clinical content at the General Hospital. As a result the students benefit from both environments.

Initially, funding for a purpose-built school was unavailable so the school has been housed in temporary buildings. A Nissen hut at the General Hospital, previously a surgical recovery ward, was converted into clinical units. These units are being used by the students to treat patients, an essential part of the course. Northampton Health Authority met the cost of equipping the converted ward. The educational part of the course is housed in temporary buildings at Park Campus, Nene College.

The temporary clinical building was opened in November 1985 by Mr Peter Brooke, at that time Minister of State for Higher Education. At the opening a public appeal was launched for monies to build a permanent clinical base for the school in the grounds of the General Hospital since the temporary building had a very short life-span, it was realised that if the school were to continue to receive validation it would have to replace this building. The 'Happy Feet Appeal' was launched, a fund raiser to the appeal appointed, and a planning group established.

The school offers a three-year full-time course leading to state registration. All students have to be 18 years of age and require five passes at GCSE and two at 'A' level. Mature students may be accepted with alternative qualifications.

The school has a staff of five full-time lecturers and one senior clinical teacher. A number of visiting lecturers also contribute to the course. These include sociologists, psychologists, pharmacists, consultants and general practitioners.

During the three years students study a range of subjects including medicine, surgery, pathology, physiology, anatomy, pharmacology as well as podology. The school has established links with Leicester Medical School where first-year students attend dissection classes. The medical school also provides external examiners to the course. At the end of each year students must successfully pass professional examinations.

During their training the students also undertake the assessment and treatment of a wide range of chiropodial conditions. The school has introduced a number of innovative practices into the area of clinical education. Students not only gain their clinical experience within the schools clinical buildings but also on placement in local and distant health authorities. The use of such industrial experience has been found to be very beneficial. The use of placements also provides a forum for ongoing discussions between the producers and the employers.

Since the school opened in 1985 over 4,000 treatments have been provided by the students in the school's clinic. Anyone may apply for treatment, which is provided free of charge. Local doctors and consultants refer a large number of patients. Patients vary from a few months to over 90 years of age. Students undertake a detailed assessment of the patient before providing the necessary treatment.

In the clinical field the school has pioneered work in the areas of paediatrics, sports injuries and surgery. In the paediatric field students go into schools, within the town, to screen school children for potential foot problems. Children found to have a problem are referred to the schools' clinic for treatment. Sports injury patients from the hospital are often referred to the clinic for treatment. The school has helped in the treatment of many of the country's top athletes, including Olympic hopefuls. As regards surgery the school was the first to become involved in ambulatory foot surgery, which enables the correction of toe deformities, etc. These deformities have led in the past to recurring problems. As this surgery is undertaken under local anaesthetic it is both inexpensive and of less risk to the patient.

The original student intake was eighteen students per year. In 1986 this rose to twenty-five per annum. The school can now cater for seventy-five full-time students. The first output of students qualified in 1988 with a 100 per cent pass rate. On qualification, students may seek posts in the NHS, in private practice or in industry. All the first output of students were successful in gaining posts.

During its relatively short life the school has been judged to have a very innovative and enterprising approach to its curriculum. This has resulted in the following comment from the Chiropodist Board, the validating body for the school: 'This school is an examplar of good practices which could be a model for other schools of chiropody, both new and long established.' The school was also a runner-up in a national competition, run by the Forward Trust Group, for innovation in management.

In April 1989 the school will move into a purpose-built building in the grounds of the General Hospital. The building will be equipped for a student intake of thirty to thirty-five students per year. Besides the clinical units the school will have consultation rooms, a gait analysis area and tutorial room. Many thanks have to go to the local and regional Health Authorities for the support they have given in providing a permanent building for the school.

The fund raisers and the students have organised many events to raise monies for the building. These events have included the auctioning of Daley Thompson's running shoes and Antoinette Sibley's ballet shoes. Princess Margaret, the Countess of Snowdon, attended a gala performance of *Coppelia*, the proceeds of which went to the school's 'Happy Feet' Appeal.

With the future of the school guaranteed with the advent of the new building the school can now look to the future. It is hoped to achieve the development of a pre-registration degree in chiropody within the next five years. It is also the aim of the school to establish itself as a research base.

POSTSCRIPT: PROPOSALS FOR A NATIONAL CENTRE FOR THE STUDY OF ABLE AND TALENTED CHILDREN

David Walmsley

Benjamin Franklin once said: 'Genius without Education is like silver left in the mine'. One of the major concerns of Eric Ogilvie has always been the problem of identifying and subsequently making provision for the able or talented child. He always felt that it was easier to recognise the disadvantage suffered by the handicapped child (since this often had visible physical and mental signs to high-light the problem which could then be tackled) than to do the same for the gifted child and to make arrangements for such a child to develop within a Local Education Authority system where a teacher might be dealing with perhaps thirty children in any given primary school class.

In 1975 Macmillan published as part of their Schools Council Research Studies a book by Dr Ogilvie entitled *Gifted Children in Primary Schools,* which described an enquiry he conducted in 1970–1 into the possibilities of producing special teaching material for individual able children of primary age within the normal class structure.

Out of the study came the idea of producing, with the co-operation of Northamptonshire teachers (especially a group of forward-looking head teachers) packaged lesson kits. The aim was to help a child with a particular aptitude in a subject to be enabled to forge ahead (with teacher support but not necessarily constant teacher supervision) on a guided 'D-I-Y' basis to explore many avenues in his or her special subject (even occasionally to the level of the pupil knowing as much as the class teacher in one area of knowledge).

Seventeen kits were prepared, these dealt with mathematics, environment and science, history and English studies. The kits were called 'SCCEP' after the name of the research project from which they had originated, namely the 'Schools' Council Curriculum Enrichment Project'. The class work was reinforced and consolidated by a Saturday morning club held at Nene College. These sessions further involved the staff there. The whole project was financed through a £35,000 grant from the Schools Council. Support came from the local authority who saw this approach to the gifted child as a valuable way to enrich the normal school curriculum within budgetary constraints.

Each SCCEP was designed to occupy a child for at least four hours every week of a term but the material was open-ended so that if need be more time could be devoted to further study if the child (or the supporting teacher) so desired.

George Ilsley (who teaches earth science at the College) once described how a SCCEP for which he was responsible was created. First of all, a definite subject and content area was selected; then the sequence of activities was drawn up and constructed. Throughout the closest contact was maintained with two practising teachers to ensure that everything contained in the pack was likely to succeed in arousing and using the child's own curiosity and interest.

For instance, SCCEP Number Two deals with the Earth in the form of a story where a visitor from space is shown the earth's structure by a couple of children. This work was designed for a gifted seven year old and tackled the understanding of sedimentary rocks with suggested experiments for the young geologist to undertake on his or her own. Here is a sample of the script:

Calcium carbonate trickles between the grains of sand and sticks the particles together in sandstone. Some sandstones have other minerals for their cement. The scientist calls this changing of sands into sandstones 'diagnosis'. On Worksheet 7 in Book 4 you will see what is called a flow chart for the making or formation of all the rocks formed from a sediment and called the sedimentary rocks.

Heady stuff for a seven year old – even a gifted one – but the evidence was that given the appropriate circumstances this sort of challenge worked. Of course it is difficult to identify a child specifically gifted in a particular subject or skill and educational tests of such things as reading ability, intelligence and study skills can only indicate 'possibilities'. In the final analysis the good class teacher's informed and instructive judgement played a large part in the matching of a SCCEP to a child.

The good class teacher with the problem of some one who does not fit into the average pattern will want to do something about it. Roy Hill who was at one time on the staff at Nene illustrated this from the musical world: 'Think how difficult it must be for the class teacher in a Middle School teaching a few happy folk songs to a class and all the time knowing that another Mark van der Weill* is sitting on the back row thinking of Mozart's Clarinet Concerto'.

All this forms a background to a paper presented to the final meeting of the outgoing Board of Governors of Nene College on the 14 March 1989, which may in some way be termed the legacy of Dr Ogilvie. This paper, prepared by John Welch (the Director of the National Association of Gifted Children) and David George (the Chairman of the National Association for Curriculum Extension and Enrichment), stated that these two organisations had decided to come together to form a charitable foundation to be based at Nene College with seven aims namely:

(1) to be the acknowledged UK champion of the need to develop child potential;
(2) to be the UK centre for information on development of child potential;
(3) to be the UK centre for research into development of child potential;
(4) to be the UK centre of expertise in the training of teachers to develop child potential;
(5) to be the leading UK developer and supplier of curriculum enrichment materials;
(6) to provide a practical environment for children; where their abilities and potential are recognised and fostered;
(7) to be the leading UK support group for the families of able and talented children.

Such a National Centre would offer:

— location in a quality educational establishment;
— comparatively central UK location with good communciations;
— shared research facilities;
— shared database facilities;
— shared administration facilities;
— a focal point for other organisations and individuals with similar aims and interests;
— a focal point for maximising publicity and public awareness.

The two founding organisations intend to draft a constitution to govern the overall direction management and funding of the proposed centre, to

* A Northampton boy now principal clarinetist with a major orchestra.

which end the sum of £30,000 has been offered by the computer company, Digital.

So far much of the work done in this field has been initiated by enthusiastic individuals and small groups or associations across the country. The time is ripe for concerted action to increase awareness of the need, to improve materials and curricula and to support teachers and parents. A centre that co-ordinates research and study would become the focal point of such action.

The emblem of the Nene College Students' Union

9 Memories of the Student Bodies

John West, Tony Rounthwaite and David Walmsley

The earliest record of students forming an association is in 1892 when the science students joined together. Meetings were of a learned nature, with lectures and intellectual soirées, plus social events of a refined nature. How long this group persisted is not known, but it is interesting that its formation should coincide with the arrival of Swaysland on the staff.

Blakeman was a great believer in a students' association, and did all he could to encourage one. By 1918 it had blossomed again and dances, concerts and hockey and tennis matches were arranged. There was also a flourishing Students' Christian Union within the Association. The Technical Committee grew tired of being badgered for grants by Blakeman and in 1923 made an annual grant of £50, on the understanding that the students would make a subscription of one shilling a year themselves. This was done. Later the shilling a year subscription was incorporated in the course fee. A Students' Council was elected to organise activities. This burst of activity lasted until 1927, when there was a break until the Association regrouped in St George's Avenue in 1932.

NORTHAMPTON COLLEGE OF TECHNOLOGY STUDENTS' ASSOCIATION *(John West)*

After the drab sulphur-ridden atmosphere of the old Technical School on Abington Square there was a blossoming of the local corporate spirit amongst students. A pride in their new home, and a sense of great days to come, inspired their thinking and prompted some of them to band together to do those things which they could not do as individuals.

It must be said that a great part of that thinking was due to the encouragement and challenge of John Blakeman himself, who always wanted the students to have their own association, and to run it themselves with the minimum of supervision from staff or the Education Committee. At the inaugural meeting of the Association in 1932, he said

'By the influence that the members can exert, the whole face of the life of Northampton can be changed.' Those who have seen students grow and take their part in the life of the town can bear witness to how sure was his vision, for it is impossible to be part of the town today without constantly meeting old students and friends of those early days who have become part of the very fabric of Northampton.

The aims and objects of the Association were:

(a) to develop the corporate life of the College and to promote good fellowship amongst the students;
(b) to organise and conduct students' activities of a social, athletic and cultural nature;
(c) to represent all the students of the College in all matters affecting their interests;
(d) to initiate and foster any project which will maintain or raise the status of the College.

How well these aims were achieved would have been readily visible to anyone taking part in the Commonwealth Week activities, held every year in November. Special events were arranged for every night, including a Gala Dance at the old Salon-de-Danse, and the week culminated in church services on the Sunday afternoon. These were held at All Saints' Church and at College Street, with officers of the Association taking part.

A tremendous amount of work was done week in and week out by a dedicated band of workers and clubs were formed within the Association for particular purposes. In the field of sports, football was very popular and at one time the College had a team in three of the divisions in the Town League. In 1951 the minor team of under-17s won the Town League Minor Cup.

The Cricket Club was formed in 1945 and after two or three years gained the Division 2 championship and promotion to Division 1. In their Report for 1952-3, they concluded with these words, 'We pride ourselves on our team spirit, and we arrive at this by mixing together socially during both winter and summer'.

A Hockey Club was formed in 1951, and finished second in their division in that first year, whilst in 1953 the Tennis Club won both the Men's Doubles and the Ladies' Doubles in Division 3 of the Northampton Lawn Tennis League. All of these activities were possible because such good playing fields had been provided by the foresight of those who planned the College building.

In fact, an excellent rapport was sustained between the Association and the Education Committee, mainly due to the encouragement and approachability of Mr. H. C. Perrin, then County Borough Education Secretary, and his Deputy (and ultimate successor), Mr. H. A. Skerrett.

They were always ready to support and encourage the aims and aspirations of the Officers and Committees of the Association through whom they provided good and sensible facilities for students, which enhanced the reputation of the College.

The Clubrooms were built and decorated by the students, with the help of a loan from the Education Committee, subsequently repaid in full within a few years, and within the rooms there were ample facilities available for all tastes. Table tennis was very popular and the College team was top of their section in the Northampton Table Tennis League in 1950.

Every Friday night, students would gather to listen to the Nene Valley Jazz Club, the only one in the town playing genuine improvised jazz, with no written music apart from piano chords. They became well-known in other districts, playing in such places as Kettering, Wellingborough and Bedford.

There were thriving clubs for those interested in chess, debating, classical music, literature and drama. The Drama Club had many successes in their productions, including *Mr Pim Passes By, Tony Draws a Horse, Kind Lady*, and a fine colourful production of *Jane Eyre*. Their greatest success was probably *Pygmalion*, which was played to capacity houses, and earned the commendation of the local press when a scene from the play appeared on the front page of the *Northampton Independent* above a similar photograph from the Repertory Theatre's production of that week, linking the two together as part of Northampton's theatrical talent. An active Christian Union met at the YMCA in Abington Street on Sunday mornings where John Blakeman was a regular attender.

The Clubrooms were in constant use and, even during the War years and the 'black-out', activity was maintained. A buffet was always available from 8.30 to 10 pm, with hot and cold beverages and snacks on sale. This service was continued throughout the 'rationing' period, when strict control and accountability had to be observed to comply with Government requirements. The Annual Commemoration Supper evolved from a sausage and mash meal to something much grander with speeches and visitors from the civic life of the town.

A part of the proceedings at Speech Day was always reserved for a full and comprehensive report from the General Secretary, and this usually received commendation from the visiting speaker who invariably expressed amazement at the width of activities generated by the students themselves.

For many years a group was formed to take place in the Annual 'Cycle' (sic) Parade and Carnival, and lorries were decorated in many weird and wonderful ways with themes as yet undreamt of! One remembers the year when around ten students carried large cardboard packing cases decorated to resemble heavy loads, bearing such descriptions as 'Education', 'Transport', 'Libraries' and other rate-hungry requirements. At the head of the procession which staggered through the whole of the parade route was a frock-coated 'councillor' complete with whip, goading on the over-burdened ratepayers of the Borough. Councillor Fred Tompkins (himself partly responsible for the setting of the rate) was so amused by this entry that he requested that a special prize of 7/6d. be given to the College group.

At an early stage of this renaissance of student pride it was felt that a College badge would be appropriate and the Borough Coat of Arms was used, (with permission), and the Students' motto replaced the usual 'Castell Fortior Concordia'. The motto was 'Omnia Vincit Juventus', which despite its doubtful Latin was meant to say 'Youth Conquers All'. The College Song contained those words (the Latin) as a sort of two-line chorus. The opening words, 'The firmer step, the wider views, mark the way for me and you,' were hardly Laureate quality but were sung with rare verve at the slightest provocation to the tune 'Gaudeamus Igitur'.

During the War years various groups were evacuated to Northampton and the Kilburn Grammar School were settled in the area. The Engineering Cadets were a new arrival at the College and they were welcomed into the Association's activities, although there was a little unnecessary friction at first. Friendships were made and maintained, and outings and visits were opened to all.

The Engineering Cadets, under the command of Major Haig, organised their own Concert Party with the professional assistance of Myer and Sidney Cipin (later well-known in Northampton as cinema proprietors). Known as 'The Norteks', the personnel of this group changed as army postings dictated but it was well known at the time for its robust humour and for the 'Will Hay' schoolmaster sketches the Cipin brothers wrote for it.

After the war with the withdrawal of many of the original founders who had been imbued with the Blakeman spirit, the ethos of the Association changed slowly and lost some of its original ideas. As the buildings were enlarged and the intake of students became greater year by year, the Association eventually became a College body known as the Students' Union, and operated under paid staff supervision.

Nevertheless, it had been a glorious two or three decades with so many students gaining confidence in their abilities, not simply from the teaching side, but from the fact that they had been trusted to run their own affairs, which they did with success and confidence. This stood many of them in good stead as they took their places in commerce and industry in the town and further afield.

*   *   *

45 Park Campus, Nene College

46 The opening of Nene College on 14 October 1975 by Lord Crowther-Hunt, Minister of State for Further and Higher Education. *Front row (left to right):*Lord Crowther-Hunt, County Councillor Mrs Dora Oxenham and Dr Eric Ogilvie; *behind:* The Mayor (County Councillor and Borough Councillor John Gardner), the Chairman of the Northamptonshire County Council (County Councillor R. E. Warwick) and the first President of Nene College Students' Union (Peter Hallam)

47 George Odey, CBE

48 Sir Kenneth Newton, Bt, OBE, TD

49 The opening of the Leathersellers' Centre on 26 May 1978. *Left to right*: The Mayor (David Walmsley), Lt. Col. J. Chandos-Pole (the Lord Lieutenant), Sir Kenneth Newton (Master of the Worshipful Company of Leathersellers) and HRH Prince Michael of Kent

50 Conversation group on the occasion of the Opening of the Leathersellers' Centre on 26 May 1978. *Left to right*: HRH Prince Michael of Kent, the Mayor (David Walmsley), Clement Davenport (Clerk to the Worshipful Company of Leathersellers), Jeffery Greenwell (Chief Executive, Northamptonshire County Council), Alan Parkhouse (Town Clerk and Chief Executive, Northampton Borough), John Gammans (County Architect, Northamptonshire County Council) and Revd John Searle (Mayor's Chaplain)

51 College of Further Education, Booth Lane, Northampton

52 Discussing Plans for the Blackwood Hodge Management Centre, *Left to right*: Dr Eric Ogilvie, Sir William Shapland and John Gammans (County Architect, Northamptonshire County Council)

53 The Opening of the Blackwood Hodge Management Centre on 19 March 1982 by the Rt Hon. Sir Keith Joseph, Bt, MP (Secretary of State for Education and Science). *In front*: Sir Keith Joseph and Dr Tony Wood; *behind to the left*: A. W. R. Fox

54 The Nene Foundation Trustees in 1978: Front row: (left to right) J. F. Thorpe, Mrs. J. Jackson-Stops, JP, The Rt Hon. the Earl Spencer, MVO, DL, The Rt Hon. the Viscount Dilhorne, PC (Chairman of the Trustees), S. F. Bennett, CBE, JP, Mrs T. G. Darby, JP, and R. E. Farren (Secretary); Back row: D. A. Walmsley, J. Mears (Mayor of Daventry), W. G. S. Edwards, M. Aldridge (Mayor of Northampton), Councillor John Poole, OBE (Chairman of the Northamptonshire County Council) and P. J. Scott (Assistant Secretary)

55 On 30 October 1975 Daniel McQuillan (aged 10) attended the official opening of the new Computer Centre at Nene College, Northampton. He demonstrated how the ICL 2903 educational system (purchased as a result of a £52,000 grant from the Nene Foundation) worked to Mr E. R. Knapp, Managing Director, Timken Europe.

56 The opening of the Timken Business and Innovation Centre on 1 November 1988, Joy Timken and Jack Timken unveil a commemorative plaque

57 The Degree Ceremony in the Derngate Centre, Northampton on Monday 13 July 1987. Geoffrey Otley (far side of stage) is directing the graduands coming forward to the Vice-Chancellor of Leicester University (Sir Maurice Shock, MA).

58 Members of the Formation Committee. *From the top of the stairs down*: Dr Eric Ogilvie, Geoffrey Otley, Tony G. Stoughton-Harris, Michael L. Dove (Chairman), Paul Southworth and Gina Ogden

59 Some of our contributors. *Front row:* Maurice Wilson and Tony Berry; *Back row:* Ron Smith, David George, Gwynneth Hood, Derek Brooks, Alan Riley and Richard Fox

Perhaps the story of the Association can best be summed up in the foreword to the 1952–53 Handbook, written by John West who was the General Secretary from 1937 to 1945.

What we have been able to give in the past days has been more than counterbalanced, always, by what we have received, and right at the outset I would like to suggest that the future of this Association is secure if those who seek to lead it will realise the tremendous opportunities of service which offer themselves in the organisation and control of such a body.

The mere history of the Association as I know it would do little to inspire or help those who are concerned for its welfare today. Whilst we may remember, perhaps a little sentimentally, the 'good old days' of building the clubrooms, painting them (and ourselves), and even the sausage and mash suppers, we realise these are simply events which have taken their place in the scheme of things, and may be classified as history, tradition, or what you will.

With a constantly changing personnel, every cycle of three or four years will see its own particular tradition, and will write its own particular story in the history-book of the Association. It will be enough if every page in that book contains as its sub-heading 'Service to others'.

The pages of this booklet will show that the Students' Association is becoming strong again and is seeking to live up to the faith and vision of its early days. The interruption of a world war has slowed down the pace of development but, from all the signs, has killed nothing.

Get into the work of the Association – it will be the better for your help – and then as you move to other spheres of interest later on, you will be able to look back on your service to your fellow students and be thankful for what it has given you.

* * *

Probably the criticism which could be levelled at the old Student Association was that it could be somewhat parochial in its outlook. However, this was inevitable when the majority of students at the old College of Technology were drawn from Northampton. When the ratio between local students and non-local students moved towards 50 : 50 – and when many students became full-time residential students then a change was inevitable. Today's Students' Union is much more of a 'business organisation' as well as reflecting the political views of young people on both local and national issues in a way that the old Student Association did not. Though even before 1975 the members of the old Student Association could be 'roused'. One can recall an occasion in the days when Alderman Fred Tollit was chairman of the Northampton County Borough Education Committee. Fred Tollit was known for driving a very old, very small car, very slowly down the road. He came to address the Students Association on an educational issue where certain decisions had been taken which had not pleased the student body. When he left the meeting he found that the four wheels of his car had been removed. The car was propped up on bricks and the wheels and their retaining nuts were neatly laid out on the ground alongside the car axles. Perhaps the reason why wrath from on high did not descend on the Student Association at that time had much to do with the fact that Alderman Tollit's own son, Michael, was an architectural student and perhaps one of his main contributions to student life were the ideas behind the unusual and striking design of the Student Building at the Avenue Campus now known as the Mandela Building.

NENE COLLEGE STUDENTS' UNION, 1975-89 *(Tony Rounthwaite)*

When the College of Technology, the Art College and the College of Education merged, three very different Students' Unions merged. The Art College students had run a small shop to provide materials at cost price to their members and operated a small common room. The College of Technology students had, over the years, organised social events which had raised funding, which initially enabled a small hut-type building to be the home of such events and later a more substantial brick-built club house. The early events featured relatively unknown groups which later became internationally famous, such as the Beatles. A small bar was included in that building known as the 18-plus Club. The College of Education Students' Union was based in the main building at the Boughton Green Road site and although a purpose-built Students' Union was top of the building programme in 1975, it became a more remote prospect over the years. In the year of merger the College of Education Students' Union had a full-time Sabbatical President, Peter Hallam, and he steered meetings of the various student bodies together to provide a joint constitution for a College with two very different sites.

The building at St George's Avenue had a full-time administrator – Ken Lewis – employed by the College with various other College staff providing administrative back-up. It was agreed that the new Students' Union would require three full-time student officers but that all staff working for the students would be employed by an autonomous Students' Union.

Ken Lewis left but no administrative continuity was provided for the first year of the new Students' Union. During this time it was recognised that a full-time officer would be required to run the trading side of the student activities and to provide continuity of advice to successive elected student officers. Consequently in May 1976 a post of Administrative Officer was widely advertised and Tony Rounthwaite was selected out of approximately ninety applicants at an interview in early July.

The whole of the administrative, financial and organisational side of the Students' Union required attention. There had been no adequate budgeting and steps were taken to introduce financial systems. A Secretary and an Accounts Clerk were appointed and staff contracts incorporating Local Authority conditions of service were implemented.

The building was dirty and neglected and a programme of alterations and improvements was commenced. Over the years plans to extend it were drawn up and the first phase was completed in 1980-1. This included new toilets, office space, a games area and improved bar storage space. Over the period from 1976 to 1989 the turnover of the Students' Union increased from about £50,000 to £250,000 on staffing hours broadly the same. Most of the staff employed have been part-time and only work in term-time, thus ensuring that service is maximised for the student body, whilst costs are limited.

The Students' Union provides many extra-curricular activities and services in ways directly responsible to the students through its autonomous government. The Union has employed about twenty staff and various casual helpers to run the bar, canteens, other trading services and to provide advice to the student members, as well as being assisted by the large number of student volunteers running clubs, societies, social events and serving on various College and student committees. The Students' Union has provided cultural, athletic and educational activities. As student numbers grew so did the scale and numbers of these activities and the clubs and societies that run them. Many of the clubs have been successful at local and national levels and brought interest, prestige and good publicity to the College. By providing such activities the Union has actively taken part in the community and involved itself in the life of Northampton. Many social events have been run by the Students' Union. They have ranged from discotheques, ceilidhs and balls through to old age pensioners parties and charity fund-raising events.

The Students' Union's main role in relation to the College as a whole lies in representing the student body. The concerns and views of the students need to be fed into the College committee structure as well as into the running of the Students' Union. All the officers of the Union have been elected and the systems and job descriptions are outlined in the constitution. Policies are developed and determined at various meetings of committees and the whole student body. The Students' Union Executive is made up of students elected annually (usually in the Spring Term) and three Executive members take a year out of their studies to work full-time for the Union, namely the President, the Vice President (Entertainment) and the Vice President (Internal). These three Executive members are usually referred to as the Sabbatical Officers. The Nene College Students' Union is affiliated to the Northants Area Council of the National Union of Students (NACWS) and to the National Union of Students (NUS).

Relaxation is a crucial part of life in an academic atmosphere. Common-room space became progressively more heavily used over the years limiting the scale and opportunity for a wider range of social activities to provide students with the chance to recharge their batteries. Over the years the Students' Union introduced a number of in-house services to make the organisation more efficient and responsive. For example, 'in-house' printing has enabled minutes, leaflets, dance tickets and internal forms to be printed cheaply and quickly. The Union has provided various trading services to its members, such as the Avenue Campus Bar and a canteen to each campus.

Many students have viewed the Union as their link with welfare organisations and agencies. Welfare information and advice is also provided for students. The Extreme Hardship Fund is largely administered by the Students' Union and many grants, housing and personal problems are processed through the Union. The Extreme Hardship Fund was set up on 6 July 1977 with David Walmsley as its first Chairman and Tony Rounthwaite as the Secretary. Representatives of the College, the Local Authority, the bank and the auditors as well as the students formed the Trustees Committee. Over 500 loans have been given to students who were in need of assistance but this was only as a last resort and alternative help was always sought first. The fund's objectives are to assist bona-fide students of Nene College who were in necessitous circumstances arising from unforeseen needs by making grants or loans.

Between 1975 and 1989 the Students' Union developed as a trading organisation and providing an administrative and information service for its members. Student activities in the form of Clubs and Societies have greatly increased and this provides an excellent basis for the Students' Union in the successor College.

* * *

Presidents of the Nene College Students' Union have come and gone but two of those perhaps best remembered were Peter Hallam, the first President, who was the Labour Parliamentary candidate for Eastleigh, Hampshire, in 1982, and Sean Silver who went with Operation Raleigh to the Solomon Islands when he worked in 90 degrees of heat and a 92 per cent humidity to build a Red Cross Health Centre for the islanders of Gizo.

Locally Tony Rounthwaite has served as a Borough and County Councillor. He has also been the Liberal Parliamentary candidate for Northampton North at two general elections. A former leading figure in student affairs was John Rawlings who was the youngest Mayor of Northampton in 1974 and also a Labour Parliamentary Candidate for South Northants.

10 Envoi: A Janus Look

Stuart Maclure

No one who has read this far can have failed to reflect on the chapter of historical accidents which brought together the disparate institutions which gave birth to Nene College. Most of Britain's major colleges have come about by a similar combination of unexpected events. Exponents of educational planning like to draw up action plans and flow charts, analysing supply and demand and locating areas of development by means of a rational examination of the balance of advantage. That may be splendid on paper in a world of blue-prints and templates, but no commentators, no matter how great their powers of rational analysis, would ever have envisaged the developmental flow chart which would gather together – over a span of more than a hundred years – Northampton's School of Art and Technical College, an annexe of the Leicester College of Education, Kirkby Fields, Liverpool (formerly a Royal Ordinance Factory hostel), the Corby outpost of the Leicester College of Education and the newly-initiated Northampton College of Education, to form Nene College in 1975. And even that was not the end of the story because Nene, itself, was soon further enlarged and enriched by the accession of the National Leathersellers' Centre and the Blackwood Hodge Management Centre, followed most recently by the Timken Business and Innovation Centre and the Northampton School of Chiropody.

All this shows, once again, that colleges are organic institutions, not machines. They have lives of their own, their own growth cycles, their own periods of vigorous development and relative quiescence.

What is clear is that 1989 is a climacteric for Nene. The Education Reform Act removed Colleges of Higher Education, along with Polytechnics, from the local authority sector. The College has become an independent 'Higher Education Corporation', governed by a board whose constitution is determined by Act of Parliament. A new Polytechnic and Colleges Funding Council has been set up to channel public funds to non-university higher education. This will be done by giving colleges and their newly constituted governing bodies the chance to bid for contracts which will pin the public money they receive to particular programmes and courses. They will be expected to compete with each other in providing value for money and in responding to the needs of industry. In the course of so doing, they are under notice to diversify their funding, and try to draw a quarter of their budgetary resources from sources of income other than the PCFC.

Therefore 1989, the bicentenary year of the French Revolution, portends a revolution in British higher education. Nene is one of the colleges with most to gain – or lose – from the change. As one of the most distinguished colleges outside the charmed Polytechnic circle, Nene is poised to move forward. But forward movement depends on seizing chances whenever they present themselves. It means spotting opportunities on the distant horizon and positioning the College to take advantage of them when the moment arrives. It means staying alive and alert, with a continuing capacity for adaptation and an opportunistic readiness to take every chance that offers.

The sequence of events which brought the College into being in the mid-1970s, gave it a splendid campus in a prosperous and expanding town. The crisis in teacher education in the mid-1970s was a blessing in disguise. It forced the College to diversify and look beyond the traditional limits of teacher training. As it happened, the College was more successful than most in its attempt to broaden its base. Today, Nene still has its teacher education, but it has a great deal more – and by that inspired combination of good fortune and good management which constitutes a sure recipe for success – the College is now extremely well placed to go from its present strength to even greater levels of excellence.

Three areas of development stand out as being particularly relevant to the Nene College of the 1990s. First, there are the courses and activities which can be grouped under the heading of 'Europe'. Second, there are those which relate to business, management and innovation. And third, there are the developing activities which serve the health professions.

The first two speak for themselves. The idea of a European business studies degree has an obvious appeal as 1992 approaches. And even if (as I suspect it will) 1992 turns out to be something of an anticlimax because nothing much will change overnight, it is as plain as a pikestaff that the days of splendid isolation are over. More and more businesses are going to need managers who combine competence in languages with acumen in business. The experience which Nene has already built up will give the college a head start in a competitive field.

Management studies is also a highly competitive field. The Sunley Trust benefaction has equipped Nene with a first-class Management Centre and made it an attractive location for post-experience courses for managers at all levels. And seeing that quality in management education depends on close working relationships with industry and commerce, Nene has an important resource on which to build.

Less glamorous than education for management, but of enormous potential importance for the future development of the College, are the foundations which have already been laid for major developments in the education of nurses and other professional support staff for the health professions. Nursing training is on the verge of a revolution that will sweep away the classic image of the bed-pan wielding student nurse, exploited by an understaffed hospital system and forced to combine learning with a heavy work-load on the wards. 'Nursing 2000' promises to professionalize the training of nurses and bring it within the regular frame-work of higher education. As and when this happens, a college like Nene, which has already begun to work in this important and rewarding field, will come into its own.

To pick out three areas that are clearly marked out for development is not to denigrate or undervalue other areas – certainly not those in initial and in-service teacher education, where rapid change is now taking place and new challenges are becoming apparent. It is simply to emphasise that the end of one chapter in the College's life is the opening of another and to remind anyone who might be tempted to forget it that the latest metamorphosis which has turned Nene College into a 'Corporation' will certainly not be the last.

Writing this 'coda' in January 1989, I am well aware that the future status of the College is, even now, a matter of keen speculation. The new governing body is confronted by competing suggestions. Should Nene go in with the University of Leicester and become part of the University Funding Council sector? Or should it respond to overtures from the Leicester Polytechnic and merge its future with that institution? Or yet again, should the governors hold back and see what life would be like if the college seeks to go it alone?

There is no doubt that Nene would be attractive both to the University of Leicester (with which the College already has connections through its degree-validating arrangements) and to Leicester Polytechnic. In the past, there has been a suspicion that, because of the established prestige of a university, any union between a college and a university would be so unequal a match as to represent at best, a takeover and at worst, an exercise in asset-stripping. No doubt the Nene Governors would be acutely conscious of this presumed danger and want to examine the small print with great care. On the plus side, however, the developments already in hand at Nene would complement those at the University of Leicester and a case can be made out for saying that a genuine synergy would be achieved. A link with the University would certainly help the University broaden its range of courses and activities – become even less like an ivory tower – and ensure for Nene a good supply of able students attracted *both* by the prestige of the University, and the mix of employment-orientated courses developed at Nene.

The Polytechnic option, too has much going for it. Nene would be a large enough institution to demand a genuine merger rather than a take-over. Nene's attempts to become a Polytechnic have been blocked so far. If the governors conclude that the only way to enter the Polytechnic ranks is by joining with another college, Leicester is only thirty-four miles away and (as with the University) there are links which would make this a logical choice.

Staying independent is the most problematic of the three options but there may be a reasonable reluctance to be bounced into a quick decision that would end the Corporation's separate existence so soon after achieving it. However, there is, it has to be said, a strong feeling 'in the trade' that the future will be with the larger, rather than the smaller, institutions. In the immediate future, student numbers can only be maintained in the face of smaller age-groups coming out of the schools, by recruiting more mature students or by making the College so attractive to students that they beat a path to Nene's door instead of going elsewhere. It is too soon to say exactly what the Polytechnics and Colleges Funding Council's attitude will be – whether they will favour promoting any more colleges to polytechnic status – but the odds are that, while the colleges wrestle with the demographic facts of life, it will be more fashionable to talk of consolidation than major expansion. This may well suggest that Nene's future lies with one or other of the Leicester options.

Nothing is harder for an institution and its governing body than to face up to the stresses and strains of mergers, which can, rightly or wrongly, be presented as leading to a loss of identity. Given Nene's site and importance, its own identity is likely to survive in any new grouping and – provided the Government's resolve to expand access to higher education holds – there must be every reason to be confident that higher education in Northamptonshire has a brave future ahead.

Appendices

Appendix I: Northamptonshire County Council, Chairmen and Officers of the Education Committee

(a) Chairmen of the Education Committee to 1974

E. P. Monckton	1903–16
H. Manfield MP	1916–20
S. J. Lloyd	1920–43
C. F. Alsop	1943–48
The Revd Canon W. Francis Smith	1948–55
W. J. Penn	1955–69
A. L. Langham	1969–74

(b) Chairmen of the Education Committee from 1974

County Councillor Mrs Dora Oxenham, CBE	1974–77
County Councillor David Walmsley	1977–79
County Councillor John Soans OBE	1979–81
County Councillor Jack Morrish	1981–85
County Councillor Mrs Gina Ogden	1985 to date

(c) County Education Officers to 1974

Byron S. Simpson, Organising Secretary for Technical Instruction	1891–1903
Byron S. Simpson, Secretary for Education	1903–04
John Lee Holland, Secretary for Education	1904–41
John Lee Holland, Chief Education Officer	1941–50
George Edward Churchill, Chief Education Officer	1950–74

(d) County Education Officers from 1974

Michael Henley, County Education Officer	1974–86
James Roy Atkinson, County Education Officer	1986 to date

Appendix II: Northampton County Borough Council

Chairmen of the Education Committee, 1903–74

Alderman E. L. Poulton	1903–07
Alderman Rowland Hill	1907–20
Alderman E. W. Sykes	1920–30
Councillor J. Peach	1930–34
Councillor W. H. Percival	1934–52
Alderman Arthur Chown	1952–55
Alderman Fred Tollit	1952–58
Alderman Arthur Chown	1958–63
Alderman Fred Tollit	1963–65
Alderman Arthur Chown	1965–67
Councillor David Walmsley	1967–74

Secretary of Education/Chief Education Officer, 1903–74

Stewart Beattie	1903–19
H. C. Perrin	1919–21
A. C. Boyde	1921–31
H. C. Perrin	1931–50
H. A. Skerrett, OBE	1950–68
Michael Henley	1968–74

Appendix III: Governors of Day School in 1895, and Technical School in 1900 and 1910

Day School Governors, 1895

The Right Hon. The EARL SPENCER, KG
The Right Hon. The LORD HENLEY, JP
Mr W. RYLAND D. ADKINS, CC
Mr JOHN DENNY, CC   County Council
Mr E. P. MONCKTON, MP, JP
Mr W. HIRST SIMPSON, CC
Mr J. RENNIE WILKINSON, JP

Sir PHILIP MANFIELD, JP
The Rev. CANON HULL, RD
Mr F. G. ADNITT, JP
Mr J. BINGLEY, JP   General Charities
Mr H. P. MARKHAM
Mr G. NORMAN JP
Mr Ald. T. WETHERELL

Mr GEORGE GIBBS
Mr WILLIAM MILLS JP
Mr Ald. H. E. RANDALL, JP   Town Council
Mr WM. TOMES, JP (The Mayor)

Mr HENRY WOODING
Mr JAMES BARRY, JP   School Board
Mr F. COVINGTON JP

Chairman: Mr H. P. MARKHAM

Clerk to the Governors: Mr J. B. HENSMAN

Technical School Governors, 1900

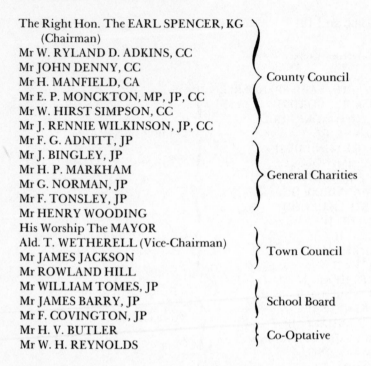

The Right Hon. The EARL SPENCER, KG
  (Chairman)
Mr W. RYLAND D. ADKINS, CC
Mr JOHN DENNY, CC
Mr H. MANFIELD, CA — County Council
Mr E. P. MONCKTON, MP, JP, CC
Mr W. HIRST SIMPSON, CC
Mr J. RENNIE WILKINSON, JP, CC
Mr F. G. ADNITT, JP
Mr J. BINGLEY, JP
Mr H. P. MARKHAM
Mr G. NORMAN, JP — General Charities
Mr F. TONSLEY, JP
Mr HENRY WOODING
His Worship The MAYOR
Ald. T. WETHERELL (Vice-Chairman) — Town Council
Mr JAMES JACKSON
Mr ROWLAND HILL
Mr WILLIAM TOMES, JP
Mr JAMES BARRY, JP — School Board
Mr F. COVINGTON, JP
Mr H. V. BUTLER — Co-Optative
Mr W. H. REYNOLDS

Clerk to the Governors: Mr J. HAVILAND, MA

Technical School Governors, 1910

The Right Hon. The EARL SPENCER, KC
  (Chairman)
Mr W. RYLAND D. ADKINS, MP, JP
Mr T. A. DICKSON   County Council
Mr H. MANFIELD, MP, JP
Mr E. P. MONCKTON, JP
Mr W. HIRST SIMPSON
Mr J. RENNIE WILKINSON, JP

Ald. F. G. ADNITT, JP (Vice-Chairman)
Sir H. E. RANDALL, JP
Mr W. MILLS, JP
Ald. W. TOMES, JP   Municipal
Mr HENRY WOODING   General Charities
Mr JOHN BALL
Mr WILLIAM HEAP

Ald. S. S. CAMPION, JP
Mr W. P. HANNEN
Mr F. H. THORNTON, JP   Town Council
Mr T. L. WRIGHT, JP
Mr G. W. BEATTIE, JP

Mr R. HILL   Town Education
Mr J. MANFIELD   Authority

Mr D. STANTON, JP   Co-Optative

Mr W. HICKSON

Special Evening and Art School Committee

Ald F. G. ADNITT, JP (Chairman)	Ald S. S. CAMPION, JP
Mr W. R. D. ADKINS, MP	Mr W. P. HANNEN
Mr H. WOODING	Mr J. BALL
Mr W. MILLS, JP	Mr D. STANTON, JP

Secretary: Mr ALFRED O. EAMER

Appendix IV: Past Governors of Northampton College of Technology, 1932–75

('Technical College Sub Committee' 1932–53)
('Governors': 1954–1975)

Mrs A. A. Adams	1932–37	(Chairman 1938–45)
P. W. Adams	1932–38	(Chairman 1932–38)
F. B. Allen	1959–60	
O. F. Bailey	1945–47	(Acting Principal – then Principal)
T. R. Bailey	1973–74	
Mrs M. M. Bartlett	1954–60	
W. J. Bassett-Lowke	1932–33	
A. H. Beavan	1973–44	(Principal Art School/College)
W. F. Belson	1939–45	(Chairman 1945)
M. W. O'Brien	1949–50	
B. V. Browne	1932–39	
H. L. Burrows	1934–46	
C. H. J. Butterfield	1932–39	
Mrs E. Chamberlain	1932–39	
A. L. Chown	1950–52, 1955–65	
Cyril Chown	1938–39	
S. Clarke	1955–64	
G. A. Clayson	1945–46	
S. E. Clayson	1951–52	
L. Danby Cogan	1945–48	
T. H. Cockerill	1971–74	(Chairman 1971–74)
W. E. Coldham	1938–45	
E. M. Collier	1973–74	
J. B. Corrin	1949–50	
M. J. Creevey	1968–69	
R. P. Cubitt	1973–74	
J. G. Dalton	1932–38	
M. J. Denney	1973–74	
J. Dickie	1974–75	
Mrs J. Dicks	1971–74	
R. P. Dilleigh	1971–72	
T. H. Dockrell	1953–74	(Chairman 1955–56, Deputy Chairman 1956–59, Chairman 1960–69)
Saul Doffman	1939–53	
H. Drage	1973–74	
P. S. Dunbar	1969–70	
C. H. Edwards	1947–54	(Chairman 1954–55, Deputy Chairman 1955–56)
Miss M. Finch	1969–71	
H. Fox	1932–38	
H. Fruish	1965–66	
G. J. Hackett	1968–69	

E. Hall	1946–47	
Mrs H. E. Hanafy	1945–46	
A. N. Harris	1954–56	
V. J. H. Harris	1960–62	
E. W. Harrison	1939–40	
H. S. Hemmings	1973–74	
M. J. Henley	1968–74	(Chief Education Officer)
Miss P. Hennings	1950–71	
Lady C. Hesketh	1968–72	
G. Hoare	1969–73	
W. H. Hollowell	1971–74	
A. A. Hope	1946–48	
R. S. Horsley	1964–65	
B. Hughes	1974–75	
S. T. James	1968–69	
M. Jones	1973–74	
S. T. Kinch	1952–65	
E. R. Knapp	1954–71	
R. F. Ledger	1960–69	
C. W. Lovekin	1965–68	
A. W. Lyne	1932–38, 1946–62	(Chairman, 1946–54)
C. McCarlie	1974–75	
P. McShane	1954–59	(Chairman 1956–59)
A. T. Mellor	1964–55	
D. Miles	1973–74	
G. Nutt	1962–74	
J. Peach	1932–34	
K. Pearson	1955–64	
W. J. Penn	1954–55	
W. H. Percival	1935–52	
H. C. Perrin	1932–50	(Secretary for Education)
W. A. Pickering	1954–56	
J. Poole	1973–74	
E. L. Poulton	1932–36	
J. Rawlings	1971–72	
G. Redfern	1973–74	
E. A. Roberts	1962–64	
T. Osborne Robinson	1954–64	
C. J. Scott	1937–38	
F. J. Sharman	1959–71	
Mrs I. Short	1969–70	
Mrs W. V. Slinn	1964–73	
H. A. Skerrett	1950–68	(Chief Education Officer)
A. J. Smart	1968–71	
L. Smith	1947–60	
R. A. Smith	1932–37	
J. R. Soans	1969–70	
A. Spencer	1973–74	

A. J. Stimpson	1968–69	
B. Tippleston	1953–55	
F. Tollit	1954–69	
Miss C. Trusler	1973–74	(Chairman 1974)
F. Tysoe	1954–59	
W. J. Walker	1946–50	
D. A. Walmsley	1968–72	(Chairman 1969–71)
Andrew Wilson	1950–52	
E. F. Wright	1971–72	

Appendix V: Nene College Governors, 1985–9

Representatives of the Authority
Councillor Mrs S. G. Ogden (Chairman)

Councillor T. G. Fordyce FCIB
(Vice-Chairman)
Councillor W. D. Morton CBE
Councillor A. W. Northen OBE
Mr D. A. Walmsley
Councillor J. G. Kane
Councillor Mrs J. M. Thomas
Councillor G. Blackwell
Councillor C. Kalyan
Mr M. L. Dove

Representative of the Employers
Mr E. R. Knapp CBE

Representative of the Unions
Mr O. Granfield

*Representative of the Social
Services*
Councillor W. G. Gee

*Representative of Art and
Industrial Design*
Sir William Shapland, FCA

Representative of Teacher Education
Dr K. M. Jones

*Representatives nominated by the
Students' Union Executive Committee*
Mr S. Baker (President)
Mr D. Greeves (Vice President –
Entertainments)
Miss B. Dowell (Vice President –
Internal)

Observer
Mr A. Rounthwaite

Co-opted members elected by the Governors
Sir Kenneth Newton, Bt, OBE, TD
The Revd Canon Frank Scuffham

*Representative concerned with training at
senior level in industry and commerce*
Mr S. Mackaness

*Representatives of the Academic Staff from
Northamptonshire Schools and from the
field of Further and Higher Education*
Mr J. Bonner (Higher Education)
Mrs P. M. Halliwell (Primary)
Mr I. Byrnes (Secondary)
Mr R. Mayhew (Further)

Director of the College
Dr E. Ogilvie

Deputy Directors of the College
Dr G. Clark
Mr A. W. R. Fox

*Representatives nominated by the
Academic Board*
Dr J. Alexander
Mr E. Watson

*Representatives nominated by the
Academic Staff*
Mrs P. Wright
Mr G. Otley

*Representative nominated by the
Non-Teaching Staff*
Mrs S. Allen

Appendix VI: Members of Staff Listed According to Faculties
Nene College Establishment

Dr E. Ogilvie
 Director
Dr G. M. Clark
 Deputy Director
A. W. R. Fox
 Deputy Director
G. Hood
 Senior Tutor
C. Bradbury
 Dean of Students
C. Paver
 Head of Academic Planning Services

M. Wilson
 Head of Learning Resources
H. Alabaster
 Deputy Head of Learning Resources
M. P. Jones
 Reader Services Librarian
C. Leach
 Technical Services Librarian
A. P. Broadway
 Head of Computer Services
S. Gilkes
 YTS Co-ordinator
M. Furminger
 Head of Innovation Centre

Faculty of Art & Design

P. Shirreff
 Dean
T. Armstrong
J. Bassett
T. J. Birch
J. Blackwood
R. Callier
J. Cook
 Deputy Dean
J. T. Czernik
B. Duffield
J. Glasman
P. Greco
J. Harper

J. Holt
A. W. Langford
M. Little
G. Meeton
Y. Mitton
J. Mooney
C. Mosley
D. R. Parker
D. W. Parrott
C. Ramsdale
M. G. Robinson
P. A. Torr
S. J. Townsend
B. Wenden
S. E. Wragg

Faculty of Education and Social Science

Dr J. L. Alexander
 Dean
A. Allen
R. E. Almond
Dr A. M. Andrew
M. D. Baldwin
Dr D. M. R. Bancroft
J. Barnes
M. Bell
Dr L. Benson
L. A. Best
R. Cartlidge
J. P. Davies
D. M. Duncan
J. T. G. George
Dr J. Gingell
F. M. Golton
Dr S. R. Harding
G. H. Hughes
M. Major
E. McDonough
Dr R. J. Mears
Dr T. Morris
D. L. Mosley
J. Moxham
R. Munro
G. Otley
 Deputy Dean

M. G. Penny
 Assistant Dean
A. Pilkington
A. D. Rae
D. Rice
J. Rogers
G. C. Rumbold
N. W. Sage
D. K. Shearing
P. Sidwell
Dr P. J. Silcock
A. Slowen
A. R. Smith
G. J. Smith
J. Spiby
J. E. Stanley
Dr M. Stowell
G. Thomas
H. Tite
M. Tolley
R. Toofanny
R. J. Walker
T. Waller
Dr M. R. Walley
P. Wells
Dr C. Winch

Faculty of Humanities and Adult Education

Dr M. Molneux ·
 Dean
R. W. E. Alder
Dr E. F. Aston
S. B. Barnes
T. D. Bell
R. A. Billingsby
Dr J. Bush
B. D. Caldwell
E. M. Carpenter
J. Cartwright
A. J. Castley
Dr R. T. Chapman
J. P. Chappell
P. M. Evans
R. Godfrey
G. Griffin
B. C. Hadkins
S. Hardy

Dr J. Harrison
Dr P. J. R. King
M. L. Llewelyn-Jones
J. S. Mason
J. S. McDonald
S. R. Moss
M. W. Pettitt
L. Reed
V. Riddell
Dr C. Ringrose
G. Savona
 Assistant Dean
I. C. Spiby
T. Tyrrell
D. L. Wagener
E. A. White
J. A. Whistle
F. A. Wragg
M. Wragg

Faculty of Mathematics, Management and Business Studies

Dr A. J. R. Berry
Dean
S. Allen
B. M. Allgood
E. G. Bellamy
T. C. Blakemore
R. A. Bolton
D. Bradshaw
Dr W. R. Brakes
P. J. Brown
E. S. Bullock
A. G. Catlow
O. W. Cleevely
M. Cook
A. C. Cozens
M. B. Cuthbert
Deputy Dean
C. R. Dedynski
J. G. Dowling
G. H. Elliott
R. P. Entwistle
J. E. Fletcher
T. Gould
J. Gribble
S. Guildford
S. M. Harland
D. A. Hayes
Assistant Dean
A. J. Hearsey
M. R. Hermann
T. W. Hiles
D. M. Hillyard
B. Hopewell

B. L. Jongman
K. Keenan
A. C. Kyriacou
J. Lacey
M. E. Lacey
Dr J. M. Mason
C. P. Meredith
P. J. M. Mothersole
A. Muff
P. F. Nalder
K. Owens
G. Parry
C. Raetschus
S. Y. Randall
Dr F. Robinson
V. L. Rowland
D. J. Shuttleworth
W. Slee
Dr M. A. Smith
J. Stephens
M. J. Sumpter
C. C. Suter
D. A. Sutton
A. J. Tattersall
J. S. Vickers
M. J. West
B. G. White
J. O. White
J. G. Wilkinson
A. C. Williams
A. F. Wilson
C. T. Wood
G. Wymant

Faculty of Science

Dr D. R. George
Dean
Dr B. R. Alcock
P. A. Alexander
R. K. Belshaw
J. A. Best
Dr S. E. Brown
Dr J. A. Campbell
A. M. Carr
N. L. Copland
D. U. L. Davighi
Dr R. Day
F. R. Dewhurst
B. J. Dunnery
G. F. Forsey

R. Graves
Dr R. J. Hall
R. Halliwell
G. V. Ilsley
M. Ilsley
C. Jones
Dr P. Jones
R. S. Kidd
Dr K. Langley
J. E. Lewis
J. McLeod-Roberts
L. Merriman
P. J. Norris
E. M. Pickles
M. V. J. Quigley

P. J. Richardson
Dr R. J. Roy
Dr W. G. Schofield
  Deputy Dean
Dr K. B. Sherwood
G. S. R. Simms

Dr V. G. F. Smith
Dr D. A. S. Symon
D. R. Tollafield
P. Tyrrell
P. T. Wright

Faculty of Technology

P. S. Knight
  Acting Dean
J. R. Appleby
H. B. Askew
K. C. Bazeley
P. Beaney
C. B. Beggs
I. T. C. Bell
Dr N. F. Boutle
M. J. Breslin
P. Briggs
R. Buckseall
B. I. Burton
B. Chamberlain
T. Coles
M. J. Collier
J. G. Cooper
R. H. Cox
W. R. Cullum
H. E. Dannatt-Brader
D. W. Dodd
M. G. Done
D. H. Elliott
J. Foreman
P. Foster
R. B. Freeman
P. R. Gilbert
D. P. Gilby
J. Ging
P. D. Golson
K. J. J. Grierson
Dr B. E. Hill
E. E. Hill
G. J. Hill
Dr D. J. Hubbard
L. J. Hyde

R. J. Irwin
P. K. Johns
H. L. Johnson
S. R. Jones
A. L. Joyce
W. G. Macdonald
S. McMath
A. D. Matthews
  Assistant Dean
E. J. Meakins
J. Mobbs
A. T. C. Newman
G. D. Prince
F. H. Richards
R. L. Southwell
R. J. Stephenson
J. R. Stevenson
G. J. Street
D. J. Stringer
M. O. Thomas
P. R. Thomas
B. E. Thompson
E. J. Tidball
D. A. Towell
R. L. Turner
R. R. Ward
G. H. Watson
B. L. Watts
T. D. Webb
B. G. White
M. W. White
R. Wilkinson
R. G. Williams
F. V. Yallop
J. H. Yates

APT & C Staffing

S. A. Allen
I. R. Ancell
D. R. Atkins
G. Atwal
R. J. Aveling
W. T. Ballard
M. J. Barber
J. E. Barnes
E. Barrett
J. M. Bell
S. E. Bevan
M. Birch
S. W. Blake
C. A. Blundell
S. Book
N. Bridel
Jean M. Brown
Jennifer S. Brown
M. A. Burnhope
L. Burrows
R. Butler
A. C. Cameron
S. R. Carter
M. Cave
A. J. Chapman
J. H. Clemas
V. K. Cocks
N. W. Cole
R. Cole
T. J. Coley
C. A. Collins
J. I. Cooper
B. K. Cox
B. R. J. Crook
B. J. Curtis
R. S. Dakin
G. M. W. Davies
L. J. Davies
M. E. Duley
W. Dunkley
M. Dunnery
P. Ellis
D. Entwistle
L. V. Flanagan
S. Fletcher
D. J. Frost
P. Gabel
J. M. Gear
A. Gibbons
A. C. Gilkes

B. Greenhalgh
Kathy J. Hall
Jane C. Hall
Linda S. Hall
Sheila E. Hall
T. J. Hammond
A. Hancock
A. P. Harding
E. P. Harding
P. Hastings-Stroud
D. J. Hendy
L. D. Henty
E. E. Hever
J. Hewson
A. E. Hickman
J. S. Hodgson
N. J. Holcombe
J. R. Hosier
M. Ingleton
R. C. Ingold
D. M. Izzard
P. M. Jewell
A. M. Johns
S. R. Jolliffe
J. Jordan
M. Jordan
A. M. Kent
C. R. King
J. King
K. A. King
C. P. Kirk
A. Knight
B. J. Knight
W. G. Kolitz
V. J. Lane
S. E. Laste
E. Lobo
J. W. Rack
B. B. Rathod
J. V. Ray
R. E. Rayner
C. Reid
J. E. Reeve
A. Revitt
I. M. Rice
A. Riley
L. J. Riley
Y. Roberts
C. D. Rout
J. W. Sharman

K. M. Shepherd
N. Singh
S. G. Slade
J. Sloan
S. B. Smart
A. J. Smith
J. R. Smith
S. M. Smith
W. C. Smith
K. H. W. Spokes
J. Stansfield
M. G. Stephenson
D. G. Stevenson
S. A. Stevenson
P. A. Stroud
E. J. Svennevik
P. Tarry
L. Lovett
S. J. Mabbutt
S. R. Maloney
P. J. Mannion
M. H. Marriott
E. G. May
E. McCloy
S. A. McGill
D. McKenzie
B McNamara
K. E. McNamara
M. McNeela
D. C. Mitchell
G. A. Moulding
J. M. Munn
G. Newbury
J. D. Newman
J. L. Nicholson
S. Noble
J. P. Norry
J. Oliff

A. D. Parmar
D. G. Parmar
J. Patel
A. F. Phillips
S. Plowright
C. J. Poole
B. W. Potter
P. E. Potter
V. H. Pritchett
J. M. Taylor
P. Taylor
B. A. Tebbutt
N. C. Tebbutt
P. J. Tebbutt
A. J. Tee
P. J. Thomson
P. A. Thurlby
T. V. M. Timberley
H. A. Tuttle
P. E. Underwood
S. D. Viccars
S. A. Vine
D. J. Walden
M. A. Warden
A. M. Watson
M. I. Watson
J. E. Watt
S. A. Webb
J. K. Welsby
J. Wetherill
M. J. White
J. Wilkins
S. A. Withers
M. I. Wolstenholme
D. A. Wood
J. A. Wood
T. Wright
C. Yeates

Domestic Staff – Park Campus

L. P. Auburn
M. Bason
A. Bourton
D. Brindisi
G. Budd
M. Bullen
C. Butler
P. Carter
M. Cartwright

J. Clarke
D. Cobley
M. A. Coleman
S. A. Coles
F. Coutts
I. Douglas
S. Draper
M. J. Flattery
P. Goodman

B. Goronwy
C. A. Harrison
S. Hawkins
C. Hayter
V. Hewitt
G. Johnson
L. Johnson
D. Jones
P. Kellett
K. Lang
J. Marriott
M. Meagher
E. Mitton
D. Neal
M. Nutt
M. Pannell
A. Parker
E. Prigmore
T. Pullin

J. Rideout
P. Robins
M. Russell
J. Shelton
C. Smith
V. Snedker
L. Solomon
B. Stones
M. Strudwick
J. Taylor
R. Tew
J. Wagstaff
I. J. Walker
A. Ward
J. Ward
L. Winter
H. Wood
J. Wood
C. E. Wright

Catering – Park Campus

S. Aitchenson
M. Bandiak
A. Brown
M. Cave
R. J. Clews
P. Coleman
A. Drage
T. Duddington
H. Harris
V. Hughes
S. McManus

E. A. May
S. E. May
B. Middleton
J. T. Nolan
D. Rose
J. K. Ryan
J. Snashall
H. Tuttle
A. Underwood
D. Williamson

Catering – Avenue Campus

J. Watt
P. Anderson
L. Gammage
T. Hammond
A. Jones
H. Mallon
N. Mallon

K. Mills
Y. M. O'Connor
J. Shally
D. Webb
D. Wilson
P. Wright

Cleaners – Avenue Campus

A. Abbott
L. Abbott
J. Alibone
H. Arnold
T. Arnold
M. Bage
C. Bain
S. Botticelli
B. Butler
E. Cato
F. Dance
H. Davies
B. Farmer
C. Higgins
C. Jelley
J. Kinsella
E. Knight
B. Laws

D. McAllister
M. Mullally
J. Norman
S. Norman
P. Perry
F. Reidy
M. Reynolds
F. Samuels
J. Scotney
G. Sharman
J. Sibley
M. Smith
L. Stojak
B. Thorpe
E. Tomlin
S. Walters
M. Wheeler
D. Wilson

Maintenance

A. Beasley
D. Gardner
F. McIlroy

Drivers

W. Adshead
T. Kaby
R. Adshead

Gardeners

R. J. Catt
A. B. Wilson

Assistant Caretakers – Park Campus

M. Cave
J. S. Hodgson
P. J. Mannion

Caretakers – Avenue Campus

W. Bradshaw
V. Chandler
P. Chapman
D. Hickie
A. Wallis
T. Wiggins
I. Hawkins

Machinist to the Fashion Course

P. A. Hardwick

Appendix VII: members of the Nene College Court, 1988-9

Roy Atkinson, MA
County Education Officer
Professor David Bellamy, BSc, PhD,
DUnivFLS, FIBiol
Botanist, explorer, broadcaster and author
Mrs Y. Bennion
Divisional Director for Industrial
Relations of the Industrial Society
The Rt Hon. The Lord Boardman, MC,
TD, DL
Director of various companies and Ex-
Chairman of National Westminster Bank
plc
T. Boswell, MP
Member of Parliament for Daventry
M. Buck, OBE, QPM, CBIM
Formerly Chief Constable and Project
Director RAC
J. L. Carr, MA
Author and publisher
Earl of Dalkeith
Trustee to 'The Living Landscape Trust'
John Dankworth, CBE, FRAM
Composer and musician
J. G. Dawson, CBEm, FEng, FIMechE
Formerly Chairman of the Civil Aviation
Authority
Sir John Dent, CBE, BSc, FEng
Formerly Chairman of the Civil Aviation
Authority
Lord Bernard Donoughue, MA, DPhil
Head of Research at Kleinwort Grieveson
Securities Ltd
Charles L. Ferguson, CEng, MIMechE
Chairman of Morgan Equipment (UK)
Ltd
Frank Fidgeon, BSc
Director of Training Services Division,
Sight & Sound Education Ltd;
formerly Deputy Chief Officer of
Technician Education Council
County Councillor, T. G. Fordyce, FCIB
Retired bank Manager; Vice Chairman of
College Governors
Professor Gerry Fowler, MA, FRSA, FBIM,
FABAC, Hon.FABE
Director, North East London Polytechnic;
Formerly Minister of State for Higher
Education
Roger Freeman, MP
Member of Parliament for Kettering

Peter Fry, MP
Member of Parliament for
Wellingborough
Jeffrey Greenwell, MA, FRICS
Chief Executive, Northamptonshire
County Council
Christian Lady Hesketh, OBE, DL, Hon.LLD
Dr Kenneth Horne, D.Litt
President, Robert Horne Group plc
Air Commodore I. Horrocks, RAF
Ministry of Defence
County Councillor J. Kane
College Governor
John Lowther, CBE, JP
Lord Lieutenant for Northamptonshire
M. S. Macdonald
Managing Director of Carslberg Brewery
Ltd
Sam Mackaness
Chairman A. J. Mackaness Ltd and of the
Northamptonshire Tourist Board
Stuart Maclure, CBE, MA
Editor of *The Times Educational
Supplement*
Tony Marlow, MP, MA
Member of Parliament for Northampton
Robert D. Moore, BA
General Manager/Chief Officer of the
Derngate Centre, Northampton
Sir Douglas Morpeth, TD, BCOM, FCA,
FRCM
Chairman of the Clerical, Medical &
General Life Assurance Society
Michael Morris, MP, MA
Member of Parliament for Northampton
South
Sir Kenneth Newton, Bt, OBE, TD
Chairman of Garnar Booth plc, Past
Master of the Leathersellers' Company
David O'Dowd
Chief Constable of Northamptonshire
J. H. Perkins
Vice Chairman of Stimpson-Perkins
William Powell, MP
Member of Parliament for Corby
Col. The Rt Hon. The Lord Pritchard, DL
Director of various companies including
Midland Bank plc and Rothmans
International plc
A. C. Richards
Chairman of Blackwood Hodge plc

Sir Gordon J. Roberts, CBE, JP, DL
  Chairman of the Oxford Regional Health
  Authority, Vice-Chairman Commission
  for the New Towns; High Sheriff
Sir William Shapland, FCA, LLD
  Trustee of Bernard Sunley Charitable
  Foundation; Member of Court of Leicester
  University; Nene College Governor
W. Sirs, JP
  Formerly General Secretary of the Iron &
  Steel Trades Confederation
A. G. Stoughton-Harris, FCA
  Executive Vice Chairman of the
  Nationwide Anglia Building Society
L. Teeman, OBE, BSc, CEng, FIEE
  Chairman of the Central
  Nottinghamshire Health Authority
Mrs Joan Tice
  Trustee of Bernard Sunley Foundation
Professor Dr H. J. Troeber Fachhochschule
  des Landes Trier, West Germany
David Walmsley, LLB
  Hon. Freeman of Northampton; Past
  Chairman of Governors; Council Member
  of Leicester University

Robert Watson
  Member of the Inner Temple; Liveryman
  of the Leathersellers' Company; Hon.
  Treasurer of the British Olympic
  Association and Hon. Secretary of the
  European Hockey Federation
The Rt Reverend William Westwood, MA
  Bishop of Peterborough
Professor R. G. White, PhD, CEng, FRAeS,
  CPhys, FInstPFIOA
  Director of the Institute of Sound &
  Vibration Research, Southampton
  University
Lord Basil Wigoder, QC
  Former Recorder of the Crown Court;
  former Liberal Chief Whip in the House
  of Lords; former Chairman Health
  Services Board; Chairman of BUPA
Brigadier P. R. G. Williams
  Commander 54 Infantry Brigade
Chairman of the College Court:
County Councillor Mrs Gina Ogden
  Chairman of the Northamptonshire
  County Council Education Committee;
  Chairman of the College Governors

Appendix VIII: College of Technology, Northampton: Full-time Staff, 1938–69

	1938/9	1948/9	1953/4	1958/9	1963/4	1968/9
Principal	1	1	1	1	1	1
Vice Principal						1
Departments						
Boot & Shoe	6	6	5	7	8	8
Building	1	4	5	6	8	10
Commerce	5	3	8	15	13	16
Domestic subjects	3	2	4	4	4	8
Engineering	3	6	9	13	23	45
General studies					12	19
Leather	3	3	3	3	4	5
Mathematics		1	1	2	5	5
Science	4	3	6	8	10	13
Total	**26**	**29**	**43**	**59**	**88**	**131**
Library					3	3
Industrial Liaison Officer						2
Administration	4	5	4	4	9	11
Audio-visual Aids						1
Caretaking	1	3	3	2	7	8
Students' Association Secretary						1

Notes:
(1) Laboratory technicians, etc., are not included, nor are members of the refectory staff.
(2) Figures for 1938/9–1963/4 taken from the College prospectuses for the years concerned; 1968/9 from establishment figures supplied by the Registrar. The departmental system in 1938/9 was rudimentary, and the staff listed in the prospectus for that year have been classified according to the system of departments evolved in the post-1945 College.
(3) This table of figures was compiled by Victor Hatley in 1969 following a conversation with the Vice Principal of the College of Technology about the development of the College since the end of the Second World War. It reveals clearly the shift in emphasis away from the teaching of boot and shoe manufacture (6 members of staff out of a total of 29 in 1948/9) and the substantial increase in the teaching of other subjects, in particular engineering (45 members of staff in 1968/9). This shift corresponds to the industrial development of Northampton and district during the same period, which was marked by the decline of boot and shoe manufacturing and the growth of engineering. The boot and shoe department in the College closed in 1975 following the retirement in the previous year of Mr John H. Thornton.

Many members of the College of Technology teaching staff were transferred in 1972 to the newly-formed College of Further Education, Booth Lane, Northampton, and this makes levels of staffing at the College of Technology between that date and 1975, when Nene College came into being, difficult to compare with the number of staff there in 1968/9 and before.

Appendix IX: The Buckley Lectures

The College is most grateful to Mr A. H. Buckley, who has generously sponored all these lectures. The first half-dozen were originally named the Miller-Buckley Lectures, after Sir James Miller (who announced them at the time of the opening of the College of Education in 1972) and Mr. Buckley. They are now known simply as 'The Buckley Lectures'.

Year	Speaker	Subject
1973	Dr N. W. Pirie	Efficient Food Production
1974	Dr David Bellamy	This is Your Environment
1975	Dr Magnus Pyke	Food and Nutrition: For Richer for Poorer
1976	Professor Denis Harper	The View from Where We Stand: Concern for our future Environment
1977	Mr Tony Soper	Nature Conservation and the BBC (A Wild Life on the Telly)
1978	Dr E. R. Laithwaite	Nature: Master Technologist
1979	Mr Jack Scott	The Weather Business
1980	The Rt Hon. Lord Sandford	Education, In, From and For the Environment
1981	Professor M. J. Pentz	Can Nuclear War be Avoided?
1982	Professor David Bellamy	Plant Yourself a Future
1983	Professor Colin Blakemore	The Perceptual World
1984	Miss Sheila Browne	Liveable Learning: A Place for the Environment
1985	The Rt. Hon. Peter Brooke, MP	The Quandary of the Environment
1986	Professor David Bellamy	The Last Resource
1987	Sir George Porter, FRS	Science and the Human Purpose
1988	Heather Couper	How Big is the Universe?
1989	The Rt Hon. Revd William Westwood, Bishop of Peterborough	Starting in a Garden – Ending in a City

Further Reading

This bibliography indicates some of the major official publications which were significant to the development of Nene College, and includes others which provide relevant background information. It is not intended to be comprehensive.

1844 Board of Education. *Report of the Royal Commission on Technical Instruction.* (Chairman: B. Samuelson). HMSO.

1889 *Technical Instruction Act.* HMSO.

1902 Board of Education. *Education Act.* HMSO.

1918 Board of Education. *Education Act.* HMSO.

1926 Board of Education. *Report of the Consultative Committee of the Board of Education on the education of the adolescent.* (Chairman: W. H. Hadow). HMSO.

1944 Ministry of Education. *Education Act.* HMSO.

1945 Ministry of Education. Special Committee. *Higher technological education.* (Chairman: Lord Percy). HMSO.

1947 Ministry of Education. *Circular 139. Plans for County Colleges.* HMSO.

1947 Ministry of Education. *Further education.* Pamphlet No. 8. HMSO.

1949 Ministry of Education. *Education for commerce.* Report on the special committee. (Chairman: Sir Alexander M. Carr-Saunders). HMSO.

1950 Ministry of Education. National Advisory Council on Education for Industry and Commerce. *Future development of higher technical education.* (Chairman: Sir Ronald M. Weeks). HMSO.

1951 Ministry of Education. *Higher Technological Education: Statement of Government Policy for development of Higher & Technological education in Great Britain.* Cmnd. 8357.

1955 Venables, P. F. R. *Technical education: its aims, organisation and future development.* Bell.

1956 Ministry of Education. *The organisation of technical colleges.* Circular 305. HMSO.

1956 Ministry of Education. *Technical education.* Advisory Panel Report. Cmd. 9703. HMSO.

1958 Ministry of Education. *Further education for commerce.* Report of the advisory committee. National advisory council on education for industry and commerce. (Chairman: J. G. McMeeking). HMSO.

1959 Ministry of Education. *15 and 18.* Report of the Central Advisory Council for Education. (Chairman: Lord Crowther). Vol. 1. Report, Vol. 2. Surveys. HMSO.

1961 Ministry of Education. *Better opportunities in technical education.* Cmnd. 1254. HMSO.

1962 Ministry of Labour. *Industrial training.* Cmnd. 1892. HMSO.

1963 Central Advisory Council for Education. *Half our future.* (Chairman· Newsom).

1963 Committee on Higher Education. *Higher education.* (Chairman: Robbins). Cmnd. 2154. HMSO.

1964 Argles, M. *South Kensington to Robbins: an account of English technical and scientific education since 1851.* Longman.

1964 Department of Education and Science. Committee on Day Release. *Day release.* (Chairman: Henniker-Heaton). HMSO.

1966 Department of Education and Science. *The government of Colleges of Education.* (Chairman: Weaver). HMSO.

1966 Department of Education and Science. *Plan for polytechnics and other colleges: Higher education in the further education system.* Cmnd. 3006. HMSO.

1966 Department of Education and Science National Advisory Council on Education for Industry and Commerce. Committee on Technical College Resources. *Report on the size of classes and approval of further education courses.* (Chairman: Pilkington). HMSO.

1969 Department of Education and Science. National Advisory Council on Education for Industry and Commerce. *Report of the Committee on technical courses and examinations.* (Chairman: Haslegrave). HMSO.

1970 Association of Training Colleges and Departments of Education. *Higher education and preparation for teaching.* ATCDE.

1972 Department of Education and Science. *Education: a framework for expansion.* Cmnd. 5174. HMSO.

1972 Department of Education and Science. *Teacher education and training.* (Chairman: Lord James of Rusholme). HMSO.

1973 Department of Education and Science. *Adult Education: a plan for development.* (Chairman: Russell). HMSO.

1973 Department of Education and Science. *Development of higher education in the non-university sector.* Circular 7/73. HMSO.

1974 Technician Education Council. *Policy statement.* TEC.

1976 Business Education Council. *First policy statement.* BEC.

1977 Manpower Services Commission. *Young people and work.* (Chairman: Holland). MSC.

1978 Department of Education and Science. *Report of the working group on the management of higher education in the maintained sector.* (Chairman: Oakes). Cmnd. 7130. HMSO.

1980 Department of Education and Science and Local Authority Associations. *Education for the 16–19 year olds.* (Chairman: MacFarlane). HMSO.

1981 Department of Education and Science. *Higher education in England outside Universities: Policy, funding & management.* HMSO.

1981 Department of Employment. *A new training initiative: a programme for action.* Cmnd. 8455. HMSO.

1983 Department of Education and Science. *Future demand for higher education in Great Britain.* Report on Education No. 99. HMSO.

1984 Business and Technical Education Council. *B/TEC policies and priorities into the 1990s.* B/TEC.

1984 Department of Employment. *Training for jobs.* Cmnd. 9135 HMSO.

1984 National Advisory Board. *A strategy for Higher Education in the late 1980s and beyond.*

1985 Department of Education and Science. *The development of higher education into the 1990s.* Cmnd. 9524. HMSO.

1985 Department of Education and Science. *Education and training for young people.* Cmnd. 9482. HMSO.
1985 Department of Education and Science. Committee of Enquiry into the Academic Validation of Degree Courses in Public Sector H. E. *Report, academic validations in public sector higher education.* (Chairman: Lindop). Cmnd. 9501. HMSO.
1986 Department of Education and Science. *Projections of demand for higher education in Great Britain 1986–2000.* HMSO.
1986 Department of Employment. *Working together: education and training.* HMSO.
1986 Manpower Services Commission and Department of Education and Science. *Review of vocational qualifications in England and Wales: a report by the working group.* (Chairman: De Ville). MSC/DES.
1987 Department of Education and Science. *Higher education: meeting the challenge.* Cmnd. 114. HMSO.
1987 Sharp, P. R. *The creation of The Local Authority sector of H. E.* Falmer Press.
1988 Cuthbert, R. (ed.) *Going corporate.* Further Education Staff College.
1988 Engineering Council. *Restructuring of engineering higher education.*
1988 Locke, M., and others. *Colleges of Higher Education 1972 to 1982: the central management of organic change.* Critical Press.
1988 National Advisory Body for Public Sector Higher Education. *Action for access: widening opportunities in Higher education.*

Works of local interest
1895 onwards *Northampton College of Technology Prospectus.* Published annually.
1914 White, A. P. *The Story of Northampton.* Published locally by W. Mark & Co. Recently reissued with an additional chapter on developments since the First World War by Victor Hatley, published by Chantry Press Ltd, Wakefield, 1986.
1930s/40s *Technical School/College Magazine.* Published annually, but with breaks in war-time etc.
1931 Thompson, Beeby, FCS, FGS. *A History of the Beginnings and Development of Scientific and Technical Education in Northampton from 1867 to 1894.* Published privately in Northampton by Archer and Goodman.
1947 Lees, T. C. *A Short History of Northampton Grammar School, 1541 to 1941.* Northampton, Swan Press.
1959 Simmons, Jack. *New University.* Leicester University Press.
1973 Ogilivie, E. *Gifted Children in Primary Schools.* London, Macmillan.
1985 Barty-King, Hugh. *The Expansion of Northampton.* London, Secker & Warberg.
— Minutes of the Meetings of:
   (a) the Northampton County Borough Council
   (b) the Northampton County Borough Education Committee
   (c) the Northamptonshire County Council
   (d) the Northamptonshire Education Committee
   (e) The Governing Bodies of the various colleges referred to in the text and of Nene College

List of Sponsors

The principal sponsors of this book are:
Nene College Governors;
The Trustees of Nene College Social Club;
Sir William Shapland; and
David Walmsley

In addition the project has been supported by the following individual sponsors:

A. B. Connections (Northampton) Ltd, Northampton
Alabaster, Mrs Heather, Northampton
Alcock, Mr Richard, Assistant County Education Officer, Northamptonshire
Alexander, Dr J. L., Dean of Education/ Social Science, Nene College
Allen, Mrs M., Creaton, Northants

Allen, Mr & Mrs P., Old, Northants
Annis, Miss P., Hanging Houghton, Northants
Antona Office Supplies Ltd Raunds, Northants
Atkin, Mr Kenneth, Kettering
Atkinson, Mr J. R., County Education Officer, Northamptonshire
Austin-Crowe, Mr Leslie, Northampton

Bantock, Professor, G. H., Leicester
Barnes, Mr D. J. C., Brisbane, Australia
Barnett, Mr I. G., Northampton
Bass, Mr James, Northampton
Beavan, Mr A. S., Biggleswade, Beds
Beavan, Mrs H. H., Letchworth, Herts
Beavan, Mr R. L., Leominster
Belshaw, Mr R. K., Northampton
Bennion, Mrs Yvonne, The Industrial Society, London
Bentley, Mr G. A., Northampton
Berry, Dr A., Nene College
Bevan-Roberts, Dr Elizabeth (formerly Deputy Principal), Leamington Spa
Bisson, Mr J. C., Northampton

Bland, Mrs M., Kettering
Boardman, The Lord, Welford, Northants
Boggan, Mr N. S., Beaconsfield, Bucks
Bonner, Mr J., Leicester University
Boswell, Mr T., (MP), House of Commons, London
Bradbury, Mr C., Dean of Students, Nene College
Broadway, Mr Alan, Head of Computer Studies, Nene College
Brooks, Mr Derek, Northampton
Buck, Mr Maurcie (QPM), Northampton
Bullard, Mr H., Northampton
Byrnes, Mr I. J., Thrapston, Northants

Campling, Dr John, Northampton
Campion School, Bugbrooke, Northants
Cannell, Mr J. W., Northampton
Carr, Mr J. L., Kettering
Chandos-Pole, Lt. Col. J. (CVO, OBE) (former Lord Lieutenant, Northamptonshire)
Chapman, Dr R. T., Northampton

Clark, Dr G. M., Deputy Director, Nene College
Clements, Revd R. R. (MBE), Heswell, Merseyside
Copland, Mr N., Northampton
Cordingley, Dr J. L., Northampton
Corrin, Mr J. B. (OBE), Northampton
Coventon, Mr W. J. E., Northampton
Cox, Philip (QC), Hon. Recorder of Northampton

Dalkeith, The Earl, Thornhill,
Dumfriesshire
Davenport, Mr M. C. Northampton
Davidge, Mr C. V. G. (OBE), (High
Sheriff, Northamptonshire 1988–89),
Little Houghton, Northants

Ellwood, Mr P. B., Barclaycard,
Northampton

Fairfields School, Northampton
Ferguson, Mr Charles, Church
Brampton, Northants
ffoulkes, Mr F. L. (OBE), Leicester
Fordyce, Cllr T. G., Northampton
Foulkes, Mr R. G. Northampton

Gardner, Mr R., Daventry, Northants
Garnett, Mr R. S. (CBE), Northampton
Gaskell, Dr M., Director-Designate,
Nene College
George, Dr D., Nene College
Godfrey, Mr B. S., Northampton
Gooding, Cllr Graeme, Northampton

Hall, Mrs J. J. D., Northampton
Halliwell, Cllr Mrs P., Northampton
Hancock, Mr F. W., Rushden,
Northants.
Harding, Dr Stephen, Northampton
Hargrave, Cllr A. J., Northampton
Harper, Professor D. R. and
Oxenham, Mrs D.(CBE), First
Chairman of Governors
Wellingborough, Northants
Hart, Lady Dorothy, Banbury, Oxon
Hatley, Mr Victor, Northampton
Henley, Mr M. J., former County
Education Officer, Northamptonshire
Hermann, Mr & Mrs M., Walgrave,
Northants

Ireson, Mr Tony, Kettering

Jackman, Mr James, Oxford
Jackson, Mr B. R., Corby, Northants
Jewitt, Mr Eric (former Principal,

De Has, Mrs D., Northampton
Dent, Sir John, Helidon, Northants
Desborough, Mr F. (former Mayor),
Northampton
Dilleigh, Mr R. P., Northampton
Dunkley, Mr C. M., Leicester University

Embury, Mr L. V. V., Chief Housing
Officer, Northampton

Fox, Mr R., Deputy Director,
Nene College
Frain, Dr J. P. A. (former HMI and
Deputy Director, Nene College),
Liverpool
Furminger, Mr M., Nene College

Goodman, Cllr Mrs Anne, Northampton
Granfield, Cllr Owen, Northampton
Greenall, Mr R., Leicester University
Greenwell, Mr J. A., Chief Executive,
Northamptonshire
Grierson, Mr K. K. J., Kenilworth,
Warwicks

Hillbourne, Cllr W., Market
Harborough, Leics
Holmes, Mr & Mrs T. F., Northampton
Hood, Miss G., Senior Tutor,
Nene College
Hooton, D. F. (TD, JP, DL),
Wellingborough
Hornby, Mrs Margaret, Guilsborough,
Northants
Horne, Dr K., Boughton, Northants
Horrocks, Air Commodore and
Mrs Ian, Salisbury, Wilts
Hudson, Mr Eric, Hartlepool, Cleveland
Hulbert, Mr & Mrs A., Wolverhampton

College of Technology),
Northampton
Jones, Miss L. M., Northampton

Kalyan, Cllr C., Northampton
Khan, Dr M. A., Leicester University
Kidd, Mr Robert, Northampton
Kitson, Mr G., Nene College

Leathersellers' Livery Company, London
Liddington, Cllr R. G., (Mayor of Northampton)

MacEacharn, Capt. Neil (CBE, RN) The Leathersellers' Company, London
MacLure, Mr S. (CBE), *Times Educational Supplement*
Mann, Mrs Dorothy, Northampton
Marlow, Mr Tony (MP), House of Commons, London
Marriott, Mrs M. P., Northampton
Mayne, Mrs L. A., (Northampton High School for Girls), Northampton
Merriman, Mrs L., Nene College
Molyneux, Dr M., Dean of Humanities, Nene College

Nardecchia, Mr J. T. (OBE), Harrow on the Hill, Middlesex
National Union of Footwear, Leather and Allied Trades Northants
Newbrook, Mr G. L., Lower Weldon, Northants

Ogden, Cllr Mrs G., (Chairman, Nene College Governors)
Ogilvie, Dr and Mrs E., Nene College
Oliff, Mrs J., Weedon, Northants
O'Rourke, Mr and Mrs A., Rothwell, Northants

Palmer, Mr N. W. (OBE, JP), Sherbourne, Dorset
Parker, Mrs L., Whitehills, Northampton
Parkinson, Rt Hon. Cecil (MP), House of Commons, London
Parthenis, Mr Alex, East Haddon, Northants
Paver, Mr C., Head of Academic Planning, Nene College
Percival, Mrs L. E., Northampton

Quigley, Mr N. V., Northampton

Knapp, Mr E. R. (CBE), Northampton
Knight, Mr P. S., Northampton
Knowsley Metropolitan Borough Council, Kirkby, Merseyside

Lock, Miss Anne R., Northampton
Lowther, Mr J. L. (CBE) (Lord Lieutenant, Northamptonshire)

Moore, Robert, D., Derngate Centre, Northampton
Morpeth, Sir Douglas (TD), London
Morris, Cllr Mrs Josephine, Northampton
Morris, Mr Michael (MP), House of Commons, London
Morris, Mr R. J. B., Chief Executive and Town Clerk, Northampton
Morrish, Jack (previous Chairman of Governors, Northampton
Mosley, Ms D. L., Northampton

Noble, Sir Fraser (former Vice-Chancellor, Leicester University)
Northampton Health Authority
Northampton School for Girls
Northamptonshire Probation Service

O'Rourke, Mr and Mrs G. T., Northampton
Otley, Mr G., Deputy Dean of Education/Social Science, Nene College

Perkins, Mrs S., Launceston, Cornwall
Pestell, Mr R. L., Deputy County Education Officer, Northamptonshire
Pettitt, Mr Maxwell W., Chapel Brampton, Northants
Pollard, Cllr George, (Chairman, Northamptonshire County Council), Northampton
Prouse, Mr A. H. W., (former Mayor), Northampton

Randall, Mrs Cheryl, Northampton
Reaks, Mr Guy, Lewes, Sussex
Ridley, Brigadier N. J. (OBE), Grantham, Lincs
Rigby-Smith, Mr I. P., Grendon, Northants
Riley, Mr Alan, Chief Administration Officer, Nene College

Scholey, Mr Trevor, Senior Inspector, Northamptonshire
Shapland, Mr W. R., Barnstaple, Devon
Sheppard, Cllr B. A. Brackley, Northants
Sheppard, Mr J., Boughton, Northants
Shock, Sir Maurice (former Vice-Chancellor, Leicester University), Oxford
Shribman, Dr S. J., Child Development Centre, Northampton
Skelton, Mr Leslie C., Northampton
Smith, Mr R. C., Northampton
Southworth, Mr Paul, President, Avon Cosmetics, Northampton

Targett, Mr & Mrs Reginald, Northampton
Taunton, Brigadier D. E. (and Mrs M. **Taunton,** (former Mayor), Duston, Northampton
Tebbutt, Mr & Mrs Norman, Northampton
Teeman, Mr Leslie, Newark

Wake, Sir Hereward (Bt, MC, DL) Courteenhall, Northants
Walmsley, Mr E. & Mrs C., Kettering
Walmsley, Mr & Mrs P. M., Stroud, Gloucs
Ward, Cllr Keith, Milton Keynes
Watson, Mr R. J. (Barrister at Law), London
West, Mr John, Northampton
White, Mrs G. M., Northampton
White, Professor R. G., Southampton
Wigoder, Lord Basil, London

Roberts, Sir Gordon, Milton Keynes (High Sheriff, Northamptonshire, 1989-90)
Robinson, Mrs Irene, Northampton
Rounthwaite, Mr T., Nene College
Royal Pioneer Corps, Simpson Barracks, Northampton

Stanley, Mr John, Ashby de la Zouch, Leics
Starr, Mr Cyril, Northampton
Statham, Major John, Launceston, Cornwall
Stimpson, Cllr A. J., Northampton
Stoughton-Harris, Mr A. G., Grendon, Northants
Sykes, Professor & Mrs L. C., Leicester
Sykes, Dr R. C. (OBE), Church Brampton, Northants
Sylvester, Mr D. W. (HMI), Banbury, Oxon

Tero, Cllr Frank, Northampton
Thomas, Cllr Mrs Janet, Northampton
Thomson, Mrs Phyllis, Northampton
Tomalinson, Mrs W. (SRN, DNG), Northampton
Troeber, Professor D. H. J., Trier, West Germany
Tudor, Revd Dr R. John & Mrs C., Purley, Surrey

Williams, Brigadier P., Eltisley, Hunts
Wilson, Mr A. F., Creaton, Northants
Wilson, Mr D., Northampton
Wilson, Mr J., Nene College
Wilson, Mr M., Head of Learning Resources, Nene College
Wise, Miss Nancy, Bradford-on-Avon, Wilts
Wood, Dr & Mrs A. J., Bedford
Woodroofe, Mr D. A., Warwick
Wright, Mrs P. T., Great Houghton, Northants

Name Index

Subject Index